KARL DOENITZ AND THE LAST DAYS OF THE THIRD REICH

KARL DOENITZ
AND THE LAST DAYS OF THE THIRD REICH

BARRY TURNER

ICON

First published in the UK in 2015 by
Icon Books Ltd, Omnibus Business Centre,
39–41 North Road, London N7 9DP
email: info@iconbooks.com
www.iconbooks.com

Sold in the UK, Europe and Asia
by Faber & Faber Ltd,
Bloomsbury House, 74–77 Great Russell Street,
London WC1B 3DA or their agents

Distributed in the UK, Europe and Asia
by TBS Ltd, TBS Distribution Centre, Colchester Road
Frating Green, Colchester CO7 7DW

Distributed in Australia and New Zealand
by Allen & Unwin Pty Ltd, PO Box 8500,
83 Alexander Street, Crows Nest, NSW 2065

Distributed in South Africa by Jonathan Ball,
Office B4, The District, 41 Sir Lowry Road,
Woodstock 7925

Distributed in Canada by Publishers Group Canada,
76 Stafford Street, Unit 300
Toronto, Ontario M6J 2S1

Penguin Books India,
7th Floor, Infinity Tower – C, DLF Cyber City,
Gurgaon 122002, Haryana

Distributed to the trade in the USA
by Publishers Group West,
1700 Fourth Street, Berkeley, CA 94710

ISBN: 978-184831-922-6

Typeset in Dante by Marie Doherty

Printed and bound in the UK by
Clays Ltd, St Ives plc

CONTENTS

LIST OF ILLUSTRATIONS AND MAPS

Plate section

Jodl signs the German surrender at Rheims. (*Keystone*)

Doenitz announces the German capitulation.

The arrest of Speer, Doenitz and Jodl at Flensburg. (*dpa/Corbis*)

Doenitz takes the oath at the Nuremberg trial.

Doenitz, shortly after his release from Spandau, on his
way to Duesseldorf to spend time with his lawyer,
Otto Kranzbuehler.

Maps in text

Pages 68–9: The Baltic Sea.

FOREWORD

by Admiral of the Fleet Lord Boyce

Barry Turner's *Karl Doenitz and the Last Days of the Third Reich* provides a masterly summation of a confusing period in the closing stages of the Second World War. It switches successfully from describing high-level strategic considerations and interplay within the Nazi and Allied leadership, to the harrowing details of individuals' first-hand experiences of war at the bottom of the hierarchical structure, with cameos of heroism, cowardice, brave offence and defence.

Captivating stories and insights into the personalities of the main players are unfolded – and nowhere is this truer, of course, than in the case of Doenitz himself. It is here that, as a submariner, I found myself most intrigued. The author has captured very well the ethos of the submarine world and its effect on the individual who lives, or has lived, within it; and the make-up of Doenitz's personality, his deep professionalism, loyalties and values, reflect this admirably. In particular, and as the book quotes him:

> I had been fascinated by that unique characteristic of the submarine service, which requires a submariner to stand on his own feet and sets him a task in the great spaces of

the oceans, fulfilment of which demands a stout heart and ready skill; I was fascinated by that unique spirit of comradeship engendered by destiny and hardship shared in the community of a U-boat crew, where every man's well-being was in the hands of all and where every single man was an indispensable part of the whole.

What he learnt about the effectiveness of submarine warfare in the First World War was to play a major part in his thinking 20 years later; and his own personal belief in the effectiveness of the submariner, hardened by his – improbably – surviving the sinking of the U-boat under his command in 1918, can be seen in the attention he lavished on the personnel in that branch of the Kriegsmarine.

His judgement on submarine warfare was sound, and the success he had in strangling the supply lines across the Atlantic nearly brought Great Britain to its knees in 1942–43 and threatened to do so again when the new generation of technologically superior U-boats was deployed in early 1945. I was interested to read of the difficulties Doenitz had in trying to get more support from the Luftwaffe for his submarine deployments – not too dissimilar from the frustrations the Royal Navy had in getting RAF support!

Having provided the nature of the background that shaped the man, and after an opening chapter on the chess-like moves for the transfer of power following Hitler's death, the narrative of unfolding events in the first half of 1945 leading up to the end of the war and immediate post-war activity can be characterised as falling broadly into four parts: action at sea in the Baltic, including Operation Hannibal; the final throes of the war on land, including the machinations of both Allied and German senior commanders; negotiations for ending the war; and Doenitz's actions and ultimate fate post war.

The importance to Germany of the Baltic – providing as it did the vital supply lines to keep the all-important, powerful and potentially war-winning industrial machine running – is strongly portrayed, as is its use to facilitate probably the biggest ever evacuation by sea: Operation Hannibal – a story probably unknown to most. The huge scale of this operation eclipses Dunkirk and the book's vivid and contemporaneous descriptions of such events as the loss of the *Wilhelm Gustloff* and 9,000 lives paint a chilling picture. Doenitz had a driving, passionate and humanitarian-based determination to save as many as possible of those in the Baltic's eastern regions trying to escape the jaws of the Bolshevik advance as it swallowed up the Baltic ports with horrendous savagery; and his belief in the importance of the evacuation – in spite of Hitler's indifference, if not objections – is later shown to be an underlying theme for his actions after the Fuhrer's death, as he tried to shape circumstances that might allow German and other refugees to avoid capture by the Soviets as they advanced through Germany from the East.

That advance, together with the similar moves by the Western Allies from the Channel and their race to cross the Rubicon-like Rhine and to reach Berlin against the desperate and unexpectedly strong defence by the Wehrmacht, as well as the effect on the civilian population, and the tensions and antipathies between key players on both sides, forms the second part and makes a story in itself – once again brought to life with recollections of individuals there at the time. Massive movements, massive loss of life and massive interplay of politics that would have far-reaching consequences make absorbing reading and lead the reader well into the other two parts of the narrative.

The descriptions of these – the manoeuvrings around Doenitz reluctantly assuming the mantle of Fuehrer, the negotiations leading to German surrender and the final scenes played out in the court at Nuremberg – provide the final pieces of evidence from which the reader can form a judgement about whether Doenitz played his war-leader part in the conflict 'fairly'. The author argues that Doenitz's incarceration as a convicted war criminal was more about politics than any crime committed, and in this connection it is interesting that the First Sea Lord supported Doenitz's appeal against conviction, and that the Royal Navy was represented at his funeral in 1980. Doenitz was a professional warrior who had total belief in his Kriegsmarine – keeping it, and himself, largely free from Nazi ideology – and an ingrained loyalty to his country. He fought a hard war, but no harder than his opposing admirals and generals, and with no worse excesses – although an accusation of uncritical devotion to a political cause would not be unfair.

Like 'old soldiers', Doenitz faded away after his imprisonment, never looking for the leadership role many expected and hoped he would take up again. But he left his own mark on European history, not least his anticipation of what he saw as the main threat to world order – Soviet expansionism; and his belief and focus on the effectiveness of the submarine as a war-fighting, potentially war-winning, machine in maritime strategy is as pertinent today as it was 75 years ago.

Admiral of the Fleet Lord Boyce

CHAPTER ONE

Berlin, 30 April 1945
1530 hours

The ruins of a once-great city were about to fall to the invader. In his Fuehrerbunker under what was left of the Reich Chancellery, Adolf Hitler could hear the gunfire as, street by street, the Red Army closed in on him. All hope was gone. With Eva Braun, his mistress of twelve years and bride for less than two days, he entered his private apartment. The door closed. Standing outside were Martin Bormann, Hitler's secretary and head of the Party bureaucracy; his long-serving adjutant, Otto Guensche; his valet, Heinz Linge; and his personal bodyguard, Rochus Misch. They waited in silence. After some minutes, Linge, with Bormann beside him, opened the door. They found Hitler face down at a table. Blood was dripping from his right temple. Beside him, a picture of his mother as a young woman; behind, a portrait of Frederick the Great. His Walther pistol was by his foot.

Eva Braun was slumped over the armrest of a couch. Linge noticed the scent of burnt almonds. Cyanide. Guensche made for the conference room where others of Hitler's entourage were gathered. On the way, he bumped into Erich Kempka, Hitler's chauffeur.

'What's going on?'

'The Chief is dead.'

Among the select few who went to view the scene were Nazi propaganda supremo Joseph Goebbels and head of the Hitler Youth Artur Axmann. Then Linge and another SS man wrapped the late Fuehrer in an army blanket and he was carried out. Hitler's bloodstained head was covered but Misch, who was standing by, recognised the black trousers: 'His legs were sticking out as they carried him past me. Someone shouted, "Hurry upstairs, they're burning the boss."'[1]

Hitler's body, along with that of Eva Braun, was carried up four flights of stairs to the emergency exit to the Chancellery garden. Put in a shallow grave, the two corpses were doused with gasoline. Returning to the bunker, Linge came back with a thick roll of papers. Bormann lit the papers and threw the torch on to the bodies. As the funeral pyre blazed, the small group of mourners, sheltering in the bunker doorway, raised their arms in the Nazi salute.

*

Three hours after Hitler had ended his life, Bormann radioed Grand Admiral Karl Doenitz, recently appointed supreme commander of all land and sea forces in northern Germany and the Baltic, along with the Netherlands, Denmark and Norway. Waiting on developments at his headquarters at Ploen, a lakeside town 150 miles from Berlin and not far from the Danish border, Doenitz had no need to be told that Berlin was lost and he fully expected to hear that Hitler was dead. But the message put before him by his adjutant, Commander Walter Luedde-Neurath, made no mention of Hitler's suicide. Judged by his own future, the news for Doenitz was more startling.

'The Fuehrer has appointed you, Herr Grossadmiral, as his successor. Written full powers follow. With immediate effect you should take all measures which seem appropriate.'

Why Doenitz? It is a question that Germany's most senior naval officer must have asked himself. He was, above all, a professional. Neither allies nor enemies ever doubted his talents as a military commander. As a political leader, however, his credentials were less apparent. A regular attender at Hitler's strategy conferences, his advice was welcomed and trusted on naval matters but he was by no means a Nazi ideologue. Until 1944 when the bomb plot to assassinate Hitler gave added value to badges of allegiance, he was not even a Party member. Others, surely, were better qualified and better placed to take on the succession. On the other hand, Doenitz must have recognised that a process of elimination had raised his status.

Hermann Goering was the first to fall from grace. The founder of the Luftwaffe and originator of the Gestapo, along with concentration camps, he was designated heir apparent in September 1939. But Goering had not lived up to expectations. His failure to bomb Britain out of the war or to break Allied air superiority had relegated him to the ranks of those who were deemed to have betrayed the Reich. Hitler bade him a chilly farewell on the evening of 20 April when Goering left Berlin for his Bavarian estate, part of the Nazi enclosure that included Berchtesgaden, Hitler's mountain hideaway.

On that night, as if to underline Goering's failure as Luftwaffe chief, British and American air forces delivered their last massive air raid on the centre of Berlin. Doenitz, with Field Marshal Wilhelm Keitel, Hitler's Chief of Armed Forces, and their wives watched the spectacle from Doenitz's service quarters. As Keitel recalled:

During this final heavy bombardment in perfect and sunny weather the already badly afflicted Reich Chancellery building escaped further damage; our own fighter squadrons did nothing to beat off the attack on Berlin, and the anti-aircraft defences were powerless against an enemy attacking from such a height. The raid lasted almost two hours, the bombers parading overhead in tight formation as though it were a peacetime air display, dropping the bombs in perfect unison.[2]

Despite everything, Goering kept faith in what he assumed to be his destiny. He waited confidently for the call to action. It came, or so he believed, on 22 April, two days after Hitler's 56th birthday. By then, the Fuehrer had come to accept what all others in his tattered administration had long accepted, that the massive counter-attack to drive the Russians from Berlin was not going to happen. Bad news had been followed by news that was even worse. The advancing Allied armies east and west, having joined forces at the River Elbe, had split the Reich in half. Everywhere, German defences were crumbling.

In maniacal rage, Hitler vented his frustration on the liars and traitors who had betrayed his mission. Then, exhausted, he declared that he would defend Berlin to the last. 'I will never leave Berlin; I will defend the city with my dying breath.' Keitel and General Alfred Jodl, Chief of Operations, were told to leave for Berchtesgaden. Hitler had no further orders to give.

'There is no question of fighting now. There's nothing left to fight with. If it's a question of negotiating, Goering can do that better than I.'

Hitler's apparent abdication soon filtered through to Goering, who responded to the invitation, as he put it in a telegram to Hitler, to 'take over, at once, the total leadership of the Reich, with full freedom of action at home and abroad'.

It soon turned out that Goering had acted prematurely. In calmer mood, Hitler either forgot what he had said or had come to regret his outburst. As one of the few close advisers left in the bunker, Martin Bormann, a long-time Goering rival, fed Hitler's suspicions that Goering had joined the ever-lengthening list of back-stabbers. Resentment at his worthless pretensions to military glory, not to mention his sybaritic lifestyle, boiled over into a vicious condemnation of the Nazi crown prince and a demand that he should resign at once from all his offices. Without waiting for a response, Bormann, presumably with Hitler's approval, ordered the arrest of Goering for high treason. For general consumption, it was announced that the Reichsmarschall had retired for health reasons.

What then of Heinrich Himmler, whose power was rooted in the SS and the Gestapo? The master of prevarication and self-delusion, Himmler had been quick to join the exit from Berlin but remained in easy reach at Schloss Ziethen, 30km north-west of the city. There he agonised over his next move.

The Reichsfuehrer relied heavily on the guidance of Walter Schellenberg, his head of foreign intelligence and the youngest of the SS generals. Possessed of a passion if not a talent for political intrigue, Schellenberg was convinced that he could move his boss into prime position for negotiating peace with honour. As early as February, the architect of the Holocaust had signalled his readiness to break ranks by coming to a deal with Count Folke Bernadotte, vice-chairman of the Swedish Red Cross, on the care of Scandinavians held in German camps. The prospect of opening direct talks with Eisenhower, touched on tangentially, was discounted by Bernadotte unless, of course, Himmler was empowered to speak for the Reich. Schellenberg was sure this could be arranged.

But despite several more meetings, it was not until Goering's downfall that the persistent Schellenberg was able to persuade his master to pursue his fantasies by turning, once again, to Count Bernadotte. The critical encounter took place at the Swedish consulate in Luebeck. With his horn-rimmed spectacles, recalled Bernadotte, the sinister Himmler brought to mind 'a harmless schoolteacher from the country'. The meeting had barely started when bombs fell and the lights went out. The strain on Himmler was all too obvious. He was 'indescribably tired and nervous', said Bernadotte, 'and fighting hard to maintain his outer calm'. But he had come to a decision. Himmler stated:

> It is very probable that Hitler is already dead and, if not, he very probably will be within the next few days. Berlin is surrounded and it is only a matter of days until it falls. The last three times we three have met you urged me to end the war. I agreed with you that the situation was hopeless, that the war must stop, and that Germany must admit she is beaten. But I have not been able to see how I could break my oath to the Fuehrer. Now the situation is different. I recognise that Germany is defeated.

He continued:

> In this new situation I have a free hand. In order to protect as much of Germany as possible from a Russian invasion I am willing to capitulate on the Western Front and to let the Western Powers' troops advance as rapidly as possible eastwards. Conversely I am not prepared to capitulate on the Eastern Front.[3]

Bernadotte knew Himmler's aims were hopeless but while refusing to contact Eisenhower, which would have compromised his neutrality, he agreed to pass on the offer, via his government, to the American and British representatives in Stockholm. When Bernadotte set off for home, Schellenberg went with him part of the way. Under orders from Himmler he was to have one last try at getting Bernadotte to appeal directly to Eisenhower.

> However [recalled Schellenberg], at our parting on the road near Waren in Mecklenburg, Count Bernadotte said to me: 'The Reichsfuehrer no longer understands the realities of his own situation. I cannot help him any more. He should have taken Germany's affairs into his own hands after my first visit. I can hold out little chance for him now. And you, my dear Schellenberg, would be wiser to think of yourself.' I did not know what to reply to this.[4]

Schellenberg drove back to Hohenlychen, the hospital and convalescent home reserved for the SS, slept for two hours, and was then called to Himmler at about 12.30 p.m. on the following day, 22 April.

> He was still in bed, the picture of misery, and said that he felt ill. All I could say was that there was nothing more I could do for him; it was up to him. He had got to take some action. At lunch we discussed the military situation in Berlin, which was steadily growing worse.
>
> At about four o'clock, having convinced him that it would be unwise to drive to Berlin, we drove towards Wustrow. In Loewenberg we were caught in a traffic jam, troops having become involved with the unending columns of fleeing

7

civilians which blocked all the roads between Berlin and Mecklenburg. As we drove on, Himmler said to me for the first time, 'Schellenberg, I dread what is to come.'[5]

Bernadotte duly reported to his foreign minister who passed on the message to the American and British representatives in Stockholm. The response was easily predicted. The Allies would accept only an unconditional surrender to the three powers on all fronts.

By now, rumours of Himmler's bid to end the war and to create, in effect, an anti-Soviet alliance, were front-page news. Apparent confirmation came with a report on Radio Atlantic, a supposedly 'free German' underground station but in fact operated by British intelligence, which spiced up Himmler's role in the negotiations with claims that his sole purpose was to supplant Hitler. And this was precisely what the Fuehrer himself concluded when news of Himmler's 'betrayal' reached him on the evening of 27 April.

It was one item in a catalogue of disasters. Early that day, Berlin's two airports, Gatow and Tempelhof, were lost, cutting off all communication and supplies by air. For Hitler's evening briefing General Weidling, Berlin's commandant, reported on the near-exhaustion of ammunition, food and medical supplies. He proposed a breakout from the 'Berlin pocket'. But to what avail? As Hitler commented, they would simply be going from one pocket to another. At midnight, Admiral Voss, liaison officer for Doenitz, telegraphed from the bunker: 'We hold on to the end'. An order was given for Himmler's arrest.

After the toppling of the two leading contenders, it was still not clear that Doenitz was next in line. But the list was shortening. Of other candidates who came to mind, Goebbels had the strongest claim, if he chose to press it. For those who knew Goebbels, that was unlikely. The man who had shaped the Nazi myth could not imagine acting independently of his proudest creation, a leader who could do no wrong.

With a stronger sense of self-preservation, Martin Bormann, the arch intriguer who had long cast himself as the power behind the throne, may have had dreams of the succession. His talent for command, however, was not obvious. As for Joachim von Ribbentrop, his defects were even more glaring. Whatever misplaced respect Hitler had once had for his foreign minister, his cock-eyed schemes for a diplomatic breakthrough had stripped him of all credibility.

That left Albert Speer. Making for Hamburg, he flew out of Berlin on 21 April. It says much for his relationship with Hitler that he was allowed to go. In his capacity as armaments minister with all-embracing control of the war economy, Speer made no secret of his conviction that having lost the war, the German people should be urged to protect whatever was left of their commercial and social infrastructure. Hitler would have none of this. For him, the only substitute for victory was annihilation. On 19 March he had ordered the destruction of all factories, water and electrical installations, railways and bridges at risk of falling into enemy hands. Four days later, the gauleiters, Hitler's regional hatchet men, were given detailed instructions on implementing the scorched earth policy.

Fully expecting retribution, Speer voiced his opposition. But the Fuehrer retained a soft spot for the youngest of the Nazi big barons and his favourite architect with whom he had planned and partly implemented a monumental rebuilding of Berlin. When Speer left the bunker, on the night following Hitler's birthday, he carried with him a written plea for common sense that he planned to broadcast from Hamburg. Enlisting the help of his friend Karl Kaufmann, gauleiter for Hamburg, Speer recorded his speech but then decided to keep it under wraps until the drama had played out in the Fuehrerbunker. As Speer noted: 'Once more Hitler had succeeded in paralyzing me psychically ... I justified my change of mind on the grounds that it would be wrong and pointless to try to intervene in the course of the tragedy.'[6]

Speer now made for Eutin in Schleswig-Holstein, where he set up a base not far from the Doenitz headquarters. But left to himself the old magnetism in Berlin recovered its power and he was soon drawn back to the bunker. He finally took his leave on 24 April.

> By now it was about three o'clock in the morning. Hitler was awake again. I sent word that I wanted to bid him farewell. The day had worn me out, and I was afraid that I would not be able to control myself at our parting. Trembling, the prematurely aged man stood before me for the last time; the man to whom I had dedicated my life twelve years before. I was both moved and confused. For his part, he showed no emotion when we confronted one another. His words were as cold as his hand: 'So, you're leaving? Good. *Auf Wiedersehen.*' No regards to my family, no wishes, no thanks, no farewell.

In his last words to Hitler, Speer talked of coming back while knowing it was impossible. But he did leave Hitler with a piece of advice that had long-reaching consequences. He suggested to the Fuehrer that in looking for a successor, Doenitz might fit the bill.[7]

In truth, Hitler was beginning to run out of options. Of the generals of any stature, most were dead or discredited. Once a favourite, Field Marshal Kesselring, commanding German forces in the south, was thought to have joined the lobby for peace at any price. A likelier prospect was Field Marshal Ferdinand Schoerner who had proved his worth by slowing the Russian juggernaut as it advanced on the Baltic states. Noted for his brutality towards his own troops when they fell short of his exacting standards, Schoerner was the last promotion to field marshal under the Nazi regime. Goebbels praised him for his 'superb political insight' which was one way of saying that he knew how to disguise unpalatable facts – making defeat sound like victory. But Schoerner was too focused for the top job, even assuming that he ever aspired to it – a long shot indeed.

Doenitz had more going for him. As chief of the German navy and as the architect of a mighty force of submarines that had constituted the single greatest threat to the Allied war effort, he had avoided the flak that Hitler had showered on the land forces. Doenitz was good at exuding confidence. Refusing to buckle under pressure, his genuine protestations of loyalty with the underlying assumption that somehow all would be well, were a steadying influence on an otherwise chaotic administration. In charge of the only military sector where recovery was remotely possible, Doenitz held out the promise of a new generation of super submarines that even at this late stage could turn the fortunes of war. His messages to his staff stressed duty, pride and honour. 'The Navy must stand as an unshakeable fighting entity. It will never bow to the enemy yoke.' Rather than submit to defeat, Doenitz professed a wish to die in battle. He refused to associate himself with Speer's plea for an acceptance of the inevitable.

Even so, Speer detected in Doenitz a rational intelligence that would, in the last resort, hold him back from the Wagnerian finale, an explosive descent into purgatory that Hitler wished on Germany. And he was right. The live Hitler held his spell over both of them. His death changed everything.

CHAPTER TWO

The briefest study of the life of Karl Doenitz is a warning, if any could possibly be needed, against an uncritical devotion to a political cause. But given the mess that was Europe during the inter-war years, many intelligent young people were drawn to an authoritarian rule as an alternative to shambolic democracy. The choice was communism or fascism. Doenitz chose fascism.

Born in 1891, Doenitz was a child of Prussian yeoman stock. As he would write in his post-war memoirs, 'My ancestors had for centuries succeeded each other as landowners and mayors of the village in the old Germanic frontier settlement on the Elbe.'[1] The young Doenitz was inspired by the Bismarckian vision of Germany as the dominant European power. This image was reinforced by a patriotic, male-orientated family, his mother having died before his fourth birthday. Karl and his elder brother Friedrich revered their father, who lived by hard work, thrift and 'duty fulfilment as the highest moral virtue'. As Karl put it towards the end of his life, 'The acceptance of discipline came quite naturally to me.' A lonely child, one who did not make friends easily, Karl's imagination was fired by the macho heroes who populated boys' books. Adventure at sea had a particular appeal. In 1910, when Doenitz was eighteen, he joined the navy as a sea cadet.

The Imperial German Navy had started in a small way as a

coastal defence force commanded by officers seconded from the army. By the early 1880s Germany was still in the minor league of naval powers. Wilhelm II, who became Kaiser in 1888, was determined to change that. The brief for Admiral Alfred von Tirpitz was to build up naval strength to match that of Britain while seeming not to challenge Britain's supremacy at sea. It was soon apparent that those were contradictory aims.

With Germany steadily chipping away at Britain's reputation as the workshop of the world, rivalry and antagonism between the two countries covered a lot of ground – and water. The first clash at sea came with Britain's war against the Dutch separatists in South Africa. Suspected of supplying arms to the insurgents, three German ships were stopped and searched. Public outrage in Germany was made to justify doubling the size of the fleet. With the coming of the First World War, active service for Lieutenant Doenitz took him to the Mediterranean and the Black Sea where an encounter with a Russian dreadnought earned him the Iron Cross. In 1916 he transferred to submarines. His leadership qualities soon gained him his first command.

Doenitz quickly caught on to the potential for U-boats to disrupt British trade routes. Even with the sinking of the *Lusitania* in May 1915 with the death of 128 American citizens, a critical turning point for US opinion on Germany, the U-boat campaign against Allied shipping was counted as a triumph for the German navy. The introduction of merchant shipping convoys with destroyer escorts cut the U-boat success rate but, as Doenitz was quick to spot, a counter-strategy of having U-boats working together to mount combined attacks (what became known as his 'wolf-packs') did much to restore the balance.

An unsought opportunity for Doenitz to contemplate the future of submarine warfare and his own future in the service came at the tail end of the war when, a month into a new command, his U-boat was sunk by British warships off Malta. It happened when he made a risky attack on a convoy while submerged at periscope depth.

> Thanks to a fault in the longitudinal stability of my boat we suddenly found ourselves submerged and standing on our heads. The batteries spilled over, the lights went out, and in darkness we plunged on into the depths. Beneath us we had water in plenty – about 1200 or 1500 fathoms of it. 180 or 200 feet, however, was the maximum depth our pressure hull permitted. I ordered all tanks to be blown, stopped, then went full astern with rudder hard over in the hope of stopping the boat's downward plunge. My First Lieutenant, Muessen, shone his torch on to the pressure gauge in the conning tower. The indicator was still moving swiftly to the right. The boat, then, was still going deeper and deeper; at last the indicator stopped quivering for a moment between 270 and 300 feet and then started to go back at speed. The blowing of my tanks with compressed air had just done the trick. But now, the U-boat was much too light. Like a stick plunged under water and then sud-denly released, it shot upwards and out of the water, to arrive with a crash on the surface. I tore open the conning tower hatch to find that we were right in the middle of the convoy. Sirens were howling all round us. The merchant ships opened fire with guns mounted on their sterns while the destroyers, firing furiously, came tearing down on us. To crash dive was impossible. My supply of compressed air was exhausted, the boat had been hit and she was making water. I gave the order, 'All hands, abandon ship'.[2]

Fished out of the water, Doenitz was taken to a POW camp near Sheffield.

He faced a year of humiliation. The news from Germany was of defeat on all fronts while from the Kaiserliche Marine it was even worse – defeat from within. A last desperate effort by the navy to score a victory at sea ended when crews mutinied against orders to sail. A sense of pride, albeit somewhat perverse, was restored when, in June 1919, the entire German fleet was scuttled as it lay at anchor at Scapa Flow. A month later Doenitz was repatriated. He later claimed that he had secured an early release by feigning insanity but given that he was inclined to embroider his anecdotes it is more likely that he simply made such a nuisance of himself that the authorities were only too glad to be rid of him.

Back in Germany, Doenitz rejoined the renamed Reichsmarine with the rank of lieutenant. On the face of it, this was not the smartest of career moves. The Treaty of Versailles tried to put the lid on German naval ambitions. While some allowance was made for balancing the Russian presence in the Baltic, there was no compromise on 'the construction or acquisition of submarines, even for commercial purposes'. The ban was total. But it was an imposition that was unlikely to stick once Germany began to regain her commercial strength. Before resuming his naval service Doenitz was confidently assured by his superiors that within two years Germany would once more have its own U-boat fleet. The promise was all he needed to sign on:

> During the war I had become an enthusiastic submariner. I had been fascinated by that unique characteristic of the submarine service, which requires a submariner to stand on his own feet and sets him a task in the great spaces of the oceans, fulfilment of which demands a stout heart and

ready skill; I was fascinated by that unique spirit of comradeship engendered by destiny and hardship shared in the community of a U-boat crew, where every man's well-being was in the hands of all and where every single man was an indispensible part of the whole. Every submariner, I am sure, has experienced in his heart the glow of the open sea and the task entrusted to him, has felt himself to be as rich as a king and would change places with no man.[3]

Throughout the 1920s intense but fruitless international efforts were made to reconcile German demands for equality with correspondingly strident appeals, largely from France, for security. Diplomatic confusion and weakness of resolve gave more than adequate cover for Germany to circumvent Versailles and rearm. For the navy, private and public finance was raised to produce a new generation of warships. At this stage, submarines were still beyond limits but under cover of a Dutch dummy company, German engineers built two submarines for Spain. Meanwhile, Doenitz was honing his tactical skills in command of torpedo boats. In one exercise, which marked him for certain promotion, he was reckoned to have destroyed an entire convoy. In 1933, the year Hitler came to power, a training centre for submariners was established at Kiel.

The breakthrough for the Reichsmarine, soon to be renamed yet again, this time to become the Kriegsmarine, was the 1935 Naval Treaty with Britain. After a lot of diplomatic huffing and puffing, the treaty represented an extraordinary climbdown by Britain. In quick order, Germany was given the go-ahead to build up its navy to 21 cruisers and 64 destroyers, around 35 per cent of Royal Navy tonnage. Such was the sense of urgency – or panic – that no one thought to consult France or Italy, the other two

European naval powers. Nor was any account taken of the views of Sweden and Denmark where there was an understandable fear of German dominance in the Baltic.[4]

By way of feeble excuse on the British side, it was said that because Germany had already repudiated the Versailles Treaty with the creation of an air force, an army of 36 divisions and the introduction of conscription, it made sense to come to a deal on relative naval strength. Supporters of the treaty argued, as Doenitz was later to claim, that it 'clearly showed Germany did not reckon with a war against England as she voluntarily renounced arming against English sea power'.[5] In that case, rather more attention should have been given to details. Incredibly, virtually no attempt was made to limit the building of submarines.

Just eleven days after the signing of the Naval Treaty, the heavily guarded sheds built at Kiel in 1934 were opened to reveal the first new German U-boats. Another eleven submarines were under construction. All of them had been commissioned well before the Treaty. The first U-boat flotilla of six vessels came under the command of the newly promoted Captain Doenitz. Soon afterwards, he was made Commander-in-Chief of the entire submarine arm. Almost immediately, he began lobbying for a bigger share of the naval budget.

British intelligence had a fair idea of what was going on. That the warning signals were ignored was the result of a fatal mix of overconfidence and ignorance. The first mistake was to assume that the development of Asdic, a sonic echo revealing the bearing and range of a detected object, had made submarines virtually obsolete. Putting its faith in Asdic, in 1937 the Admiralty declared that 'the U-boat will never again be capable of confronting us with the problem we faced in 1917'.

But Asdic was an imperfect device. What was thought to be a

U-boat on the offensive was just as likely to be a school of fish or a wreck. Then again, Asdic could not identify a submarine on the surface or even underwater at close range. The shortcomings were all the more consequential given that the submarine, despite its name, was still essentially a surface craft which submerged only to avoid danger or, a rarity, to make a daylight attack.

It was the submarine's efficiency as a surface craft that had been raised to a point where the machines were virtually unrecognisable to veterans of the First World War. Torpedoes no longer left a tell-tale swell when launched or an easily observed wake on course to their target. Magnetic firing devices allowed for detonation under a ship's keel where the torpedo could do maximum damage. With more efficient batteries, the U-boat was able to stay underwater longer and operate noiselessly. Long-range radio allowed tacti-cal planners to coordinate activities at sea from their land-based headquarters.

But the British and American navies were slow to catch on to the submarine as a war machine of enormous potential. Doenitz was way ahead in his thinking when he argued, with Britain in mind, that his submarines were capable of starving an enemy into submission by cutting off food imports and other supplies by sea. The figures supported him. In 1939 Britain was importing by sea an annual total of 55 million tons of supplies, including all its oil and half its food and raw materials. The Merchant Navy had around 2,500 ships at sea at any given time. All were vulnerable to U-boat attack.

A strong but not always tactful advocate for his cause, Doenitz touched on the sensitivities of senior officers of the old school who favoured a battle fleet on the British model. Leading the con-servatives was Erich Raeder, Commander-in-Chief of the German navy and soon to be Grand Admiral, who professed admiration for Doenitz and who, indeed, did most to give the younger man a higher profile, but who could never quite make the leap in strategic imagination that was second nature to Doenitz.

That said, Raeder's position was not entirely irrational. The case for accommodating the submarine force within a wide range of naval weaponry rested on the assumption, shared by Doenitz, that war with Britain was not an immediate prospect. Rather, the focus was on France as the likeliest adversary. Thus, if war did come it would be fought on land and in the air with the navy in a supporting role. In this scenario, the surface fleet would have more to do than the submarines.

In arguments with Doenitz over funding priorities, Raeder could declare convincingly that it was hard enough competing with the Wehrmacht and Luftwaffe for scarce resources without parading divisions within his own ranks. Assured by Hitler that if there was to be war with Britain it would not break out before 1944 at the earliest,[6] Raeder put his faith in the 'Z Plan' to expand Germany's surface fleet to a point where it could contend with the Royal Navy on equal terms. He was supported by Hitler who visualised great battleships as symbols of Nazi power. The fault in Raeder's strategy was in taking Hitler at his word.

So it was that in September 1939 when Germany invaded Poland and Britain and France declared war, the Kriegsmarine was far from ready to do battle. Just a month earlier, Doenitz had staked his reputation on the claim that with 300 ocean-going U-boats and without any assistance from the army or air force, he could force Britain into early submission. Successful exercises in the Baltic and Atlantic had so impressed Raeder that he agreed to amend the Z Plan to give Doenitz what he wanted. But before decisions could be translated into action, the Z Plan was consigned to the archive. With a meagre 56 submarines, ill-suited to action beyond coastal waters, and only 49 of them ready for operational duties, there was little chance of Doenitz meeting his monthly target of sinking 600,000 tons of British shipping – the total calculated to bring about a decisive victory.[7]

The most effective U-boat available to Doenitz was the Type VII. It could accommodate twelve to fourteen torpedoes, had a diving time of 20 seconds and a maximum speed of 16 knots. But it could carry no more than 67 tons of fuel oil, which limited its radius of action to 6,200 miles.

Doenitz was further constrained by technical faults with the firing of torpedoes. Detonators had a high failure rate while steering fins were found to be vulnerable to changes in air pressure when submarines were diving or surfacing. The higher the pressure in the chamber, the deeper a torpedo ran. As a result, torpedoes often passed harmlessly under their targets.[8] On 31 October, Doenitz reported in his war diary, 'At least thirty per cent of our torpedoes are duds'. It took a change at the top of the Torpedo Inspectorate for the problems to be recognised and rectified, a process that dragged on for more than a year.

The challenge for Doenitz to deliver on his promises was all the greater for the lack of a naval air arm. This meant that the Atlantic shipping routes had to be reconnoitred by the U-boats alone. 'Yet,' wrote Doenitz, 'the number of U-boats was too small for the complete surveillance of the open sea … once contact was made with a convoy the attack succeeded every time. The difficulty lay in the finding and not in the attacking.'[9] As chief of the Luftwaffe, Hermann Goering was disinclined to make concessions. While he offered to provide nine long-range reconnaissance squadrons, the promise was not kept. Raeder was told bluntly that he would 'never have the naval air force he so much desired'.[10]

Despite the limitations, Doenitz, a rear admiral from October

1939 (he was promoted to vice admiral a year later), pitched in with whatever was to hand. In the first four months of the war, 47 British and French ships were lost to German U-boats, surface raiders and mines. With properly functioning torpedoes the number would have doubled.

Guenther Prien, captain of *U-47*, was the first of Doenitz's new breed of young and daring submariners to sink a British merchantman. The *Bosnia* was caught off the north coast of Spain on 5 September. The crew was picked up by a Norwegian ship as the *Bosnia*, having caught fire, was finished off by a torpedo. Prien claimed two more British steamers before returning to base at Wilhelmshaven. Patrolling off the Hebrides, the *Ark Royal*, Britain's most modern aircraft carrier, had a narrow escape when three torpedoes from *U-39* exploded prematurely. The *Courageous*, a First World War cruiser rebuilt as an aircraft carrier in the 1920s, was less fortunate. Three days after the attack on the *Ark Royal*, *U-29* came so close to *Courageous* it could hardly miss. With two torpedoes finding their mark, it took only fifteen minutes for the ship to capsize with a loss of 519 lives.

Doenitz had bigger targets in his sights. He needed a master stroke to set against the sinking of the *Athena* on the very first day of the war between Germany and Britain. The *Athena* was a medium-sized passenger liner on its way to Montreal with a full load of passengers only too eager to get away from Europe before the real fighting started. Captain James Cook assumed immunity from attack for an unarmed vessel. Germany had taken a pledge against unrestricted submarine warfare and Hitler was wary of upsetting neutral countries, the US in particular.

Unfortunately, the message had failed to get through to Fritz-Julius Lemp, captain of *U-30*, who judged the *Athena* to be fair game. She succumbed to a single torpedo. Most of the

118 passengers who died were trapped between the lower and main decks after the stairways collapsed. Among them were 28 Americans. Propaganda efforts to cover up for the Kriegsmarine including Goebbels' claim that the liner had been sunk on Churchill's orders to sway neutral opinion against Germany did nothing to stem the flood of hostile commentary from across the Atlantic. Memories of the *Lusitania* were still fresh.

The objective Doenitz had in mind, one that would restore the prestige of his service and his own standing with Hitler, was no less than to strike at the British fleet at its main anchorage at Scapa Flow. Guenther Prien was selected to lead this bold, some might have said suicidal, mission. *U-47* set out from Wilhelmshaven on 8 October to make a surface crossing of the North Sea en route to the Orkneys. There were seven entrances to the Flow, all heavily defended, but air reconnaissance had shown a gap 50 feet wide at Kirk Sound between the island of Mainland and the islet of Lamb Holm. Cables obstructed half the entrance but there was just enough space for a submarine to squeeze through. This the *U-47* did around midnight on 13/14 October.

Since the Home Fleet was out at sea in a fruitless search for the German navy, there were fewer targets than Prien had been led to expect. But the *Royal Oak*, a semi-retired battleship which lacked the speed for front-line duty, was at anchor, her crew blithely unaware that they were in easy range of *U-47*. Four torpedoes struck home. The *Royal Oak* exploded, turned turtle and sank, taking with it over 800 seamen. With a 10-mile-an-hour current running against *U-47*, Prien had more trouble getting out of Scapa Flow than getting in.

Prien was well on his way home when the Admiralty acknowledged belatedly that the *Royal Oak* had met its end not by accident, as first assumed, but by design. Churchill recognised 'a remarkable exploit of professional skill and daring'. So too did Doenitz, who was on the quayside at Wilhelmshaven to welcome the crew and to bestow on each of them an Iron Cross – Prien's being the Iron Cross, First Class. They all then flew to Berlin for a victory parade through the streets. The 'Bull of Scapa Flow', as Prien was now known, was received by Hitler who upgraded his decoration to the Knight's Cross of the Iron Cross, Germany's highest military decoration.

Prien became the first German war hero, feted wherever he went. An autobiography, suitably embellished by ghostwriters, was wildly popular. Under Prien's command, U-47 went on to sink 31 Allied ships before she was reported missing in March 1941. What happened precisely has never emerged but the entire crew were presumed to have died. Prien was aged 33.

While Doenitz was rapidly gaining credibility he had yet to be given the freedom to mount random attacks on merchant shipping. But it was not long before neutral sensitivities took second place to the main objective of cutting the British lifeline to the US. In January 1940, Hitler agreed to the sinking of neutral ships without warning where the sinking might be attributed to mines.[11] With the occupation of Norway and the fall of Holland and France in May 1940, the Kriegsmarine came into possession of ports that extended U-boats' operational range by bringing them closer to Atlantic shipping. Said Doenitz, 'The sea routes were now, so to speak, at the front door'. More U-boat commanders joined the ranks of national heroes. Volunteers lined up to join a service that had the pick of naval talent.

In charge of training was Hans-Georg von Friedeburg. Promoted to rear admiral in 1942, Friedeburg was to have a leading role in the winding-up of the Nazi regime. For now, however, it was his job to keep up the supply of dedicated officers and crews for the newly commissioned U-boats. Doenitz had high regard for his 'true friend and loyal subordinate' who proved to be a 'particularly gifted organiser and a man endowed with an exceptional capacity for work'.[12]

By the end of May 1940, U-boats had sunk 241 ships totalling 853,000 tons. In June alone another 250,000 tons was sent to the depths. Given the small number of U-boats at sea and their less-than-perfect weaponry, this was quite an achievement. From July to the end of 1940 was known as *die Glueckliche Zeit* ('the happy time') for German submariners as they scored a succession of hits against British shipping. The victims included the *Empress of Britain* which, at 43,200 tons, was and remains the largest ship ever sunk by a submarine.

Inevitably, the kudos went to a handful of U-boat 'aces' who qualified for the distinction after sinking 50,000 tons. Following Prien came Otto Kretschmer, known as the 'Wolf of the Atlantic', being among the early practitioners of 'wolf-pack' tactics, Doenitz's answer to the growing strength and effectiveness of convoy escorts. Submarines were deployed in groups to disrupt convoys and disperse their destroyer escorts. Another leading ace was Joachim Schepke, who sank seven ships totalling over 50,000 tons from one convoy in four hours.[13]

If celebrity status was hard earned, so too was the high regard in which all young submariners were held. What it meant to sign on for U-boat service was vividly demonstrated in a lecture given by Wolfgang Lueth, an ace commander credited with sinking 47 ships amounting to in excess of 225,000 tons. He spoke at Weimar on 17 December 1943. Doenitz was in the audience.

Lueth wasted no time on preliminaries. 'It is my job to sink ships,' he announced before pitching into his experiences of four years at sea. Life aboard he described as 'unnatural and unhealthy'.

There is no change between day and night, for the lights burn all the time inside the boat. There are no Sundays and no weekdays, and there is no regular change of seasons. Life is monotonous and without rhythm. Added to this is the change of climate, which affects even the healthiest man. The boat passes from the trade wind zones to the tropics, from humid regions to clear weather zones, touching one climate zone after the other on route to and from her zone of operations. There is no regular time for sleeping, since most of the fighting is done at night. The stench on board, the racket and the motion of the ship all affect morale.

Success was the great morale booster:

At one time I ran smack into a convoy in the middle of the night. I barely dodged a destroyer and sneaked close by a steamer into the middle of the convoy. Visibility was poor. I slowed down. After I had given my orders, I called the chief engineer to explain what was going on above. He then relayed the information to the crew over the loud-speaker. Since the men knew what the game was I did not have to drive them on. Before the boat turned for the attack I called down: 'The run starts!' This not only gives the crew a heightened feeling of confidence, but also prepares them for the climax of the attack. When the torpedo is on its way I add: 'It will be at least forty seconds before it hits!' When the entire boat counts together, the victory bottle is uncorked in anticipation and the victory march is prepared for playing over the loud-speaker. The seconds pass. And if after two minutes there is still no explosion, the waiting ended with 'Shit!' If we manage to keep on the surface, a few deserving crew members are allowed to come up on the bridge for a moment to watch the sinking steamer. By day, while at periscope depth, there are always opportunities to let some of the men look through the periscope. In the heat of battle such things are not possible.

For the daily routine, Lueth tried to maintain the rhythm of life on shore.

Since the change from day to night cannot ordinarily be felt on a submarine it must be brought about by artificial means. During supper the dim lights are switched on, and we have evening concert on records from half an hour before the watch changes until half an hour afterwards. Sunday is always a special occasion and begins with a recorded programme, initiated regularly by the song 'Yes, this is my Sunday fun, to stay in bed at least until ten'. The evening concert always ends with 'Abendlied' sung by the Regensburger Domspatzen. I tell my men: 'If you do put on a clean shirt every once and a while, don't do it on Tuesday or Friday; do it on Sunday, so at least some of you will run around in Sunday clothes.' Every man brings along enough illustrated magazines so that it is possible to distribute six new ones every Sunday. We arrange it so that the last papers are given out when we reach port.

But there were limits:

I have not permitted the men to hang pictures of nude girls on the bulkheads and over their bunks. If you are hungry you wouldn't paint bread on the wall. It is also advisable to leaf through the books aboard every once and a while, time and again you turn up one which can be thrown overboard because it appeals only to man's lower instincts. … Similarly, it is forbidden to hang the picture of the Fuehrer on the left side of the bulkhead in the officers' mess and on the right side one of a girl from a box of candy which they bought in Paris. That shows bad taste. The same is true if they like to listen to American and British jazz. Whether they like it or not has nothing to do with the matter.

Conditions were hardest on U-boats adapted for long voyages.

This [adaptation] was achieved by storing diesel oil in tanks meant for drinking and washing water, trimming and ballast, and in jerrycans stuffed into every cranny on the outward voyage. One of the two lavatories aboard had to be used as a food store on the way out. Drinking water was carried in cans, making the crammed 750-ton boats even more uncomfortable.[14]

The compensation for devotion to duty at sea was the chance to 'live like a god' between patrols. With pay and allowances double that of other seafarers, submariners could afford the finest food and wine in the French hostelries along the coast. Rest and relaxation centres were set up in requisitioned hotels and chateaux. 'Live and be merry' was the philosophy, with the inevitable addendum, 'For tomorrow, well, who knows?'

America's entry into the war was a golden opportunity for Doenitz to show what his submariners could do, given the necessary resources. Operation Drumbeat targeted shipping along the east coast of the United States. The US Navy was caught totally unprepared:

> The U-boats found that conditions there were almost exactly those of normal peace-time. The coast was not blacked-out, and the towns were a blaze of bright lights. The lights, both in lighthouses and on buoys, shone forth, though perhaps a little less brightly than usual. Shipping followed the normal peace-time routes and carried the normal lights. Although five weeks had passed since the declaration of war, very few anti-submarine measures appeared to have been introduced. There were, admittedly, anti-submarine patrols, but they were wholly lacking in experience. Single destroyers, for example, sailed up and down the traffic lanes with such regularity that the U-boats were quickly able to work out the time-table being followed. They knew exactly when the destroyers would return, and the knowledge only added to their sense of security during the intervening period. A few attacks with depth charges were delivered by American patrol vessels; but the attackers did not display the requisite perseverance, and the attacks were abandoned too quickly, although quite often, thanks to the shallow water, they stood a good chance of succeeding. The aircraft crews employed on anti-submarine work were also untrained.[15]

Merchant vessels used open radio, frequently signalling their positions, an invitation to U-boats to manoeuvre to maximum advantage. The war diary of Lieutenant Commander Hardegen made his voyage across the Atlantic sound like a holiday outing.

It is a pity there weren't a couple of mine-laying boats with me on the night I was off New York, to plaster the place with mines! And if only there had been ten or twenty boats with me here tonight! They would all, I am sure, have had successes in plenty. I have sighted something like twenty ships, some blacked out, and a few tramps. They were all sticking very close to the shore.

Life was made easier for submariners by the introduction of the *Milchkuh* or Milch-cow, a tanker submarine designed to refuel U-boats at sea, enabling them to stay on active duty for longer periods. How it worked was described by Heinz Schaeffer.

We were cruising parallel to the supply boat, perhaps ninety yards away. A line was fired over us by pistol, and this was followed by the hose and a towing-wire. We breathed again as the precious fluid began to flow in. Altogether we took in twenty tons of it, not to speak of bread, potatoes, vegetables and other food in watertight sacks. The whole thing went off perfectly, though it was our first experience.[16]

Despite huge losses of unprotected shipping, the US Navy was slow to react. In the first quarter of 1942, U-boats sank 216 ships (1.25 million tons) in American waters. More than half of these were oil tankers. In June alone the Allies lost 145 ships, the highest number of any month since the start of the war. The highest tonnage lost in any single month – 700,000 tons – came in November.[17] By the end of the year when German U-boats were sinking an average of 100 Allied ships a month, Doenitz could claim economic superiority over the enemy in that he was sinking Allied ships faster than they could be built. Over the year, imports to Britain fell to

33 million tons, down 40 per cent on 1939. Fuel supplies dropped by 15 per cent, forcing the government to draw on its strategic reserves. If openly admitted, the move would have shattered home morale.

Having declared that 'all ships, with a few exceptions, could be regarded as enemy',[18] Hitler backed plans for increased U-boat production and technological advances including high-speed submarines and a remotely controlled torpedo. From May 1942, Doenitz, who now had 200 U-boats under his command, was able to take advantage of direct contact with Hitler. He reported that the Anglo-American lifeline across the North Atlantic was close to breaking point. Raeder made unsuccessful efforts to rein in the ambitions of his closest associate. Then, in January 1943, after an unsuccessful attack on a British convoy in the Barents Sea drove Hitler to fury against the surface fleet, Raeder resigned. He was succeeded by Doenitz who took the rank of Grand Admiral while keeping control of his beloved submarines.

Doenitz did not have it all his own way. As he reported to Hitler in August, a third of his U-boat strength had been lost since the start of the war.[19] After a poor start, the Allies gained a technological edge starting with air superiority. With extra fuel tanks and equipped with radar, the four-engined B24 Liberator had the range and capability to cover the mid-Atlantic 'air gap' where hitherto U-boats had been free to operate on the surface knowing there could be no threat from above. Since the fully armed Liberator also carried 24 depth-charges, the rules of mid-Atlantic warfare had to be revised.

The German answer to the Liberator was the Kondor, another long-range bomber able to guide U-boats to their targets and to join in the attack. Doenitz was able to persuade Hitler to put two Kondor squadrons under his direct control until Goering discovered what was going on and overruled the navy. Back under Luftwaffe control, the Kondors were reduced from a major force to a minor irritant. Post-war, Doenitz asserted that 'the lack of an extensive naval air arm proved to be a decisive disadvantage for the German conduct of the war at sea'.[20]

The only comfort for Doenitz was the relatively small number of Liberators coming on stream. Well into 1942, only half a dozen or so were available for Atlantic duty. Three out of four sinkings were in the Atlantic air gap, still at 600 miles in late 1942. But the gap narrowed appreciably after aircraft carriers were allocated escort duties and also with the mass production of escort vessels. As significant was the adoption of more sophisticated radar and underwater sound detection. Airborne radar allowed air attacks on submarines at night with aircraft flying in to close range before releasing bombs along searchlight beams directed on to the target.

However, for several months the advantage remained with Germany by virtue of the sheer number of submarines Doenitz was able to deploy. When the Battle of the Atlantic (a phrase coined by Churchill) approached its peak in early 1943, 30 new submarines a month were coming into service. Despite severe losses, the U-boat force remained highly trained and dedicated. As they crossed the Atlantic gap, Allied convoys were almost bound to encounter a 'wolf-pack' of German submarines. The Germans' preferred tactic was to sail towards a convoy in daylight but go for the kill at night. As many as ten or even 20 submarines would engage in a single operation, often mounting a series of attacks for up to eight days and over a thousand miles. The tally for two years of intense submarine warfare was the loss to the Allies of 8 million tons of shipping.[21]

A major breakthrough for the Allies came courtesy of the cryptologists at Bletchley Park who cracked the German Enigma codes.

Messages between Doenitz and his commanders were now open to inspection, a task simplified by Doenitz's style of leadership which kept him in frequent contact with his commanders at sea. The more messages that were sent, the easier it was to interpret strategic moves. As the success rate for U-boats fell, various theories were advanced by way of explanation. More sophisticated radar was judged to be the likeliest catalyst but fears of treachery were strong enough for an intensive inquiry to be mounted. When no evidence of leakage was found, Doenitz remained unconvinced. 'What do you suggest now?' asked Admiral Godt, his chief of operations. 'Should I investigate *you* or will you investigate me?' Still, Doenitz could not bring himself to believe that Enigma was vulnerable ('Out of the question,' he declared). It was not until 1974 when the relevant papers were released by the UK Public Record Office that he recognised that British intelligence had indeed broken the Enigma code:

> So that's what happened! ... I have been afraid of this time and again. Although the experts continually proved – with conviction as it seemed – that there were other reasons for the suspect observations, they were never able to dispel my doubts completely ... Only after the war did I feel reasonably reassured by the lack of any reports from the Allied side ... Well, now you historians will have to start right at the beginning again![22]

The climax of the Battle of the Atlantic came in March 1943 when, over two weeks, two Atlantic convoys, one overtaking the other, were attacked day and night over hundreds of square miles, by 38 submarines. Of 92 ships, 21 were sunk with a loss of 146,000 tons, an all-time high for one continuous U-boat action. The tally on the

German side was the destruction of just one submarine, and that by a Sunderland bomber. The Kriegsmarine was jubilant, the Royal Navy devastated. What was particularly galling for the Admiralty was that for all the secrets given up by the Enigma decrypts, with so many U-boats at sea it was near-impossible to divert shipping out of trouble.

But the U-boat mid-March victory, though record-breaking, was also the last of its kind. With more long-range aircraft made available to patrol the Atlantic, the air gap was finally sealed. Moreover, as the cryptologists dug deeper into German naval strategy, greater skill was applied to exploiting the intelligence gained. When, in May, 41 submarines, one third of those at sea, failed to return, Doenitz ordered the remaining U-boats to withdraw from the North Atlantic. 'It is impossible to foretell,' he admitted, 'to what extent U-boat warfare will again become effective.' At the end of October, the total tonnage of Allied naval construction passed the total of Allied shipping sunk worldwide in four years of war.

Kriegsmarine morale was not improved by the fate of the battleship *Tirpitz*, immobilised in its Norwegian fjord by a British midget submarine and subsequently destroyed by Lancaster bombers. Germany's other prestigious battleship, *Scharnhorst*, went down in November. Leading the force that sank *Scharnhorst*, Admiral Bruce Fraser composed a memorable epitaph:

> Gentlemen, the battle against *Scharnhorst* has ended in victory for us. I hope that any of you who are ever called upon to lead a ship into action against an opponent many times superior, will command your ship as gallantly as the *Scharnhorst* was commanded today.

This was a critical time for Doenitz in his relations with Hitler.

With rivals at court who were only too happy for the navy to be taken down a peg, the failure of his U-boats to deliver a knock-out blow was liable to expose him to one of the Fuehrer's lengthy tirades against military incompetence. He courted danger when he proposed countermanding Hitler's order for doing away with the surface fleet, the pride and joy of Doenitz's predecessor. Initially, Doenitz went along with the idea. Ever since the sinking of the *Bismarck*, the Kriegsmarine's prestige symbol, in May 1941, Germany's big ships had proved to be an expensive luxury. Resources, declared Hitler, could be better used elsewhere. But Doenitz soon realised that breaking up the surface fleet would itself be expensive in time and labour while handing a propaganda weapon to the Allies. He advised Hitler to backtrack, something he was averse to doing under any circumstances. 'He was at first extremely immoderate but in the end he very grudgingly agreed, and I was ungraciously dismissed.'[23]

The decisive moment came soon afterwards when Doenitz had to face Hitler with the news that a large tanker bound for occupied Greece had been intercepted and torpedoed by a British submarine near the Dardanelles. Hitler flew into a rage. 'The British, of course, can do it, but our boats off Gibraltar don't sink a thing.' With an attentive audience of senior Wehrmacht officers, Doenitz made his response.

'My Fuehrer,' I retorted sharply, '*our* U-boats are fighting against very great sea powers. If, like the British off the Dardanelles, they had no anti-submarine forces to contend with, they would achieve at least an equal success. Off Gibraltar I have stationed the most outstanding of my U-boat Commanders, and they, let me tell you, are a great deal better than the British!'

There was a dead silence. Hitler went red in the face, but after a few moments he turned to General Jodl, who had been in the middle of submitting a report, and said quietly: 'Carry on, please!'[24] And that was it, apart from a friendly breakfast à deux. A bold move paid off in that there was no further interference by Hitler in naval affairs.

But in taking credit for protecting the independence of the Kriegsmarine (he even managed to keep the service clear of insidious intrusions by the Nazi ideologues), Doenitz may have overestimated his role in the greater scheme of things. By the spring of 1943, the fortunes of war had turned against Germany and its allies. Losing the Battle of the Atlantic was bad enough but it shrank in significance against the Japanese defeat in the Pacific when, in the Battle of Midway, the American navy inflicted irreparable damage on the Japanese fleet. Now it was the land war that preoccupied Hitler. While the victory at El Alamein in November 1942 had ended the Axis threat to Middle Eastern oil and opened the way to the Allied invasion of North Africa, it was followed by even worse news from the Eastern Front. The five-month battle for Stalingrad, one of the bloodiest in history, ended in February 1943 with the surrender of the Axis forces to the Red Army. In retrospect, it was seen as the decisive turning point of the Second World War. In Hitler's inner council, Doenitz was inevitably sidelined. While planning for a renewal of the Atlantic War, he could do no more than wait on events.

CHAPTER THREE

Work started on a new generation of U-boats. Doenitz took his inspiration from Hellmuth Walter, an inventor-engineer who was commissioned in 1933 by the Kriegsmarine to produce an experimental streamlined submarine, fuelled by hydrogen peroxide. The prototype was capable of speeds as high as 28 knots and could stay submerged for as long as the crew could endure the stale air.

In November 1942, Doenitz called a conference at his headquarters in Paris to map the progress of the Walter U-boat and to plan for its launch. To his surprise, he was told that the end product was nowhere near ready for service. Other priorities, expounded by powerful lobbies, had brought development of the Walter U-boat to a virtual standstill. It could be years before the designers and engineers caught up with demand. Doenitz looked to ways of accelerating the process. One suggestion was for adopting the basics of Walter's thinking to enhance the performance of existing U-boats, for example by doubling the number of batteries carried to increase underwater speeds.

Another idea was to adopt what became known as the snorkel, the brainchild of the Dutch submarine commander Jan Jacobs Wichers. The snorkel was simplicity itself. Two concentric pipes, one inside the other, about the same length as a periscope, were fitted to the deck. The inner pipe expelled exhaust from the diesel engines while the outer pipe sucked in air. This meant that the U-boat was no longer compelled to surface to recharge its batteries which, in turn, enabled it to attack while submerged at periscope depth. The snorkel was not in itself sufficient to restore U-boat superiority but it was enough of a threat to ensure that there could be no letting up on the costly provision of Allied convoy escorts for the rest of the war.

Meanwhile, the ocean-going Type XXI, the forebear of all modern submarines, and the smaller, coastal Type XXIII went into production. The aim was to have the first off the assembly line by the end of 1944. On Hitler's orders U-boat construction was given top priority but Doenitz had to endure the frustrations of an overstretched war economy. Shortages and mismanagement were endemic. Engineering companies with no experience of shipbuilding delivered components that bore little relation to the overall design.

A sense of order was imposed after Doenitz came to a deal with Albert Speer, Reichsminister of armaments and production, to take control of production. The result was a dramatic improvement in the supply of standardised prefabricated units sent to the shipyards for assembly. The Allies' carpet-bombing of Hamburg, Bremen and Danzig* where most of the work was done caused disruption, though the new U-boats were given better than ordinary protection by their 'pens' of reinforced concrete. The XXI held out great promise. Fitted with an anti-radar-coated snorkel head with radar search aerials, it had ultrasensitive hydrophones with a 50-mile range for locating ships, a supersonic echo device to give the course, range and speed of targets and an impressive

---

* Now Gdańsk.

range of weaponry including torpedoes which could be fired at targets at any angle.

Of the XXI and XXIII, 98 were commissioned in the second half of 1944 and 83 in the first quarter of 1945. Of all new U-boats coming into service the monthly average for 1944 was 19.5, an extraordinary achievement bearing in mind that the only higher figure (19.9) was scored in 1942 when the bombing of German industrial plant was relatively light.

The production of minesweepers and E-boats was also impressive. In 1944, 87 minesweepers and 62 E-boats were delivered, against 52 and 41 in 1943 and even fewer in earlier years. Doenitz gave full credit to Speer. 'He alone was in a position to make available alternative industrial resources when the original factories had been bombed out.'[1]

Doenitz was on leave in June 1944 when the Normandy landings gave notice that the biggest ever invasion force had burst into occupied Europe. Returning to his HQ, his fear was of being overwhelmed by the sheer number of Allied vessels at sea. He had 73 U-boats within range of the mass of cross-Channel troopships but, of these, only 25 were fitted with snorkels. After ordering seventeen U-boats to attack the invasion force, the rest were directed to the Bay of Biscay to guard against possible landings on the French Atlantic coast.

His message to crews was pitiless. 'Each soldier and each weapon destroyed before reaching the beachhead diminishes the enemy's chance of victory. A U-boat which inflicts losses on the invasion forces fulfils her highest mission and justifies her existence, even though she herself may be destroyed.'

Nine days after D-Day three snorkel boats sank an American landing ship and two British warships. On 25 June, Lieutenant Heinz Sieder in *U-984* damaged a frigate, evaded detection for four

days and then scored four crippling hits on separate American supply ships a few miles from Portsmouth, using his snorkel to escape.

Ernest Cordes in *U-763* was able to avoid the consequences of
a serious navigational error. Having sunk a freighter on 5 July and
fired five torpedoes at a military convoy and missed, *U-763* escaped
a massive hunt to take refuge at what Cordes initially thought was
the island of Alderney in the German-occupied Channel Islands. It
was in fact Spithead Bay near Portsmouth. His snorkel saved him
as he crept out to sea, firing a torpedo at a passing destroyer (it
missed) before docking undamaged at Brest on 14 July. His War
Diary tells a sorry tale of life on a U-boat.

> It is nearly thirty hours since the boat was last aired. The
> first cases of vomiting occur and I issue each man with a
> potash cartridge [air-filter]. Breathing becomes distressed.
> The enemy search group is still active … during the thirty
> hours of pursuit, 252 depth-charges were counted in the
> near vicinity, sixty-one at medium range and fifty-one at
> long range.[2]

By July, Allied bombing was so intense that U-boats on the French
coast were restricted to their bomb-proof pens. Doenitz ordered
their withdrawal to Norway. Their combined tally since D-Day
accounted for five warships, twelve merchantmen and four landing
craft. It was little enough to show for the sacrifice of 20 U-boats
sunk or otherwise put out of action and close on 800 lives.

More of a threat to the Allied supply chain was the motor torpedo boat or E-boat. In the first half of 1944, operating from the
Dutch coast, German E-boats sank 31 ships. The British response
came from Coastal Forces with its own motor torpedo boats
(MTBs) based mostly at Great Yarmouth in Norfolk and Felixstowe

on the Suffolk coast. As a young war correspondent, Tom Pocock saw them in action.

Ferocious battles took place at high speed and close range. It was a curiously old-fashioned form of warfare, fought with dash by both sides. In the balance of the weaponry there was a touch of medieval trial by combat. E-boats and MTBs were about the same size; wooden boats of little more than one hundred tons with a crew of thirty-odd, but their armament and capabilities were as different as those of gladiators with trident and net, or sword and armour. Armed with torpedoes, or mines, and few guns, the E-boats could make more than 40 knots, whereas the British, heavily armed with torpedoes, depth charges and perhaps a dozen guns, could not manage 30. If the E-boat came within range of the MTB it could be instantly shot to pieces. Since it could not be caught in pursuit, the British would lie in wait with engines stopped in the hope of interception.[3]

Having regrouped in Norway, more U-boat campaigns were launched against Allied shipping in the Channel. To succeed, crews had to endure long periods submerged. When a corvette and four merchantmen were destroyed not far from Liverpool, it was by a U-boat that sailed 2,500 miles out of 2,729 underwater. It returned to Trondheim unharmed. In the last four months of 1944 U-boats sank sixteen ships in British waters. Warning of the new generation of U-boats to come, the Admiralty conceded that the snorkel made U-boats virtually undetectable.

The failure to repel the Allied invasion forces led to prolonged sniping between the Wehrmacht and the Kriegsmarine. Doenitz was blamed for allowing the trans-Atlantic build-up of the vast quantities of weaponry and support needed to overwhelm the German defences. General Hans Speidel, Chief of Staff for Field Marshal Rommel and for his successor Field Marshal von Kluge, went further by accusing Doenitz of 'turning against the Army'. The disappointing U-boat performance he could forgive, but not the refusal to throw into battle the 5,000-strong Marine Security Unit based in Paris, or the underestimating by half the range of Allied naval guns which hit targets 25 miles inland.[4] For his part, Doenitz blamed the Wehrmacht for the 'premature surrender' of Cherbourg with its harbour installations damaged but not beyond repair. Operating from Norwegian and home bases extended by more than a thousand miles the U-boat voyage to and from operational areas.

There was no let-up in the speed and ferocity of the Allied invasion as forces broke through German defences to sweep across France and Belgium. Caught in a pincer movement between American forces curving round from their advance and Canadian and British troops moving down from Caen, the German Fifth and Seventh Armies were trapped and destroyed. Paris was liberated on 24 August.

Doenitz concluded, and he was not alone, that 'the war could no longer be won by force of arms'. But since the Allies were in no mood to negotiate, 'there was nothing for it but to fight on'. This fatalistic appraisal was softened when, by September, it was clear that the invasion had run out of steam. Supply lines had become dangerously extended and battle-weary troops were in need of respite.

Allied hopes of an early breakthrough were not easily abandoned. Operation Market Garden, a combined ground and airborne attack across 60 miles of enemy-held territory, was conceived by Field Marshal Sir Bernard Montgomery as a speedy conclusion to the war. The airborne troops would be dropped at Arnhem in Holland to secure a Rhine crossing. An infantry follow-up could then bypass the Siegfried Line defences to make directly for the great German industrial cities of the Ruhr. The plan foundered. After nine days of close fighting, which virtually wiped out the British First Airborne Division and inflicted heavy casualties on the American parachutists, the operation was called off.

The ability of the Wehrmacht to challenge the odds was proved again 80 miles south of Arnhem, at Aachen, the first German city to fall to the Allies but at terrible cost to American forces. It was the same story in Italy, the only other front where Allied progress might reasonably have been expected. After the capture of Rome in June, Allied forces moving north had bumped up against a stubborn German defence of the Po Valley.

Preparation for a full-scale assault on the German frontier was hampered by the destruction of past battles. The French railway system had been devastated first by Allied bombing and then by the Germans in retreat, while many of the Channel ports had been shelled or sabotaged beyond immediate use. Ahead was the Siegfried Line with its networks of pillboxes and minefields and mile after mile of deep trenches that had to be cleared step by step. As winter approached it was clear that German resistance would not be broken easily. Everywhere the Allied advance was on hold.

The Eastern Front was another matter and it was here and on the Baltic that Doenitz now focused his attention. For much of the war the Baltic was a German lake. After the invasion of the Soviet Union in 1941, territory to the east including Ukraine and the Baltic States – Estonia, Latvia and Lithuania – were expropriated by the Reich. Flanked on the west by occupied Denmark and neutral Sweden, the northern stretch of the Baltic was secured by an alliance with Finland. The only shipping access to the Baltic was by the easily policed Danish straits and the Kiel Canal, both connecting to the North Sea.

Doenitz was obsessed with the need for Germany to remain dominant in the Baltic. And for good reasons. Merchant convoys crossing the Baltic were the lifeline for German forces on the Eastern Front. Sea traffic from Sweden to Hamburg and other north German ports carried high-grade iron ores and speciality steels including the major supply of ball bearings. By this route, some 11 million tons of iron ore was imported annually. Further support for the war machine came from the Nave region of northern Estonia where huge deposits of shale oil, estimated at 5–6 million tons, had been discovered. By 1943, production was an annual 100,000 tons; and this was only the start.[5]

In the wider context of the war at sea, the Baltic was critical to naval strategy. It was where the Kriegsmarine had its power base. Submarine research and innovation were concentrated here, along with the training of U-boat crews. To lose the Baltic, declared Doenitz, would be to lose the war. Hitler agreed. The Baltic had to be defended at all costs.

The supreme test came after the siege of Leningrad was lifted in January 1944. Thereafter, the Russian juggernaut was on the move, annihilating three army groups and rolling back the German front line by up to 500 miles. In mid-September, the Red Army broke through to the Gulf of Riga. Estonia was cut off and had to be evacuated. Finland was forced to change sides. The following month the German Army Group North found itself trapped in the Kurland (Courland) Peninsula of Latvia, isolated from Army Group Centre as it withdrew to the coastal strongholds of Lithuania and East Prussia. Having regained Ukraine, the Red Army swept on into Poland.

Doenitz was summoned by Hitler to attend a conference

on the Soviet threat. The Fuehrer wanted to know what effect a Russian breakthrough would have on naval operations in the Baltic. Doenitz responded that the greatest danger was a direct breakthrough south of Kurland. This would make it impossible to continue to carry supplies by sea to the northern group of armies. Lining up with Hitler, he was all in favour of holding on to Memel,* against the advice of General Reinhardt, commander of Army Group North, who urged evacuation to strengthen the defences of Koenigsberg** and the nearby port of Pillau.***

At the same time and in defiance of Hitler, Doenitz was in favour of abandoning Kurland. 'The carrying of supplies was nothing but a burden to the Navy,'[6] he commented, doubtless adding under his breath that holding on to Kurland had no strategic value. The generals agreed but, as ever, Hitler baulked at surrendering territory even for the best of reasons. Doenitz gave what support he could to the beleaguered German forces by stationing offshore such heavy ships still in commission – *Prinz Eugen, Luetzow, Scheer* and *Hipper* – to direct their guns over the heads of the defenders to bring a hail of shells down on the enemy. Just how effective this could be was proved by the *Prinz Eugen* when it sailed into the bay of Riga to support a counter-attack to restore the link between the Riga garrison and the German front in Kurland.

On 20 August at 7 a.m. the cruiser fired her first ranging shots. The gunnery-officer was in constant telephonic communication by ultra-short wave with the carrier-aircraft acting as spotter and hovering above the target area, as well as with advanced army-observation posts and the spearhead

* Now Klaipėda.
** Now Kaliningrad.
*** Now Baltiysk.

of the German tank units. The target, invisible from the cruiser, was the town of Tukkum, situated some fifteen miles inland, a railway-junction where the Russian opposition had stiffened.

The first rounds from the *Prinz Eugen*'s 8-inch guns were well aimed:

> As she continued to fire round after round, the observers gave 80 per cent direct hits. The cruiser was not even firing from a fixed position, but steaming to and fro. Nevertheless there was no doubt the *Prinz* was firing with great accuracy.[7]

Incredibly, though the cruiser was vulnerable in narrow and shallow waters, there was no retaliation either from the air or at sea. The bombardment continued unhindered until late afternoon when the *Prinz Eugen* had exhausted its ammunition.

There was a repeat performance in October when the *Prinz Eugen* was joined by a flotilla of light cruisers to take turns in shelling the Russians moving in on Memel. Again, though Russian submarines were thought to be in the area, no attempt was made to stop the onslaught. Hard-pressed troops took heart.

> Russian tanks had reached the hill to the south of our camp. Our soldiers who had been in the path of their advance had done their duty before they died. Then a heavy bombardment from the sea had struck the tanks as they slid over the dunes. Several tanks to the south of us went up in flames. The Russians were even forced to retreat a little, fighting as they went. The bombardment from the sea continued. Through the darkness and fog we could see the luminous discharges of the guns. With daylight, we were

able to see the source of our help through heavy curtains of smoke. Two warships were standing close by the shore. One of them was the *Prinz Eugen*. The other was a ship of the same size. To the desperate defenders of Memel, they were a source of support we had never hoped for. The tanks respected their large guns, and kept their distance.[8]

However, the Russian aircraft that did get close could hardly miss.

A barge packed with men had been bombed amidships. We were summoned from our rest period to deal with the mess. I shall omit the details, the memory of which still nauseates me. Our boots were red with blood. The human refuse which we threw off the front of the half-submerged wreck drew a throng of fish, and the smell of bodies torn open by gaping wounds is beyond expression, even though the water washing over the carnage diminished it somewhat.[9]

Ironically, the heaviest damage to the Kriegsmarine was self-inflicted. On its way to lay mines off Swinemuende, the *Leipzig* sailed at night without lights. Visibility was further reduced by dense fog. At 8.04 p.m. she was struck amidships on the starboard side between the bridge and the funnel. At first, it was assumed to be the result of a well-aimed torpedo. But it soon became apparent that something more substantial was responsible. The *Leipzig* had been rammed by her sister ship *Prinz Eugen*.

Locked together, the two cruisers drifted in the Baltic for fourteen hours until two tugs arrived to pump water out of the *Leipzig* in an attempt to keep her afloat. Then while the tugs held the *Leipzig* stationary, the engines of the *Prinz Eugen* drove her astern. Beating expectations, both ships stayed afloat and both were back in action within a month, though the patching-up of the *Leipzig* allowed only for light duties.

'Thiele's fighting squadron', named after Admiral August Thiele commanding the battle group, continued its support of land forces with heavy bombardments from offshore. When in November, after a seven-week battle, the Russians were close to taking the Sworbe peninsula at the south end of the island of Oesel, Estonia, the Kriegsmarine gave heavy gun support to the evacuation of troops and equipment. This time, the Russians retaliated with their onshore batteries, though with limited success. Having the advantage of a longer range, the cruisers withdrew to a safer distance. Russian torpedo aircraft and high-altitude bombers then went into action, the chief target being the *Admiral Scheer* with its powerful 11-inch guns. Turning and twisting, the *Admiral Scheer* dodged torpedoes and bombs to return safely to her base at Gotenhafen.*

After the Sworbe evacuation General Heinz Guderian, Chief of the General Staff of Land Armies, sent a heartfelt message of thanks to naval personnel for the 'self sacrificing support they have given us in a united struggle against overwhelmingly superior enemy forces'. On the Baltic at least, relations between the Kriegsmarine and the Wehrmacht remained strong. To hold on to the Baltic ports, the German surface fleet fired more shells than in all its other operations put together.

At the tail end of 1944, the Russians took stock of their successes. With the Allied advance to the Rhine so fiercely contested, the hope was for the Soviet Union to lighten the pressure by a quick resumption of its offensive. But the Red Army was not about to repeat the classic error of outdistancing its supply lines. Time was

---

* Now Gdynia.

needed for a build-up of tanks and artillery that would annihilate the German Baltic forces and carry the Russians across the river Vistula, at a kilometre wide one of the strongest natural defences guarding the eastern approaches to the heartland of the Reich.

Hitler and his generals spent the lull in the proceedings debating their options. The frustrations of the professional military were palpable. Hitler simply refused to recognise the enormity of the Soviet threat. Never one to hide his contempt for the Red Army (a 'useless rabble' he called them in one of his less excitable moods), he nonetheless credited his fellow dictator with a tendency to act rationally – a case of the pot failing to recognise that the kettle was equally black. Military logic suggested that Stalin's first priority would be to sweep up the 200,000 German troops in the Kurland Pocket, directed by Hitler to fight to the last. Thereafter, it was East Prussia that Hitler thought to be most at risk.

Guderian, though, with first-hand experience of the Red Army, believed otherwise. He was inclined to hedge his bets. The likeliest prospect was seen as an attack to the south towards Vienna, barred by five redoubts between the Vistula and the Oder. This meant that the Russians had five great battles ahead of them to get within striking distance of Berlin. Failure at any stage would be the signal to begin the rollback. Confident that the Eastern Front could be held, Hitler turned his attention to the West. With the Allies held down at the Siegfried Line, Hitler had time to reinvigorate the Wehrmacht. He did so with ruthless energy. Reserves of manpower were discovered by the simple expedient of lowering the recruitment age while roping in those hitherto let off as too old or unfit to wear uniform. It was an awesome thought that a battered Germany, beset on all sides by powerful enemies, still had 10 million men in uniform, two-thirds of them in an army backed by formidable military hardware.

Hitler had something more ambitious in mind than a defensive war, but there were few that he trusted to share his plans. After the July plot on his life he was wary of declaring himself openly, even to his senior commanders, who had no inkling of Operation Watch on the Rhine (later Autumn Mist), until 22 October, barely a month before the intended start date. It was then that Hitler called together the Chiefs of Staff of Field Marshal Karl von Rundstedt, recently recalled from retirement to take up his old job as Commander-in-Chief West and of Field Marshal Walther Model, commander of Army Group B which straddled the Western Front.

The strategy, to sweep through the Ardennes forest on a 60-mile front along the Belgian and Luxembourg frontiers and then, having crossed the Meuse, make straight for the Channel coast to take Antwerp, was nothing if not audacious. If successful it would disrupt the Allied troop supply, extend German control of the Netherlands and split the British and Canadian armies in the north from the Americans in the south, allowing both to be encircled. With Antwerp recaptured there would be no Allied escape by sea. Three armies were to be thrown into the assault. After a breakthrough by the infantry, the tanks would follow at speed, bypassing strongly held towns and villages, a tactic which had been used to great effect on the Eastern Front.

But there were glaring deficiencies. Many of the troops were fresh to battle and inadequately trained, essential equipment had still to come on stream and air support was minimal. Only a quarter of the fuel needed could be guaranteed; advancing units were expected to capture supplies from the enemy. Moreover, fighting conditions in winter over a heavily wooded and mountainous region were hardly propitious. But Hitler was adamant. Even if he could not destroy his enemies, cutting them off from their supply lines via Antwerp would, he calculated, weaken Allied resolve and even conceivably lead to a negotiated peace on the Western Front so that Germany could concentrate on the threat to the East.

Rundstedt and Model did their best to persuade him otherwise. The two leading commanders in the field, General Hasso von Manteuffel who led the Fifth Panzer Army and General Sepp Dietrich of the Sixth Panzer Army, also voiced their fears. But Hitler's orders were 'irreversible'.[10] His only concession was to postpone the attack until 16 December when poor weather was expected to offer protection against aerial bombing.

The Wehrmacht started with another advantage. The strategy adopted by the Allied Supreme Commander, General Dwight Eisenhower, of advancing on a broad front inevitably left some sectors light on manpower. In the Ardennes, General Omar Bradley's Twelfth Army Group covered 80 miles of Belgian–German border with just one armoured and three infantry divisions. Two of these had lately arrived fresh from the United States and the other two were exhausted by their recent bruising encounter with the enemy in Huertgen Forest. Though perilously overstretched, his troops, many of them fresh arrivals, were encouraged to think that a weakened enemy was unlikely to mount a winter campaign in such unfavourable territory. The morning of 16 December proved just how wrong received wisdom could be.

At 5.30 a.m., German artillery opened up a 45-minute barrage, destroying communication links between Allied commanders and their forward observation points. When the guns stopped, searchlights pierced the night sky, the beams bouncing off the clouds to create artificial moonlight. Made ghostly by their white combat gear, the ranks of infantry, fourteen abreast, rushed the American lines. The surprise was total.

American forces crumbled across the entire 80-mile front. By the time the high command realised that they were not dealing with localised attacks but a full-scale offensive, the German push had extended fifteen miles into Allied lines. Fifteen thousand GIs had been captured, thousands more lay dead or wounded in the snow, while others wandered aimlessly, cut off from their own lines and having no idea how to find them. Despair for the Americans equalled jubilation for the Germans, whose morale rose to giddy heights.

'The Americans are on the run,' wrote a German soldier to his wife. 'We cleared an enemy supply dump. Everybody took things he wanted most. I took only chocolate. I have all my pockets full of it. I eat chocolate all the time, in order to sweeten this wretched life ... Don't worry about me. The worst is behind me. Now this is just a hunt.'

It took a change of command at the highest level for the Allies to regain the initiative. With the risk of the German advance cutting off Bradley's headquarters in Luxembourg, on 19 December Eisenhower handed over the northern front, including the Ninth and First Armies, to Montgomery's Twenty-First Army Group, leaving Bradley to concentrate on the southern sector.

Barring the way to Antwerp, Montgomery threw the bulk of the American First Army and much of the Ninth into the battle area. British and Canadian forces were used as a backstop to hold the line of the Meuse. There were sound reasons for this, not least the wish to avoid the administrative complications of thrusting the British troops into the centre of an American army. But it was a decision that was to damage Montgomery's reputation with his US colleagues who resented his boast of a British victory achieved, as they said, on the backs of American casualties. Of more than 30 Allied divisions engaged in the struggle, nine-tenths were American.

The high point of German success was Manteuffel's breakthrough to within striking distance of the Meuse and his encirclement of General McAuliffe's 101st Airborne Division, known as the 'Screaming Eagles', who had raced to protect Bastogne, one of the road junctions with the potential to determine the outcome of the campaign. With the growing strength of German artillery within range of the town, McAuliffe was given two hours to surrender or face 'total annihilation'. Knowing that Patton's Third Army was charging to the rescue, he held his nerve.

The Third Army's race north, up from Luxembourg, was a spectacular demonstration of mobile warfare. More than 130,000 tanks and trucks, in double-banked columns, took part in the 'round-the-clock trek' over icy roads. They were kept going by six new supply points holding 235,000 rations and 300,000 gallons of petrol. 'The troops in heavy great coats still caked with the mud of the Saar were huddled against the wintry cold that knifed through their canvas topped trucks while the tank commanders, their faces wrapped in woollen scarves, huddled in the turrets of their Shermans.'[11]

Four days after the Third Army started its 130-mile 'fire call' run, the tanks of the Fourth Armoured Division were in Bastogne.

The Rundstedt offensive reached its limit on Christmas Eve. Today, in the Belgian village of Celles, a swastikaed tank serves as a monument to the Germans' point of return. But Allied optimism had taken a hard knock. On 4 January 1945, Patton noted in his diary, 'We can still lose this war. The Germans are colder and hungrier than we are, but they fight better.'

As Patton broke through to relieve Bastogne, American forces in other sectors were pushing the Germans back over territory they had so recently occupied. Clear skies opened German supply lines to intensive air attack. Five thousand Allied bombers took to the air to set ablaze the roads all the way to the Siegfried Line. Rundstedt urged a withdrawal to strong defensive positions but

Hitler, still seeing attack as the best defence, ordered a diversionary offensive in the north of Alsace. Operation North Wind would, he calculated, divert Patton from his Ardennes counter-attack, freeing Manteuffel to resume his advance towards Antwerp, the great prize that Hitler refused to accept was now beyond reach. North Wind began on New Year's Day. It failed utterly.

As German forces gave way in the West there came news of a renewed offensive on the Eastern Front. The sheer overwhelming power of the Soviet attack was a nightmare shock, not least to the civilian population who had clung to the reassurances of the gauleiters that Hitler would never fail them. On four fronts over 4 million men and 9,000 tanks supported by 40,000 artillery pieces confronted a force that was barely half the strength. With his sights on the Vistula river, Marshal Konev lined up his artillery wheel to wheel, with up to 300 pieces for each kilometre of his planned advance. Moved into place under cover of fog and blizzards, the noise of weaponry on the move to its assembly points was covered by deafening music relayed over loudspeakers.

In the early hours of 12 January, the Russian artillery opened up on the Fourth Panzer Army and its right-flanking Seventeenth Army.

> The air incandesced with an unnatural light, and before long a sky of fire and smoke lowered over the country on the west side of the Vistula. The frozen soil was torn up hundreds of times over, houses flared like torches, bunkers collapsed, roads were broken up and men were ripped apart.[12]

At first light Konev's First Ukrainian Army Group braved a heavy fog and a snowstorm that took the breath away to attack across the upper Vistula towards Cracow and Silesia. The first two lines of German defences were overrun in a single day; the third and strongest line, protected by a deep belt of minefields, was crossed a day later. In 48 hours, the Red Army advanced 25 miles on a 37-mile front. Another day extended the front to over 70 miles. Cracow was within striking distance.

The opening offensive in the south was followed by a double attack from two narrow bridgeheads across the Vistula. Marshal Zhukov's First Belorussian Army Group was able to break through twelve miles of deep defences before fanning out to sweep round Warsaw, opening the way to Berlin. Warsaw, a decimated city, its people and buildings crushed by Nazi vengeance, was taken on 17 January.

Two days after the fall of Warsaw, Cracow and Lodz were captured. The plains of western Poland were now wide open. The Russian tide rolled forward at up to 40 miles a day, sweeping the Germans from Poland, except for the neck of the corridor leading to Danzig. By the end of January, the great industrial region of Silesia, with its tank and aircraft factories little touched by Allied bombing, was in Russian hands.

On 16 January, still unwilling to acknowledge the magnitude of the Soviet offensive, Hitler moved his headquarters to the Chancellery bunker. 'It was a smart move,' was the bitter comment of one of his adjutants. 'You just had to take the suburban train for a short journey from the Eastern to the Western front.'

'The war is lost,' declared Albert Speer. He reckoned without the February thaw. 'The splashing in the gutters sounds to our ears like choirs of angels,' wrote Wilfred von Oven in his Berlin diary.[13]

The melting snows made the grass airstrips in Poland unusable and turned dirt roads into rushing streams. The smooth-running operation that had kept Russian forces well supplied descended into muddy chaos. The fighting continued but with greater hope on the German side that the Russian advance could be halted and, eventually, reversed.

The defence of East Prussia devolved on General Georg-Hans Reinhardt, who was compelled to spend too much of his time arguing with his Fuehrer about the deployment of forces over a 360-kilometre front. Constructive suggestions from Reinhardt for strengthening the line by withdrawing to stronger natural defences were consistently rejected by Hitler who saw only war maps designed to give a rosy image of the campaign. Frustrated by incompetence at the top, Reinhardt relied increasingly on his own initiative.

As a result, on 13 January, when Marshal Chernyakovsky led the Third Belorussian Front into East Prussia, he had a harder fight on his hands than he expected. After the opening barrage fell on outer defences already vacated by Reinhardt, the Russians came up against stiff opposition from well-prepared forces barring the way to Koenigsberg, the regional capital. But by 20 January the pressure of numbers was overwhelming. Concentrating his strength on the weakest points of the German front, Chernyakovsky's forces smashed their way through to within striking distance of Koenigsberg, itself close to Pillau, one of the major ports for evacuation. Koenigsberg was awash with refugees who had been pouring in ahead of the Russian advance. In the hospitals 11,000 wounded and injured waited for treatment, mostly in vain.

The civilian population had taken too much time to realise the peril coming to them. Faith in the invincibility of the Wehrmacht, fed assiduously by the Nazi propaganda machine, supported a policy of 'wait and see'. It was not until convoys of troops, recently cheered on their way to the front, came racing back through towns and villages that panic took hold. In temperatures well below freezing and with heavy snowstorms slowing the bedraggled processions of horse and hand carts, the fear was of being overtaken by Russian tanks making speedy progress over flat frozen ground.

Most at risk were the indigenous Germans of East Prussia, where they formed the large majority. But elsewhere on the Baltic there were many of German antecedents who had done well out of the war at the expense of their fellow Estonians, Latts, Lithuanians and Finns. But whatever their national allegiance, few were prepared to take their chances with a military bent on wiping out the memory of humiliating defeats earlier in the war. The Wehrmacht had been none too scrupulous in its first encounters with the Red Army. Now that fortunes were reversed, revenge was the driving force. Those who suffered the attentions of the triumphant Red Army were liable to greet death as a welcome release.

German propaganda made the most of Russian atrocities, hoping to build up a tide of fury that would stiffen resistance. Pictures of the massacre at Nemmersdorf, an East Prussian village recaptured by the Wehrmacht, were shown widely in print and at cinemas. But the results were not at all what Goebbels intended. Though Nemmersdorf entered the public imagination as a symbol of Soviet barbarism, the rapes and the murders in cold blood of between 60 and 70 civilians instilled not so much a desire for retaliation as a fear of suffering the same fate.

A panic to escape took hold of entire communities. Before long, the great East Prussian migration stretched back from Koenigsberg and Pillau to the Oder River, 250 miles of snowbound roads and tracks. 'In endless procession the horse-drawn wagons moved, at times three abreast. Beside them, men and women dragged along on foot.'[14] No one could possibly make an accurate count but it was a fair guess that over 2 million refugees were on the move. Among

those who took night shelter from Russian artillery at Kahlberg*
to the north of Koenigsberg was a woman who had just lost her
child. A family she had met on the way stayed with her.

The young woman whose child had died complained of
fever and pain in her back. In the morning, her pain was
so violent that they could not go on. They stayed in the
dunes, listening to the distant rumble of the Russian artillery, afraid the Russians might break through to the Gulf
of Danzig and cut them off.

In the afternoon the young woman died without another
word. They made a bier of branches, and buried her in a shallow grave in the sand. Then they moved on. They passed a
heap of nearly fifty vehicles lying about on the road, tipped
over, shattered, or burned. Among them dead horses, and
people trying to repair or salvage. An air attack had hit them
last night. Some army trucks stood nearby, burnt to a crisp –
probably they had called down the catastrophe.[15]

On 23 January, the Red Army reached the mouth of the Vistula
where it joined the sea at Elbing.** This cut the land route between
East Prussia and the West. After the departure of the last refugee
train the only cross-country escape was over the frozen Vistula
Lagoon to Danzig or Gotenhafen. Under frequent attack by Soviet
bombers and fighter aircraft, without camouflage or shelter,
thousands began the long trek. With overladen heavy wagons the
chance had to be taken that the ice would bear the weight. It was
a gamble that too often failed.

---

* Now Krynica Morska.
** Now Elbląg.

The ice groaned and creaked. To the right and to the left lay the victims of other days: sunken wagons with all their load, the frozen carcasses of horses – and some men and women, dead, grotesquely twisted. The girl tried to look straight ahead. But she saw it all.

Soft parts of the ice had been covered with planks. But that meant little. The girl passed wagons that had broken through not more than an hour ago. There were many stops – more vehicles broke through the ice, they were being unloaded and, if possible, pulled out again.

The wagon ahead of her broke through after half an hour. One of the women who had walked alongside had fallen into a hole – now they were fishing for her with poles. The coachman had cut the harness of the horses, and the dripping animals were trying to struggle out of the water in deadly fright. But the wagon was lost. She and those who followed drove round it.

At seven o'clock Russian planes swooped down on them. They attacked further ahead. She saw them dive, and heard the clatter of the machine guns and the dull explosions of their small bombs. There was a panic, horses tore loose, distance was not kept, and a whole row of wagons broke through the overburdened ice. Some horses drowned. The shrill voices of women called for help. Some women, silent with a despair beyond words, circled round holes in the ice that had swallowed a child, a mother, a husband. Or they ran to the next wagon and, on their knees, begged: 'Please don't leave us …' But who could help among all those who barely got their own carts through?[16]

If an exodus by land was all but impossible, there remained the chance of an escape across the sea, assuming, of course, that ships could be made available to lift the host of refugees now congregating along the shore. As the land route closed, Doenitz gave the order to begin evacuation by sea to ports beyond Soviet reach. Codenamed Hannibal, it was to become the biggest ever seaborne rescue.

CHAPTER FOUR

W hy did Hitler sanction Operation Hannibal? He was notori-
ously unfeeling when it came to protecting civilian lives.
In so far as he had a coherent view of the plight of refugees it was
that they should stand and fight. To attempt to escape was to invite
a deserved retribution. What changed his mind? The chances are,
nothing did.

Though refusing to the last to give up territory gained earlier
in the war, when annihilation was a near certainty he could be persuaded to sign evacuation orders. He was doing so as early as October
1944. But it was the fighting men, not civilians, that he wanted to
save, those who could live to fight another day in defence of the
Reich. Doenitz had a ruthless edge but he was more the humanitar-
ian. Even so, he managed to get away with Operation Hannibal only
when all hope was lost of holding the Baltic coast and only then by
disguising his intentions under cover of military necessity.

Supplies had to be carried to the military. If, for the return
trip, ships took on human cargo, who was to argue? Certainly not
the Fuehrer, whose state of nervous collapse was becoming more
apparent by the day. The launch of Operation Hannibal was not the
only significant event of 23 January. On that day, with even German
commentators conceding that the war had reached a decisive stage,
Hitler made the bizarre decision to place his interior minister and

SS chief, Reichsfuehrer Heinrich Himmler, a functionary with no military knowledge or experience to speak of, in command of the new Army Group Vistula, with orders to frustrate Russian efforts to take East Prussia. The madness of desperation was all too obvious. Himmler's appointment was short-lived. His abject failure to mount an effective counter-offensive was the beginning of the end for Hitler's closest confidant.

Leading from the front of Operation Hannibal was the recently promoted Rear Admiral Konrad Engelhardt. An energetic and experienced sea transport officer who had seen wartime service in France, Italy, Africa, the Crimea and the Baltic, Engelhardt exercised wide authority over merchant as well as naval shipping. In seafaring matters his orders took precedence over those of the Wehrmacht, though relations with the land forces, the SS in particular, were edgy. Engelhardt reported to Admiral Oscar Kummetz – the senior naval officer in the western Baltic region whose excusable failure to destroy a British convoy in a closely run Battle of the Barents Sea in late 1942 had led Hitler to his decision, later rescinded by Doenitz, to scrap the German surface fleet – and to Admiral Friedrich Burchardi who was responsible for the eastern region, including the coast of Prussia.

The three worked well together, with Kummetz and Burchardi happy to delegate to a colleague of proven organisational flair. They had known for some time what was likely to be required of them. While the official line up to the end of 1944 and even beyond was of an imminent change of fortune on the Eastern Front, a counter-attack that would turn the Russian tide, behind closed doors and out of Hitler's earshot, the high probability of further retreats from Baltic strongholds was accepted and built into contingency plans. From the autumn of 1944, Engelhardt began building up a fleet of evacuation and supply ships.

Since, apart from submarines, no new vessels of any worth were in production, Engelhardt had to draw on merchant shipping which for one reason or another was out of commission. Much of it was held back by commercial operators who were unwilling to risk their assets in a free-for-all with the Russians. Engelhardt had the power to requisition whatever he needed but there were strong forces of obstruction, particularly when civil administrators, sporting their Nazi insignia, had to be cajoled or bullied to cooperate. Though invariably taking care to protect their own escape routes, they feared above all the accusation from on high that they were submitting to defeatism.

Engelhardt also had his eye on one-time cruise liners now used as military or civilian staff accommodation ships. Secure in their moorings, these floating hotels gave more attention to domestic arrangements than to preparing for a return to the open sea. To get them back into working order, Engelhardt had to find deck and engine crews and to plunder what was left of oil and coal reserves.

Not least of his worries was squaring matters with Doenitz, who had a proprietorial interest in the accommodation ships. Most of them were reserved for U-boat instructors and their cadets, the pride of the Kriegsmarine and the best hope of forcing concessions from the Allies as they faced up to the potential of the new generation of submarines. Doenitz temporised. The U-boat training divisions were to be moved west to Luebeck. Once this had been achieved, the ships were to be handed over to Engelhardt for refugee and troop evacuation. For his own headquarters, Engelhardt found an unseaworthy but otherwise functioning ship which he had towed to Flensburg.

In selecting his staff Engelhardt had more regard for efficiency than for numbers. His liaison officer, Lieutenant Commander Eschricht, stayed close to Kummetz to feed updates on movements across the Baltic. Field officers were based in Hamburg, Stettin and Danzig with staff empowered to uncork the bottlenecks at all the embarkation points. It was an administrative structure that proved its worth time and again.

By the end of 1944, Engelhardt had at his disposal 22 liners each over 10,000 tons. The largest was *Cap Arcona* at 27,564 tons but others were well over 20,000 tons. In the same class 25 cargo ships were made ready to join the Baltic ferry service. It was impossible to keep track of the number of small boats involved. Ranging from ice-breakers to fishing smacks, they set out alone or in convoy on course for one of the supposedly safe German ports or for occupied Denmark or neutral Sweden where extra mouths to feed were seldom welcome.

An ongoing concern was the prospect of doing battle with the Soviet navy. Now that Russia controlled the entire coast along the Gulf of Finland there was a real possibility of submarine attacks on German convoys. The threat to Kriegsmarine U-boat bases and training areas had also to be taken into account.

Large-scale evacuation began with shipping out some 60,000 residents of Memel and about the same number from other vulnerable spots along the Baltic coast. And that was only the start. In November, there were over 700 crossings without a single loss. It was much the same in December, though one trawler was sunk by a random air attack.[1]

The sights and sounds of battle were never far away. While Soviet aircraft showered German defences with phosphorus bombs, the heavy cruisers *Luetzow* and *Admiral Scheer* stood offshore to deliver salvoes of 280mm shells over the heads of the land forces to inflict devastation on the Russian lines. The range was all of 22 miles. Through the range finder observers on the *Admiral Scheer* could see long columns of refugees moving slowly across the frozen Curonian Lagoon to the long, narrow sandspit connecting to Pillau and Koenigsberg.

So intense was her firepower that the *Admiral Scheer* was eventually forced to withdraw to Kiel to have new liners fitted to her guns. When the ship left Gotenhafen in early March, she took with her 800 refugees and 200 wounded. It was her last service to the Reich. In Kiel dockyard, she was easily spotted by RAF air reconnaissance. A succession of attacks left her unscathed but on 9 April 1945 her luck ran out. A stick of bombs hit the water close against her side. The explosion tore away her plating. The *Admiral Scheer* keeled over and sank within minutes. She remained in shallow water for the remainder of the war. (In the process of rebuilding the port, the post-war administration filled her berth with rubble from bombsites. So it was that the *Admiral Scheer* earned the distinction of being the only ship of the Kriegsmarine to be buried on land.)

With the loss of the *Schleswig-Holstein*, sunk outside Gotenhafen, and the *Admiral Hipper*, put out of action while in dry dock at Kiel, the sea-to-land battle was left to the *Luetzow* and the *Prinz Eugen*, the only two remaining naval heavyweights, with support from the old battleship *Schlesien* and the light cruiser *Leipzig*.

Luetzow met her end anchored at Swinemuende. At 5 p.m. on 16 April, the crew were at their evening meal when warning came through of the approach of eighteen Lancaster bombers.

> With the sound of men's clattering, trampling feet as they hurried to their guns there now mingled suddenly the barking of the light flak from destroyers in the vicinity of the *Luetzow*. At once the alarm-bell's 'Fritz ... Fritz ... Fritz' shrilled through the cruiser. The men left on the mess-decks

sprang to close the armoured deadlights over the scuttles – but several of them never got so far.

Suddenly a great quivering shock went through the ship – then a second, duller thud – and immediately a third. The men's quarters, where they had been having supper only five minutes before, were now in utter chaos, and the ladders to the upper decks were torn away. As sailors and cadets pulled themselves, aching, to their feet – the ship listing heavily to port – from somewhere or other there was a shout: 'Get on deck, we're sinking!'.

Thick reddish-brown smoke billowed out to meet the men now hurriedly seeking a way out to safety. The *Luetzow* was heeling over more than ever on her side. In this oblique position her bows protruded queerly from the water, while the quarter-deck was many feet lower and in parts already awash. One bomb had dropped into the marshy ground between ship and land and splashed a fountain of black, sticky slime over the ship, through which the men were now wading ankle-deep.

'All hands abandon ship – except flak and damage-control personnel!'

Already a second wave of bombers could be seen approaching. Hundreds were still swimming in the water or running to take cover in the near-by woods when the next series of heavy bombs exploded round the ship.

But somehow the *Luetzow*, though listing heavily to port and with a huge gash in her side, was not yet done for.

Eleven days later a great deal had been done to the *Luetzow*.

Great wedges of timber had been hewn and inserted in order to close up the underwater leaks in her side. A salvage-vessel had managed, through successive processes of clearing and flooding, to raise the vessel from its crooked position so that it now lay straight on the canal bottom. More could not be done; the *Luetzow* would never float again.[2]

But her guns were still in order. They were firing again on 28 April when the Russians broke through at Pasewalk. Then on the night of 1 May, a fire broke out. Unable to bring it under control the crew abandoned ship as shells began to explode. By morning the *Luetzow* was a wreck beyond salvage.

The pattern was for refugees closest to the Russian advance to be brought south to Pillau, Danzig and Gotenhafen, there to be offloaded on to larger ships for the Baltic crossing. Put like that, the procedure might seem to have been reasonably straightforward. It was anything but. For one thing, in the middle of a hard winter, the ports were ill-equipped to cope with the thousands of refugees thronging the holding areas. Makeshift shelters and soup kitchens could do little to ease the suffering of women, children and old people who made up the bulk of the migration. Soviet air attacks added to the terror and the chaos. In one of the worst attacks early in the year, an ammunition dump in Pillau blew up. Hundreds were killed or injured. Hospitals were overwhelmed. Ambulances with their wounded were left by the roadside. Over one night the refugee population of Pillau increased by some 28,000.

The threat from the air intensified over the spring. The supply of American-built bombers and fighters was welcomed by the Russians though the shortage of experienced pilots tended towards easy targets such as crowded ports rather than ships at sea.

The Baltic Sea, where Operation Hannibal was played out

A much greater menace to shipping came from below the surface where Russian submarines, having broken through the German blockade of the Gulf of Finland, were increasingly active. Equipment was not of the best – faulty torpedoes were like on-board time bombs – and crews lacked training. But they proved to be quick learners. Their hunting ground was the open sea. Operating chiefly at night, the U-boats kept clear of the shallow coastal waters where they could be easily spotted. Any remaining doubts as to the hazards of running the gauntlet of the Russian submarine patrols were silenced once and for all in late January with the sinking of the *Wilhelm Gustloff*.

Gustloff had been the Nazi Party leader in Switzerland who had met his end with five bullets to the head, fired by a young Yugoslav Jew. Until his assassination, few in Germany had ever heard of this minor politician but the manner of his departure made him a folk hero worthy of a state funeral and a lasting memorial. In May 1937, his widow launched the new liner that carried his name. Designed as a floating holiday camp for members of Strength Through Joy, a Nazi leisure organisation that aimed to extend middle-class holidays to the workers, it had a crew of 400 catering for around 1,500 passengers. Soon after the outbreak of war, having been converted into a hostel for cadet submariners, the *Gustloff* sailed to Gotenhafen where she remained in dock for four years.

The command of the *Gustloff* was a prime example of the difficulties faced by Engelhardt and his colleagues in persuading the services to work together. As master, the 67-year-old Friedrich Petersen did not get on with Commander Wilhelm Zahn, the senior naval officer of the submarine training school. With the launch of Operation Hannibal, it was Zahn who gave the order for the ship to be made ready to sail within 48 hours. Petersen resented the assumption that he had nothing to contribute. Zahn was not strong on tact.

In the last days of January, the *Gustloff* was preparing to take on board 1,500 submariners and their families along with several thousand (no one could be sure quite how many) refugees and wounded soldiers. At the dockside, enduring snow and icy winds, long cordons of refugees waited to hear if they were to be among the passengers. There was a thriving black market for places at the head of the queue.

The precious pieces of paper, printed in Gothic type on the ship's own press which in peacetime had provided its special newspaper and menus, were headed: 'Identity Pass for MS *Wilhelm Gustloff*'. They carried the stamp of the headquarters of the U-boat Training Division along with the owner's name and reason for being on board. U-boat personnel claimed them as of right for their families; refugees with local and Nazi Party influence schemed for them; and those with money tried to buy them. In the early stages those who had managed to acquire passes went aboard in orderly fashion, while the refugees packed on the quay looked at them with bitter envy. But as thousands more refugees poured into the dock area the tension mounted, and the *Wilhelm Gustloff* was tugged a few metres away from the quay to prevent the refugees rushing the gangways or sneaking aboard during the night. Those with passes boarded a ferry at the other side of the harbour and climbed a guarded gangway on the starboard, seaward side.[3]

Nonetheless, embarkation was soon close to breakdown. 'You

really had to fight a way through to the ships,' recalled Fritz Brustat-Naval.

> I remember forcing a way through with a squad of wounded soldiers who were being evacuated and when we got there the ship was still very bureaucratic and passes had to be shown. The whole area was full of refugees and cluttered with horse-drawn covered wagons which had brought them thousands of miles through the snow. What I remember best was all the horses and dogs which had come overland with the treks and had been abandoned by their owners because they had nothing to feed them on. They were all over the city centre and the dock area.[4]

Another witness claimed that the docks held over 60,000 refugees.

As soon as the gangways were let down people raced forward and pushed their way in. 'In the confusion a lot of children got separated from their parents. Either the kids got on board leaving their parents on the harbour or the children were left behind as their parents got pushed forward by the throng.' In the rush to get ready to sail, corners were cut. One young passenger noted the shortage of lifeboats. There were davits for eleven lifeboats on each side of the sun deck. But several were empty while the boats that were in place were full of snow with their launching ropes frozen to their pulleys. The crew was severely undermanned. The few petty officers struggled to maintain discipline.

On the morning of 29 January, the *Gustloff* was more or less ready to sail. On board were 1,626 naval and military personnel and 4,424 refugees, though those figures were soon invalidated by last-minute getaways who scrambled up nets put down to lift them off small boats. There were more than 3,000 of them.

But where were the escort ships? The *Robert Ley*, the *Pretoria* and the *Ubena*, each carrying up to 7,000 passengers, had already made a successful crossing but they had sailed in convoy with a full escort. With the build-up of Operation Hannibal, there were simply not enough warships to go round. Apart from the *Gustloff*, other liners were standing by for orders to sail. No one could say how long they would have to wait. Commander Zahn took the initiative. The *Gustloff* would sail on 30 January.

The plan was to make for Hela,* there to rendezvous with the *Hansa*, also loaded with refugees, and for the two ships to enlist an escort of torpedo boats and recovery vessels. When the *Gustloff* left Gotenhafen, it was accompanied by a single mine-sweeper, which took up its position ahead of the ship, pushing its way through chunks of ice floating in the water. An hour later, the *Hansa* was spotted. But when flag signals were exchanged (security demanded radio silence) it was to find that the *Hansa* had engine trouble. A lengthy delay was in prospect.

It was now that a critical and, as it turned out, fatal decision was made by the district commander of submarines who retained the final authority over what was still technically one of his accommo-dation ships. There was no way of telling how long it would take for the *Hansa* to repair her engines. Meanwhile, both the *Hansa* and *Gustloff* were anchored in daylight off a coast that was vulner-able to Russian air attack. The decision was to halve the risks by ordering the *Gustloff* to proceed alone.

Tossed about on a rough sea with a load of nervous passengers eager to be on their way, the reaction to the news on board was one of relief. On the bridge, Zahn was less phlegmatic. It was no comfort to hear that the *Gustloff* was to have two escort vessels;

---

* Now Hel.

both were small, old and ill-equipped torpedo boats. Not long after the *Gustloff* resumed its voyage one of the boats started taking in water and had to turn back. With Captain Petersen and Zahn arguing over tactics – the latter wanted 16 knots on a zigzagging course while Petersen asserted that 12 knots was the maximum possible speed and that zigzagging was beyond the capacity of a large, overloaded liner – neither was aware that the navigation lights of the *Gustloff* had been spotted by a Russian submarine.

It took two hours for the *S-13* to catch up with the *Gustloff*. The target was only 1,000 metres away when Captain Marinesko gave the order to fire. Three torpedoes found their mark. One passenger, thirteen-year-old Guenther von Maydell, showed remarkable composure for his years. 'What shall we do?' a woman cried. Guenther told her to put on a coat and a lifebelt, and she rushed off to find her daughter who had gone to another cabin with some friends. Guenther, who had got to know the topography of the ship, then went off in search of his mother. Reunited, the two of them

> ran up the frozen and sloping deck to one of the lifeboats where sailors were already trying to operate the winches. It was an almost impossible task, for the machinery was frozen stiff and the scratch crew was ill-trained to get lifeboats away smoothly in such conditions.

But they managed to scramble aboard one of the boats. As for the rest:

> The privileged passengers with cabins of their own, even crowded ones, were the most fortunate, for at least they were on the upper decks within easy reach of the open

air and the boats. For the mass of refugees packed into the public rooms on the lower decks things were more desperate. Few of them knew anything about the layout of the ship, and hardly any had bothered to look for the emergency exits which had been carefully signposted by the crew before sailing. They had been glad to get passage on an escape ship, and for the many who had never before been to sea there was no means of knowing how to get out.[5]

Sigrid Bergfeld was pushed forward to one of the lifeboats. But she held back for a woman carrying a baby. The woman got in and they began lowering the boat. Sigrid watched it capsize as it hit the water. The woman and her baby disappeared.

Faced with the horror of drowning in icy water, there were those who chose a quicker way to die. Heinz Schoen, a survivor who subsequently interviewed other survivors, told what happened in a lower-deck cabin when a sailor forced open a jammed door.

On the floor lay the bodies of a woman and a small child. In the centre of the cabin was a naval officer holding a still smoking pistol while a terrified five-year-old boy clutched his father's leg. 'Get out!' ordered the officer, staring vacantly at the sailor.

Another sailor named Dorch heard a woman shout at her husband, 'Put a quick end to us all'.

There were three shots as the man killed his wife and two children, then silence when his weapon jammed as he tried to end his own life. He shouted to Dorch to borrow his pistol but then lost his balance and fell into the sea.

It took the *Wilhelm Gustloff* 70 minutes to sink. After the first shock, the ship stabilised. Those who were still clinging to rails and ropes hoped that the liner might stay afloat long enough for rescue ships to appear out of the night. But then, under pressure of thousands of tons of water, the bulkheads and watertight doors gave way. The ship tipped slowly over on its side. Eva Luck, a sixteen-year-old, with her mother and six-year-old sister were hurled off the deck.

The funnel was lying almost parallel with the sea. People were jumping in. I could hear the ship's siren and felt the ice-cold water round my legs. I reached out to try and grab my sister. I felt nothing but the water as it swept me out and over the side.

Order prevailed on the Bridge. Forty-five minutes after the torpe-does had struck,

With the wheelhouse indicator recording a list of twenty-five degrees and waves hitting the Bridge windows, Commander Zahn supervised the destruction of the ship's codes and papers. Then Steward Max Bonnet appeared, still wearing his white jacket. With enormous difficulty he managed to carry his tray. 'A final cognac, gentlemen,' he said. They drank and threw down the glasses.

For a few seconds the thick glass of the Bridge windscreen cleared and they caught a surrealistic glimpse of a couple of men climbing into a raft. Within seconds a huge wave seized the toylike craft and hurled it at the superstructure of the Bridge.[6]

Zahn survived. So too did Captain Petersen, who found a place in one of the few serviceable lifeboats.

The only ship of any size within rescue distance was the *Admiral Hipper*, carrying around 1,500 evacuees. As her escort she had a torpedo boat – *T-36* – loaded with military stores and another 250 refugees. A distress signal brought them and other support vessels hurrying to the stricken *Gustloff*. There was little they could do. *T-36* picked up some survivors but the *Hipper*, fearing that she might be the next victim of Russian submarines, detected nearby, could not wait. In making good her escape the *Hipper* ploughed her way through the floating dead and dying. In what was to be the biggest human loss in one sinking in maritime history, over 9,000 perished. Those saved numbered between 1,000 and 1,300.

News of the fate of the *Wilhelm Gustloff* was announced by Doenitz on 31 January at the Fuehrer's conference on naval affairs. Regretting the losses but taking some comfort in the knowledge that many other overloaded ships had made successful crossings, the Grand Admiral could not resist taking a stab at the Luftwaffe.

Russian submarines are able to operate undisturbed in the Baltic Sea only because there are no German aircraft there to combat them. Because of the shortage of escort forces the Navy must restrict itself to direct protection of convoys. The only practical defence against submarines is the radar-equipped aircraft, the same weapon which enabled the enemy to paralyse our own submarine warfare …

Ten days later, Captain Marinesko and his *S-13* U-boat came across another sitting target. This time it was the *General von Steuben*, a former trans-Atlantic liner carrying some 3,500 refugees and wounded. She sailed from Pillau on the evening of 9 February, escorted by an old torpedo boat and an even older minesweeper. Between ten and eleven o'clock the *Von Steuben* entered the stretch of water where the *Gustloff* had met her end. Hoping for better luck, her captain ordered full speed, such that the escort had trouble keeping up. In the event it was good that they were able to do so. They would soon be needed.

> The chronometer on the Bridge pointed close to one o'clock when a muted explosion rocked the vessel. The alarm sounded. For a short moment, the liner sailed on as if nothing had happened. On the upper deck, the gun crews were racing to their turrets. Then the ship stopped. What followed took only a few minutes.
>
> In the glare of the spotlight of the minesweeper and of the distress rockets rising from her Bridge, the *Steuben* began to go down, prow first. The captain, who immediately realised that his craft had been hit by torpedo from starboard, tried to lower the lifeboats on port – but there was no time for that.[7]

Those who escaped from the upper decks crowded together on the stern of the liner as it rose higher. In seven minutes, the stern rose vertically out of the water and the *Von Steuben* went slowly down into the sea. While the torpedo boat dropped depth charges to drive off the Russian submarine, the crew of the minesweeper were hanging off the sides grabbing at survivors as they floated past. Three hundred were saved.

Despite the loss of the *Gustloff* and the *Von Steuben*, the evacuation balance sheet for February showed a massive net gain. Over half a million refugees were carried safely to the West.

There were many hair's-breadth escapes. In early March when Soviet forces were within striking distance of Stolpmuende, the town was cleared of 20,300 refugees in two days. Fourteen middling-size ships headed west accompanied by a fleet of fishing trawlers, tugs, pilot boats, ferries and motor launches – in fact, anything that could float and looked seaworthy. Commander Kolbe who had organised the operation was the last to leave.[8]

Around the same time, 75,000 troops and civilians were lifted off the island of Wolin. Of the bigger ships, the *Deutschland* alone carried 11,000 refugees. The rumble of Soviet artillery, like an approaching storm, was getting louder as the ship weighed anchor.

Koenigsberg, capital of East Prussia, declared by Hitler to be an 'invincible bastion of the German spirit', was next in the Soviet firing line. By late January, the Nazi hierarchy had made good their escape. Among them was the infamous Erich Koch, gauleiter of East Prussia, who had spent the new year whining to Hitler that the Wehrmacht were not doing enough to save him while he was spreading propaganda lies to keep the people in place. Koch was already at sea on the way to Denmark when, on the streets of Koenigsberg, loudspeakers blared out the message that it was now every man, woman and child for themselves. The rush to get to Pillau with the chance of finding a place on one of the evacuation ships soon turned to panic as thousands began the trek by road only to be mown down by Soviet planes or blown to bits by Soviet artillery. Though outgunned and under siege, Koenigsberg defied expectations by holding out until early April.

Fighting along the coastal region of East Prussia known as the Heiligenbeil Cauldron, the German Fourth Army managed to keep control of around 50 kilometres of shoreline up to 20 kilometres deep. On the seaward side was the Curonian Lagoon where, until the end of February, the ice was strong enough to bear refugees as they crossed to the relative safety of the sandspit that stretched from Elbing almost to Pillau.

In mid-March, when coastal traffic was no longer practical, German troops joined the civilian refugees in the rush for whatever craft were still able to get close to dry land.

A motley collection of German army units, survivors of other battles, came together in Koenigsberg where the commandant, General Otto Lasch, managed to put together a fighting force of sufficient strength to mount a counter-attack to reopen the land corridor with the West. Made to realise that the conquest of Koenigsberg was not to be a walkover, the Russians took time to reassess their strategy. This gave Lasch the chance to strengthen his main line of defence along the city perimeter marked by twelve sturdy 19th-century forts.

Some sense of order was restored to Koenigsberg. A steady stream of refugees took the opportunity to make for Pillau, though numbers fell when news came through of the sinking of the *Wilhelm Gustloff*. With the lull in the fighting, there were those who were persuaded that things were getting back to normal. Why take the risk of drowning in the high seas? The illusion of security was soon dispelled. On 2 April, Russian shells rained down on the German defences.

The German positions were smashed, the trenches ploughed up, embrasures levelled with the ground, compa-nies buried, the signals system torn apart, and ammunition stores destroyed. Clouds of smoke lay over the remnants of the houses of the inner city. On the streets were strewn fragments of masonry, shot-up vehicles and the bodies of horses and human beings.[9]

When a crowd of survivors set off on the road to Pillau they were strafed by machine gun fire and mortars. Many were cut down as they tried to get back into the city. German resistance was now reduced to a few pockets. At the harbour in Pillau,

everyone was pushing their way towards the ships. There some appalling scenes. Humans turned into animals. Women threw their children into the water, just so they could come along. The general confusion was then increased by fully disoriented troops streaming into the town and houses, mingling with the refugees and pushing their way onto the ships. To get through the barriers to the ships, soldiers snatched children off their mothers, saying they wanted to take their family on board. Others dressed in women's clothing to try and get away on the ships. If they were discovered during the patrol, they were brought on board and after a brief trial were shot by court martial. The first of these deserters were hung from lampposts with signs around their necks to serve as a deterrent.[10]

A rather more cheerful image of the evacuation has been left by Martin Bergau who praised the German navy for 'an amazing job … thousands were saved at the last minute'. The writer was carried to Roenne on the Danish island of Bornholm.

We got some Danish money, and I bought myself a huge piece of cake with cream. Here it was peacetime, we didn't need to black anything out. We could hardly believe that this was possible. The next day I went down to the beach with some companions. The March sun was warm enough for us to take off our pullovers. I was shocked to see that my lovely marine pullover was almost crawling, it was so full of lice. The others noticed the same thing. The straw camp was obviously seething with lice. I made a fire with dried driftwood and burned the 'lousy pelt' with indignation, thinking to myself: 'If your mother knew that you had lice she'd die of shame'.[11]

It was now abundantly clear to Lasch that Koenigsberg was lost and that fighting on served no purpose except to increase the death count. After his offer to surrender was accepted, around 35,000 German soldiers were marched into captivity. They had endured a three-month siege.

The houses burned and smoked. The Russians were adding to the stuffed furniture, musical instruments, kitchen utensils, painting and china which they had already thrown from the windows. Shot-up cars stood between blazing tanks, and items of clothing and equipment were strewn about. Drunken Russians staggered around. They fired in wild abandon, or tried to ride bicycles – and then fell off and lay bleeding and unconscious in the gutters. Weeping and struggling girls and women were dragged into the houses, and children called after their parents. The sights were intolerable. We marched on.[12]

While Koenigsberg was in its death throes, what was left of the German Second Army led by General Dietrich von Saucken was battling mud and rain in an attempt to build up the defences of

Danzig and Gotenhafen. An East Prussian by birth and dedication, Saucken was a professional soldier who was ready to follow Hitler's orders to create 'fortresses' of the two cities. At the same time he was determined to do whatever was necessary to save the 1.5 million civilian refugees and the 100,000 wounded soldiers waiting to be lifted out of harm's way. Under heavy air attack, the evacuation across the Baltic continued by day and night.

Meanwhile, forward observers in the marshland south-east of Danzig and in the wooded hills to the west were in radio contact, directing supporting fire from *Schlesien*, *Prinz Eugen* and *Leipzig*. As the Russians closed in, Saucken urged his troops to greater sacrifices. Luck favoured the attackers when a young girl, a member of the Polish resistance, smuggled through to the Russians a map of the Gotenhafen defences. On 15 March, the first Russian shells fell on the city.

Identifying the weak spots in the German barricade, the Russians were able to fight their way into the suburbs. By 26 March they were in the city centre where the guns could be directed at the refugee ships trying to leave the harbour.

A gun would fire, then came the explosion of the shell, and another craft capsized and went to the bottom with its load of fascists. Another shot, then another – and a barge flared up and heeled over.[13]

By then, the defenders had given up on trying to hold Gotenhafen. Harbour installations were destroyed as the survivors who could walk straggled along the coast towards Danzig.

No one could have counted the crowds in the cellars of Danzig. The highway from the city to the harbour was hemmed with corpses – not just of people who had died of cold or exhaustion, but now also of those who had fallen under the machine guns of the Russian planes. Wagons were standing there with horses dead in their harness, and here and there a woman or a child still crouched on top of a wagon as they had died. But when the word of the arrival of a ship spread, a new stream of refugees rushed out to the harbour.[14]

The city was gripped by battle fever with the SS wandering the streets meting out death sentences to any who seemed reluctant to throw themselves into the slaughter. Waves of Russian bombers flew low over the endless processions of refugees. 'This is what hell must be like,' said a witness of the massacre.

Danzig was lost. On the night after the fall of Gotenhafen, the last transport left the harbour. The following day Russian tanks entered the city. Under cover of darkness, a unit of the German Fourth Ranger Division came to rest at a village on the Vistula delta.

In front of us … we could see the dispatch riders of the various units. Girls from Zoppot and Danzig were sitting in some of the sidecars. They had been with the troops for some days now, and nobody objected to that. We noted the dearly beloved of the dispatch rider from the Pioneers – she was a pretty railway conductress, and he was determined to marry her at the first opportunity.

There was something sinister about the way the narrow gables of the old houses soared into the sky. They were thin, and they seemed to sway in the wind. The thought was still in my mind when someone yelled a warning from in front: 'Watch out! The wall's coming down!' I saw the motor cycles buzz into confused movement in a fraction of a second, and then the wall broke into several pieces in the air and crashed on the crowd. There was a roar, a crack, a violent gust of air – and then an impenetrable cloud of dust. I stood as if paralysed on the running board.

We all hastened to the scene of the catastrophe, where the debris lay nearly one metre deep over the motor cycles. All the soldiers were safe – for years now their reactions had been honed to lightning speed, and they had been able to leap to one side. But the girls had not moved from the sidecars and they were all buried. Cold sweat ran down our backs as we began to dig like madmen. The little Pioneer dispatch rider seemed to be out of his mind. We helped him to lift his dead bride from the sidecar. With extreme care he proceeded to wash her face, which was covered with a thick layer of dust.[15]

To the rear, Danzig burned.

All along the Baltic coast, isolated pockets of German resistance came under sustained attack. The small port of Kolberg was typical in so far as its military presence was pathetically modest while its refugee population was pathetically large – not much over 2,000 troops to protect nearly 70,000 refugees. Since the local Nazi administration refused to act because it had no higher authority telling it what to do, the commandant, Colonel Fritz Fullriede, took charge of the refugees, guiding them in manageable numbers to the quayside where the Kriegsmarine was operating a ferry service to Swinemuende to connect with ships on hand for the Baltic voyage. As luck would have it, the first load of passengers to depart Swinemuende just missed a raid by

American bombers, adding their support to the Soviet campaign. It was a narrow escape.

> We steamed out again at fifteen knots. We had just passed the lighthouse when we heard the roar of a carpet of bombs landing on the town and harbour of Swinemuende. A high white wall signified where a line of bombs descended on the exact place where we had turned. The paralysing tension gradually relaxed, and while we were repassing the moles on the way out two refugee children appeared on deck. They were holding hands and laughing with joy. That made us happier than anything for a long time.[16]

The evacuation continued until 18 March when the few remaining troops and civilians left Kolberg. Among the last out, Fullriede made it back to Berlin where he was awarded the Knight's Cross of the Iron Cross.

With the Russian occupation of all the major Baltic ports, the only hope for refugees was to make for the sand dunes of the Hela Peninsula. Barges and fishing boats were sent from Hela to the mouth of the Vistula to clear pockets of wounded and helpless. Engineers built jetties along the banks of the river so that rescue vessels could dock even at low tide. With Soviet shore batteries opposite Hela keeping up a heavy barrage and fighter bombers terrorising overcrowded boats waiting to leave, some 250,000 refugees were picked up from around the bay to be delivered to larger transports waiting outside the shallow waters. In Operation Walpurgisnacht, 8,000 men of the 7th Armoured Corps were rescued from Gotenhafen by a flotilla of 60 landing craft and other small boats. Having taken them across the bay to Hela, the same flotilla returned to collect 30,000 civilians.

Stettin was another beleaguered settlement whence the citizens departed en masse. A convoy of small ships, braving artillery fire from the advancing Red Army, set course for the West. Stettin fell on 26 April. As the refugee crisis boiled over, relations between the Kriegsmarine and Party administrators who, even as they made good their escape, were still proclaiming the ultimate Nazi victory, deteriorated to the point of open conflict.

In Danzig Bay, torpedo boat *T-28* – commanded by Lieutenant Hans Temming – noticed a small steamer under way north, decks empty. *T-28* hailed the steamer, asking where she was headed, and if she had any refugees on board. The steamer responded that she had Gauleiter Forster on board and was under way for Hela. *T-28*, awash with refugees, then requested that the steamer heave to and take some of them aboard her. The steamer failed to answer to this. *T-28* then coldly announced that if the steamer did not stop, the T-boat would sink her. *T-28*'s crew began to clear a gun. Whereupon the little steamer hove to and took off a full load, continuing to Hela. The Gauleiter was not again seen or heard from.[17]

With growing confidence, Russian air and sea raiders exacted an increasing toll. Thirteen German transports were lost in the first week of April alone.

There was one more disaster to rank with the loss of the *Wilhelm Gustloff* and the *General von Steuben*. On the evening of 16 April, the *Goya*, a modern freighter designed to carry only cargo, took on board over 6,000 passengers who were packed into the holds, shoulder to shoulder.

Goya had already completed four such runs before her luck ran out. Russian submarines were lying in wait west of Hela. At just before midnight Captain Konovalov, commander of the minelaying submarine *L-3*, gave the order to fire two torpedoes. The *Goya* broke in half and was gone in less than seven minutes. Only 170 lives were saved.

The sinking was reported to the Fuehrer's naval conference on 18 April. Doenitz, as was his habit, gave the positive side of the story.

> In connection with the loss of several hundred persons in the sinking of the steamship *Goya*, the C-in-C, Navy, points out that personnel losses in the transports in the Eastern areas up to this time have been extremely small, i.e. 0.49 per cent. These unfortunate losses seem very large every time a ship is sunk, and it is easy to forget that at the same time a large number of ships with numerous wounded and refugees aboard reach port safely.

It was no less than the truth. The success rate of the big ships taking part in Operation Hannibal was impressive. The *General San Martin* and *Eberhard Essberger* came through relatively unscathed after making thirteen and twelve crossings respectively. After seven runs, the *Deutschland* could boast 70,000 grateful passengers. Another 67,000 gave thanks to the *Essberger*.

Operation Hannibal was at full pitch when Doenitz heard that he was to be the next Fuehrer. It was not the only matter of concern to bear in on him.

CHAPTER FIVE

A s the Red Army penetrated into eastern Germany, Allied forces in the West advanced on a broad front stretching from Kiel in the north to Salzburg in the south. On 9 February, British and Canadian troops broke through the outer defences of the Siegfried Line to catch their first sight of the Rhine.

In the war of words fought in the newspapers and on radio, both sides exaggerated the strength of the Wehrmacht: the Germans to keep up morale, the Allies because they feared that if the Third Reich was known to be tottering, their own people would weaken in their resolve to achieve unconditional surrender. So it was that with some 80 German divisions facing some 80 Allied divisions the length of the Western Front, the combatants were seen to be evenly matched. The truth was otherwise.

Everywhere the German defences were suffering chronic manpower shortages and mounting supply problems. Allied air forces had brought chaos to the transport network and there was not nearly enough fuel to keep the tanks and munitions trucks rolling. By the beginning of February, oil production was down to four synthetic oil plants and reserves were all but exhausted.

The contrast on the Allied side could not have been more stark. American war industries were now at peak production, feeding the military machine in the Far East as well as the forces on both

European fronts. Moreover, in planning the final push into the German heartland, Eisenhower could count on a steady build-up of manpower. The flood of new recruits was a mixed blessing – their level of training was the despair of veterans – but there was no denying strength in numbers, which were now so great that a new American army, the Fifteenth, was created.

But the Reich still had plenty of fight left in it. Despite the best efforts of the US Army Air Force and RAF (nearly 700,000 tons of bombs were dropped in Germany in 1944) Speer's armaments and production ministry had been adept at disguising the scope of the damage and, on occasion, at improvising a seemingly miraculous recovery. In early 1944 every known aircraft plant in Germany was hit and assumed to be put out of action. Yet in that year the Luftwaffe was reinforced by nearly 40,000 new aircraft of all types, compared to under 16,000 in 1942 before any of the plants suffered attack. The explanation had to wait until after the war, when it became clear that Allied bombs were more effective in destroying buildings than the machine tools inside. In answer to the bombing campaign, the Speer ministry had set up *Jaegerstab* or 'Fighter-Staff', teams of technicians and managers who created a network of small specialised production units which were virtually immune to attack. The paradox was the inability of the Luftwaffe to take full advantage of its change of fortune. Many of the new aircraft were grounded for lack of fuel or trained pilots.[1]

By January 1945, work on jets, especially the ME-262, the most advanced aeroplane in the world, was progressing well. By May 1945, 1,400 jets had been produced. That they did not deliver the expected punishment was less to do with shortages than Hitler's ill-timed directive to convert the ME-262 to a fighter-bomber. The consequent delay in getting the prototype off the drawing board robbed the Luftwaffe of its last chance for a comeback.

Few outside the Allied command understood the potential, or even knew of the existence, of jet aircraft. But in Britain, practical experience introduced a large part of the population to the destructive power of unmanned rocketry. Having come through the Blitz and beaten off the threat of invasion, the all-but-exhausted citizens were now kept on edge by the prospect of being blown to bits by a *Vergeltungswaffe* or V1, soon known on the receiving end as a flying bomb, doodlebug or buzz bomb. These long-range missiles were all the more terrifying for their erratic aim. A long drawn-out screech announced their arrival. When the sound stopped, it was only a matter of seconds before they nose-dived to the ground, shattering whatever was in their path.

Over seven months until March 1945, 2,511 Londoners were killed and 5,869 seriously injured in rocket attacks. The human cost was small by comparison with the bombing of Germany but that did not stop the war-weary citizens of London and other cities worrying about what else they might have to endure.

The answer came with the launching of the V2, capable of rising to an altitude of 50 miles, the very edge of space, and of reaching a target nearly 124 miles away in six minutes. Flying at 3,600 miles an hour, it was too fast to be destroyed by anti-aircraft fire. When nearly a hundred of the V2s had done their worst, German radio reported that London 'was devastated' by the weapon, a claim that was quickly denied, though there was no disguising the fear that, even at this late date, rocketry was a serious threat to Allied hopes of a speedy victory. At a remote settlement on the Baltic island of Usedom, the 34-year-old Dr Wernher von Braun was at work on a V2 with a booster rocket that would take it across the Atlantic.

Those at the front had no need to be persuaded of the power of German technology. Wehrmacht tanks were far superior to anything on the Allied side and in capacity, if not in numbers, were getting better all the time. In early March, after the US 227th Infantry overran the town of Oberembt, a captured Tiger tank was found to have the heaviest calibre weapon so far encountered in any of the fighting, a 380mm howitzer, with a seven-foot barrel. 'It fired projectiles apparently rocket propelled, five feet long and 15 inches in diameter, weighing 800 pounds. A hoist was used to load the huge gun.'[2]

Fresh recruits who had been encouraged to think they had the best equipment of any of the combatants were soon disillusioned. Many discovered the hard way that among the most effective weapons of the war was the German 88mm cannon. Relatively small and manoeuvrable, it could be used as an anti-tank, anti-personnel or even as an anti-aircraft weapon. The 88, which was usually mounted on a tank, had other merits.

> It had flash arrester for one thing. But not only that, but it had a lower trajectory than our shells. Higher velocity, lower trajectory. They were deadly accurate.

German machine guns were also judged to be superior.

> Our machine guns were firing at the rate of 600 rounds a minute, theirs were at 1,300 rounds a minute. Brr! And if they were under continuous fire, every half a minute or every minute, they would have to replace their barrels; their barrels would be red hot. So red that you could see 'em at night time.[3]

Stories circulated of weapons so powerful as to negate all the assumptions of conventional warfare. Goebbels was only too ready to feed the rumour network suggesting, for example, that American and British bombers would soon be made ineffectual by a mysterious searchlight beam that would paralyse their engines. There was no truth in this or in reports of a mysterious new compound: 'One jet of it will be enough to burn a man to death. It will penetrate the tiniest gaps in the armour of tanks and will make superiority in armour useless.'[4]

Quite apart from helping to demoralise the enemy, the purpose of such fantasies was to persuade the German people to keep faith with military technology. As long as they believed that deliverance was at hand, if not this month, then the month after, the longer they would be ready to hold out against the invaders. Given enough time, argued Goebbels, who successfully fed the line to Hitler, divisions would open up between the Allies, allowing for a negotiated settlement that would favour the Reich or at least ensure its survival.

Much of this was delusion – as Doenitz, for one, was well aware. He alone of Hitler's staff kept his head. His reports were always encouraging, and with some reason. Of all the 'miracle' weapons on which so much was staked, it was the advanced U-boat that gave the Allies most cause to worry. The strength of the German U-boat force rose from 432 in December 1944 to a peak of 463 three months later. Even so, Doenitz suffered agonies of frustration:

During the last weeks of the war we suffered heavy losses in our own ports and coastal waters as the result of the ever-increasing pressure of the enemy's air forces on the shrinking area of territory in German hands.

When the new types XXI and XXIII were undergoing their trials and their crews were being trained a series of teething troubles came to light, as was only to be expected with types which had been constructed on a new principle. These defects admittedly delayed both trials and training, but the final results were most satisfactory. The maximum underwater speed of the type XXI was 17.5 knots. At the high underwater cruising speed of 5.5 it was almost silent. Its radius of action was so great that it could range over the whole Atlantic and could go as far as Cape Town, remain there for three or four weeks and then return to base without having to refuel. With new instruments and a new system of torpedo fire-control, this boat could do all its firing calculations blind and could fire from a depth of 150 feet.

Type XXIII possessed the same characteristics, except that as a smaller vessel its maximum underwater speed and radius of action were both proportionately smaller.[5]

Doenitz was convinced that his new generation of U-boats would put an end to Allied defences against the submarine enjoyed since 1943. His British opposite number agreed. Admiral of the Fleet and First Sea Lord, Sir Andrew Cunningham, warned that the new U-boats could inflict 'merchant shipping losses of the order of 70 rising to 90 ships a month ... which could in turn prejudice the maintenance of our forces in Europe'.

The casualty figures went some way to realising Cunningham's worst fears. In early 1945, high-speed U-boats went into action off the English east coast, inflicting serious damage before withdrawing several miles to observe the depth charge counter-attack at a safe distance. Seven supply ships were lost in January, eleven in February, and ten in March. It says much for Doenitz as a military leader that by the end of the war, the German submarine fleet was a potential world-beater. However, in February 1945 it was not at sea but on a river that new hardware was most needed.

The Rhine is one of Europe's most formidable natural barriers. Over a mile wide in parts, with a flow powerful enough to sweep away unpractised navigators, the Rhine had long been Germany's strongest protection. Before 1945, the last army to have crossed the Rhine was led by Napoleon.

A three-line defence network of concrete pillboxes, anti-tank ditches and minefields guarded the approaches to the Rhine. The West Wall or Siegfried Line ran through the Reichswald Forest, itself a formidable barrier. There was also the Hochwald, more forest, with 'layback' defences covering the approach to the Rhine at Xanten. For Hitler the Siegfried Line was much more than an impressive piece of military engineering. He saw it as an impenetrable line of concrete fortifications. Behind it the Reich, so he confidently predicted, was secure.

The first and by far the strongest assault on the German-held positions along the Rhine was launched at the northern end of the Allied line. This was Operation Veritable, led by Montgomery's Twenty-First Army Group. The main thrust of the attack was to come from the Nijmegen area through the forests of the Reichswald to clear the way to the industrial Ruhr. The general charged with bringing it off was a feisty Canadian, Henry Crerar.

Crerar had the Canadian First Army, including the British Thirty Corps under General Brian Horrocks, in all 300,000-strong, to achieve his objective. A second-stage attack, Operation Grenade, fell to General William S. Simpson's US Ninth Army. After crossing the River Roer, Simpson was to drive north-east to crush German resistance in the Duesseldorf, Krefeld, Muenchen-Gladbach region before linking up with the Anglo-Canadians at Wesel. An essential preliminary to Grenade was the capture of seven Roer dams to stop the Germans opening the floodgates. This task was allocated to General Courtney Hodges' US First Army.

Operation Veritable got under way in the early morning of 8 February. During the night heavy bombers blasted Cleve, Goch, Weeze, Udem, Calcar and other communication centres behind the Reichswald. After they had done their work, the artillery was called into play. For the infantry who had to follow through, rain and mud were as much the enemy as the Germans behind their anti-tank ditches, wires and mines.

After two days of Veritable the first of the three Siegfried zones was pierced and 1,800 prisoners taken. But Montgomery's battle timetable was already in the bin. The entire operation had not been expected to last more than four days. Instead, on an advance of just 20 miles, the only worthwhile objective in sight was the capture of Cleve. With all its handicaps, the Wehrmacht was still proving to be an indomitable enemy. The overwhelming force that Montgomery had amassed found itself up against four parachute, four infantry and three Panzer divisions. Of these, the most daunting were the troops of the First Parachute Army, who enjoyed the title only as a courtesy; neither the aircraft nor the time had been available to teach them how to jump. But these young men 'fresh from a Luftwaffe that had ceased to exist', were among the best at the Wehrmacht's disposal, ready to fight to the last man for a cause which still held their undiminished loyalty.

Up against their stubborn refusal to accept the inevitable, it was not until mid-February that the Allies were able to claim possession of the Reichswald and ten miles of the west bank of the Rhine. Having captured Kessel and Goch against heavy opposition, the Canadians and British were across two of the three main defensive belts of the Siegfried Line. The next objective was Calcar and then Xanten where the third fall-back of the Siegfried Line ran through the densely forested Hochwald guarded by the elite Panzer Lehr Division. Crerar decided to take them head-on in a daring attack called, appropriately, Blockbuster.

Blockbuster was launched on 26 February. At 4.30 a.m., after a 45-minute artillery barrage, Canadian forces attacked under artificial moonlight. It turned out to be an inauspicious beginning as crews struggled in icy rain to free their vehicles from glutinous mud.

As the German artillery opened up (Montgomery said later that it was the heaviest 'volume of fire from enemy weapons ... met so far in the campaign') the forward troops were pinned down for hours on end, some 'up to their necks in icy water'. It took two days for the Canadians to reach the outer fringe of the Hochwald. Unfortunately, this was precisely where the German forces were concentrated. It was not until 4 March that they were able to clear the Hochwald. After Xanten fell on the 8th, fighting around the city continued for two more days.

After Xanten, Thirty Corps turned east towards Wesel, where the enemy west of the Rhine was confined to a fast-shrinking bridgehead. Meanwhile, the US Ninth and First Armies had joined bridgeheads across the Roer, creating a front 30 miles long and seven miles deep. They now began the push towards the Rhine across the Cologne plain.

Muenchen-Gladbach and Krefeld, important industrial centres, fell in the first week of March. In stark contrast to the reception given to the conquerors on the Eastern Front, there was almost a sense of relief at the rumours of an imminent arrival of the Americans. Marie Therese Fuegling, an art student who had been put to work on a farm before returning to her parents in Krefeld in late 1944, recalled life in the city in its last days under Nazi rule.

People prayed a lot, even those who hadn't done so for a long time. We lived our lives in the cellars, with makeshift beds and cooking facilities. For days we had no electricity, water or gas. Women and the foreign forced labourers had to dig trenches. On the radio there was no end of motivating slogans – telling us to hold on and goading us into werewolf action, meaning that the enemy had to be vanquished with claws, teeth and any method possible. Cowards and traitors were threatened with the death penalty. There was talk of a wonder weapon which would annihilate the enemy at the last minute.

In Krefeld the frightening question was raised of whether we should be declared a fortress – anyone in their right mind knew what this would mean and wanted as quick an end as possible. Our anger wasn't even directed at the Allies, but at our own leaders who had brought this disaster upon us. But of course one could not say that out loud. Any criticism was seen as 'subversion of the fighting forces' and was met with death. Yet while the leadership appealed for our courage and stamina with serious threats, many men from the upper echelons had already made off over the other side of the Rhine.[6]

As the two major cities straddling the Rhine, Duesseldorf and Cologne were destined for a period of divided rule. As their western suburbs were penetrated by American forces, the bridges to the east bank heaved under the force of tons of dynamite, sending smoke and debris high into the air. The Duesseldorf-Oberkassel bridge was one of the first to go. All that was left was a few iron girders sticking out of the river. Soon afterwards water, electricity and gas supplies to the west were cut off.

Germany's third-largest city and the biggest prize so far in the Allied list of gains, Cologne was entirely bombed out. Two hundred and sixty-two air raids had killed 20,000. The last raid was on 2 March, four days before the First Army captured the left bank of the city. (The right bank remained in German hands until 21 April.) Military and civilians joined the rush across the river before the five bridges were destroyed. One badly damaged bridge fell without the help of explosives. 'It was just after 5 a.m. and the bridge was full of traffic – men, horses, carts, refugees and tanks – the weight plunged the whole lot into the river.'

Bonn was next to fall. For the older citizens, handing over their city to the invader and doing so willingly, in some cases enthusiastically, was a strange sensation.

> Mother stood in the kitchen and said to me with a strange faraway look – 'When World War I was over I was 18. The Germans still had a love of their Fatherland in those days – they weren't happy to see foreign soldiers turning up. But us today – we're glad to see them finally arrive. They may be our victors, but they are also our liberators from Hitler's terror regime.' A memorable day – then we had to think about it – what day was it exactly? 'The 9th of March? Well it's your birthday!' – we'd almost forgotten – 'Happy Birthday.' We carried on with the cleaning up. It was my 14th birthday.[7]

Along the entire left bank of the Rhine, the third week of March was largely spent mopping up remnants of German forces hanging on to isolated positions. Their withdrawal across the river was badly managed, not for any fault of military planning but because Hitler was demanding a fight to the last while refusing to believe that anything more than a revival of the fighting spirit was needed to roll back the Allied advance. The result was not so much conflicting orders as no orders at all. German units in the last line of defence were ill-informed and ill-prepared for action. Often it came as a traumatic shock to discover that the enemy was in their midst.

By 25 March every part of the west bank of the Rhine was in Allied hands. It had been a long and costly fight. Against some 16,000 dead on the Allied side, the Germans lost some 90,000 of their best soldiers. Moreover, in March alone, over 340,000 German soldiers were taken prisoner.

It was, said Horrocks, 'unquestionably the grimmest battle in which I took part' and Eisenhower told Crerar, 'Probably no assault in this war has been conducted in more appalling conditions', adding that these last weeks had been among 'the most anxious of the entire campaign'.

There was some surprise at the rarity of any civilian hostility. Having been warned so often that all Germans were mad fanatics bent on destruction, the appearance of white flags hanging from windows with recognisably ordinary women and children peeping out from behind the curtains took some getting used to. Not surprisingly the mood on the other side of the Rhine was less euphoric. In the post-mortem, which sent Hitler into paroxysms of rage, the future of Field Marshal Karl Gerd von Rundstedt, Commander-in-Chief West, was hardly at issue. Dismissed without ceremony, he was replaced by Field Marshal Albert Kesselring, a former Luftwaffe Chief of Staff and, subsequently, commander of German forces in the Mediterranean. Kesselring had secured his reputation with a masterly defensive campaign in Italy. Now he was called up to adapt his skills to defending what was left of the Reich.

The Americans were first over the Rhine, though it was not supposed to be like that. The next phase of Eisenhower's grand plan was for a full-frontal assault across the river led by Montgomery's Twenty-First Army. It was scheduled for 23–24 March. While Montgomery was building up his infantry, armoured and airborne forces, his American colleagues made several unsuccessful attempts to frustrate German efforts to destroy the bridges after troops had withdrawn to the east bank.

Setting off fuses was a matter of close timing. Hitler's preference was for keeping the bridges intact for what he imagined as the glorious return of his armies. On the other hand, if any bridge was captured the officer responsible would answer with his life. General Alfred Schlemm of the First Parachute Army, who had faced the Anglo-Canadian onslaught, had nine bridges in his sector. As he told his post-war interrogators, 'I could see my hopes for a long life rapidly dwindling.'

American luck turned at Remagen, an ancient town on the edge of the Rhine midway between Koblenz and Bonn. On the morning of 7 March, advance units of the Ninth Armoured Division discovered, much to their surprise, that the Ludendorff railway bridge at Remagen, though damaged, was still in use. Men and vehicles were moving gingerly over planks slung across the rail track. Once the Americans were spotted, the withdrawal, along with preparations to blow the bridge, took on a frenetic urgency. When American tanks started firing across the river, the order was given to set off the explosives. But nothing happened. Something, probably an American shell, had broken the circuit. A volunteer went out on to the bridge to light the primer cord of a demolition charge placed where it would cause the maximum damage.

There was a sudden roar as timbers shot into the air, and the bridge seemed to rise from its foundations. All the

Germans on the east side of the Rhine breathed a tremendous sigh of relief.

But they reacted too soon. A moment later, their relief turned to horror as they watched the bridge slowly settle back on its foundations.

It was still standing![8]

Braving ferocious machine gun fire, American infantry moved in on the bridge, cutting demolition wires as they went. Only a few managed to hold their positions once they were across but it was enough before reinforcements arrived.

Meeting Hitler in Berlin on 9 March, Kesselring, known to his troops as Smiling Albert because he was always breaking out into a cheerful grin, found the acid test of his sense of humour. Remagen was his first priority. The enemy had to be held back, he was told, until 'new fighters and other novel weapons could be employed in overwhelming numbers'. As Kesselring recalled:

Hitler largely blamed the Luftwaffe for previous defeats; but he had now personally taken over its technical direction and guaranteed success.

The Commander-in-Chief of the navy, Admiral Doenitz, would soon make his new U-boats felt and would substantially relieve the situation. He was full of praise for the superhuman efforts and endurance of the people at home.

Arms production was coordinated in the hands of Saur of the Armament Ministry, in whom he had implicit confidence that he would satisfy the essential requirements of our armies in the field. There would, however, have to be some diversion of production to new units being formed, which would be the best the German Wehrmacht had seen during the war. He himself would be responsible for getting first rate leadership. So it was once again a battle for time!

Hitler's exposition, which lasted hours, was remarkably lucid and showed an astounding grasp of detail. My mission was clear: Hang on![9]

If Kesselring was inspired by this diatribe, it did not take long for him to come back to earth. It was now 11 March. Belatedly, he realised that there were simply not the men, military hardware or fuel to mount a successful counter-attack to recapture the bridge. But he had a fall-back plan. Before leaving Berlin, he had persuaded the commander of Luftwaffe West to put all his efforts into destroying the Remagen bridge before the Americans could consolidate their positions.

As Kesselring later conceded, he had not reckoned on the rapid success of the American armoured forces, the war-weariness of the German troops and the inability of the Luftwaffe to deliver the promised knockout blow. On 15 March the Luftwaffe sent in their strongest force so far – 21 bombers, including several jets, but American anti-aircraft defences brought down sixteen. Bombs falling near the bridge shook its foundations but the structure held – just. Heavy weapons, including a 17cm railroad gun, were unable to get the bridge in range. It was the same with the V2s, eleven of which were aimed at the bridge. All missed.

By now, the Americans were pouring in all the troops they had within manageable distance. By 16 March, nine days after the Americans entered Remagen, three corps of the First Army were within striking distance of the Frankfurt autobahn. Their bridgehead was 25 miles across. But the frequent vibrations from near-misses, plus wear and tear from the constant stream of heavy traffic, took its toll on the bridge. The end came at mid-afternoon on 17 March. The main span suddenly rotated, then crashed vertically.

Interrogated after the war's end, Goering claimed that events at Remagen 'upset our entire defence scheme along the river'. Moving reserves to the Remagen bridgehead weakened the defence of the Rhine to the south between Mainz and Mannheim where Patton was to make his breakthrough. 'All this was very hard on Hitler,' added Goering.

Remagen was indeed a terrible blow to German morale. If the enemy could not be held back on one of the more impenetrable sectors of the Rhine, what chance was there for the depleted Wehrmacht to check the massive assault planned in the north? To make matters more problematic, General George Patton now decided to get in on the act. Angered that it had been the First Army with the painstaking and cautious Hodges in command that had won all the plaudits for Remagen and made doubly furious by the prospect of his great rival, Montgomery, taking credit for the northern crossing, Patton embarked on his own adventure to show that 'I can outfight that little fart any time'. A day before Montgomery was to embark on Operation Plunder, a division of the Eleventh Infantry Regiment of the US Third Army took to the assault boats at Oppenheim and simply paddled across the Rhine without meeting any real opposition. Patton was ecstatic but was cautious on parading his achievement, urging his commanding officer Bradley to keep the news to himself 'until we see how it goes'.

Bradley could hardly wait to put the knife into Montgomery. Two months of mounting resentment at the way Montgomery had treated him over the Ardennes offensive found its release in a stinging communiqué with its none-too-subtle reference to Monty's elaborate preparations. 'Without benefit of aerial bombing, ground smoke, artillery preparation and airborne assistance, the Third Army at 2200 hours, Thursday evening, 22 March, crossed the Rhine.'

Eighteen hours after the first assault craft of the Fifth Infantry Division had landed on the east bank, a treadway bridge was carrying traffic. A second bridge was in place the following day. By 27 March, five divisions with supporting troops had crossed these bridges. The entire Sixth Command Division crossed in less than seventeen hours. Patton was on his way. His tanks entered Darmstadt on 25 March. The following day they reached Frankfurt.

It was undeniable that German defences had been weakened by the transfer of tanks and infantry to plug the Remagen gap but the best of what was left of the Wehrmacht – the Fifteenth and Fifth Panzer Armies and the First Parachute Army – was concentrated on the vulnerable stretch of the Rhine between Wesel and Arnhem to the north. Everybody knew that this was where the main Allied attack was to come. To 'crash the river' here, as Bradley urged, was a risk too far. It was unwise to underestimate the strength of German opposition. Montgomery was not about to repeat that mistake. At the same time, there was justification in the American complaint that Montgomery took so long in preparation as to lose every element of surprise. A dense smokescreen along the river may have hidden the precise disposition of nearly a million troops but the Germans had a fair idea of what was going on and had plenty of time to dig in. Their orders were to hold on until, in Kesselring's words, 'our new fighters and other novel weapons could be employed in overwhelming numbers'.[10] It was, as he knew very well, a forlorn prospect against 'the enemy's extraordinary superiority in men and materiel on the ground and his absolute ascendancy in the air'.[11] Over the entire front, Kesselring could count on no more than 100 combatants to every kilometre.

Montgomery's grand slam, codenamed appropriately enough,

Operation Plunder, was scheduled for the night of 23–24 March. After a massive air and artillery bombardment intended to shatter enemy morale and open up gaps in their defences, the British Second Army, commanded by Lieutenant General Sir Miles Dempsey, was to cross the Rhine on the left of the Allied advance, aiming to seize Rees and Wesel. Simultaneously, Simpson's US Ninth Army would attack on the right between Wesel and Duisburg. Both crossings having been made by troops in amphibious vehicles and landing craft, the engineers would move up with ferries and Bailey bridges. It was then up to the tanks to carry forward the attack on the east bank. They were to be helped by a daylight air drop by General Ridgway's Eighteenth Airborne Corps, codenamed Operation Varsity.

The combined attack of infantry, armoured and airborne forces aimed at creating a bridgehead 40 miles long and ten miles deep within 24 hours. Thereafter, the objective was to encircle the industrial cities of the Ruhr before breaking out on to the north German plain. Straining a sporting metaphor, as was his inclination, Montgomery talked of 'going into the ring for the final and last round'. In a personal message from the Commander-in-Chief to be read out to all troops he promised to 'continue fighting until our opponent is knocked out'. The last round, he said, 'is going very well on both sides of the ring' (a reference to Soviet successes) 'and overhead'. He prophesied 'the complete and decisive defeat of the Germans' as a certainty.

The artillery, over 5,000 guns, opened up at 5 p.m. on the evening of 23 March. 'Came the hour and the world exploded. The noise was ear-splitting and got worse as the German guns hit our side of the river.'[12] Miles to the rear, the ground shook so violently, farm animals broke loose from their stalls, causing as much damage as enemy shells.

The first crossing began just before 9 p.m. Early on, every yard had to be fought for, but in less than 24 hours troops were able to cross the river without much opposition. It was now not altogether clear that Operation Varsity was necessary. But the greatest ever mass display of air power went ahead on the 24th. Starting at 9 a.m., some 1,500 bombers and transporters with 1,300 gliders in tow took to the air. When they all met up over Brussels, the US Seventeenth Airborne Division and the British Sixth Airborne Division formed two unbroken aerial convoys stretching 150 miles. They carried twelve parachute battalions (six US, one Canadian and five British) along with 800 vehicles and artillery pieces with backup equipment. A swarm of American and British fighters, over 1,000 in all, manoeuvred round the heavy aircraft to give protection against the feeble attentions of the Luftwaffe, while over the drop areas, countering a more serious threat, the bombs fell on German flak batteries to the north and west of Wesel.

'The sky was black with planes and gliders, moving over in a continuous stream for two or three hours,' recalls A.E. Baker, a wireless operator. 'While the Armada was passing overhead I sat on top of a tank listening to the American forces radio. One of the tunes they played was *String of Pearls*. Every time I hear it now I picture the Airborne going over.'[13]

By 1.00 p.m. it was all over. Richard Hough, a fighter pilot whose job it was to identify and destroy the flak batteries that were giving so much trouble, was convinced that the battle had turned out badly for the Allies:

The kaleidoscope of falling planes and men, gliders landing seemingly without plan if they were not shot out of the sky first, of smoke of every shade and hue, and sometimes the sharp blaze of flame from building or machine, all seen from the solitariness of a fighter's cockpit, left me stunned and anguished.[14]

Eisenhower's report to the Combined Chiefs of Staff told a happier story: 'Some losses were sustained from A.A. fire over the target, but the total of 46 planes destroyed was remarkably low.' But he made no mention of the number of gliders lost or of total casualties.

Estimates of losses of men and machines vary wildly. At least 100 aircraft and gliders were destroyed. Over 1,000 men of the Sixth Airborne Division were killed or wounded. Most of the equipment carried by the gliders was lost.

In part an ego trip for Montgomery – intended perhaps to wipe out the memory of Arnhem – Varsity has been justified as the final undeniable demonstration of an inevitable Allied victory. But it was Ridgway who got closest to an objective judgement on the last big airborne assault of the war. 'We learned a lot,' he concluded, 'but the knowledge cost us dearly.'[15]

There could be no doubt in anyone's mind that the Rhine had been well and truly breached. Even German newspapers recognised what was coming. 'It is very difficult to be an openly declared, courageous Nazi today, and to express one's faith freely,' conceded a leading article in the *Voelkischer Beobachter*, adding, 'We have no illusions now.' The Swedish newspaper *Expressen*, which had a correspondent in Berlin, reported that 'panic has struck military circles'.

By the early hours of 25 March, while the troop-carrying ferries were lumbering back and forth across the Rhine, the first two Bailey bridges were almost in position. By nightfall the two floating bridges were in constant use and others were under construction. On the far bank the Americans and British had linked up near Wesel to create a bridgehead 30 miles long and seven miles deep.

Kesselring had hoped to be able to hold Wesel and other strongholds long enough for reserves to be brought up but the impetus of Montgomery's advance was too fast for him. Four days after the first assault troops had set foot on the left bank of the Rhine, German defences pulled back fifteen miles to a line between Bocholt and Dorsten. By now American, British and Canadian forces were consolidating in massive strength, with Montgomery able to count on up to 20 divisions and over 1,000 tanks.

Two days of fighting broke the new German positions. With the capture of Dorsten and Bocholt the whole front collapsed. German losses in prisoners alone averaged 10,000 a day. With the end of March, Simpson's Ninth Army, on the right of the Twenty-First Army Group, was spearheading towards Magdeburg on the River Elbe, not much more than 77 miles from Berlin. Another part of the Ninth Army had sheared off to begin an encirclement of the Ruhr industrial region, an objective achieved when it met up at Lippstadt with the US First Army, closing up from the south. The Second British Army made for Hamburg at the mouth of the Elbe, while Crerar's First Canadian Army was 'to open the supply route to the north through Arnhem'. Once over the Rhine, the way into Germany was through a belt of wrecked towns and villages, victims of artillery and aerial bombing and now 'only gaunt and blackened walls and heaps of rubble'.[16]

After the wreckage came open countryside where the war had so far intruded only marginally on ordinary life. The contrast was surreal. As BBC correspondent Chester Wilmot noted:

Today we drove for mile after mile, past farms where the peasants were still working in the fields, through villages where women were doing their washing or tending their gardens; they hadn't felt the shock of battle.

We saw them standing by the roadside with their white flags in their hands, and soon, as the traffic streamed by, the Germans began waving and smiling ... not really in welcome but as an expression of their relief that the war for them was over and that the battle had swept past them so quickly and painlessly.[17]

In the south, the US Third Army was surging forward to outflank Frankfurt. The city fell on 29 March, by which time the Third had linked up with the eastward-thrusting First around Giessen. This brought within easy reach the Kassel-Wuerzburg autobahn, a prize much savoured by Patton whose tanks, two abreast, could then roar on to Hannover.

Opposition was so light that he was able to send out armoured columns as if on training exercises. A few roadblocks were lightly defended and there was the occasional sniper to contend with, but more often the surprises were pleasant ones – an important bridge thought to have been destroyed but captured intact, a supply dump with arms and ammunition waiting to be purloined, whole companies of German troops in search of someone to accept their surrender. In one week the First and Third Armies handed in 70,000 prisoners.

Though reporters made much of the challenge of keeping up with Patton, he was never far away from the press. Like Montgomery, he was in love with headlines, though rather better than his bête noire at coming up with quick quotes to support his image as a war leader. Presiding at a ceremony to open the Roosevelt Railroad Bridge near Mainz, he was invited to cut the ribbon with a large pair of scissors. He gave them back demanding 'a goddamned bayonet' adding he wasn't 'a goddamned tailor' – as if anyone in their wildest imagination supposed he might be.

Further south again the French First Army was evoking the days of Napoleon with a Rhine crossing aimed at Karlsruhe with Stuttgart as the ultimate prize. Acutely conscious of the supporting and thus secondary role Eisenhower had in mind for General de Lattre de Tassigny, his political master in Paris had feared a last-minute change of plan that would deprive France of sharing in the Rhine offensive. So that there could be no misunderstanding de Gaulle sent his own unambiguous directive to de Lattre. 'You must cross the Rhine even if the Americans are not agreeable and even if you have to cross it in boats. It is a matter of the greatest national interest.' This was all very well but where were the boats to come from? Putting out the call for anything that would float and carry men and equipment, de Lattre put together a motley fleet ranging from stormboats, propelled by outboard motors and each capable of taking just six men, to rubber dinghies that had to be paddled across. Given the firepower that the enemy brought to bear on the French sector, it was a miracle that any of the assault force survived. Of 90 vessels, 54 were hit and over 40 were sunk. But two narrow bridgeheads were secured and, by 31 March, French troops were fanning out to capture more than 20 towns and villages. It was the day, said de Lattre, when France 'succeeded in raising the stone under which Germany had sought to entomb her'.[18]

As the Allied advance accelerated, Kesselring found his imme-diate prospects 'anything but pleasing'.[19] On paper, he had three army groups at his disposal: in the north Army Group H, led by General Johannes Blaskowitz, comprised the First Parachute Army and Twenty-Fifth Army; in the centre defending the Ruhr Field Marshal Walter Model's Army Group B had the Fifth Panzer Army, Seventh Army and Fifteenth Army; while to the south Army

Group G, commanded by General Paul Hausser, consisted of the First and Nineteenth Armies.

Just a few months earlier any one of these Wehrmacht units would have been a match for the toughest Allied assault but now they were in disarray, undermanned and with little armour, at risk of degenerating into a demoralised rabble. The rate of desertion was high and Kesselring resorted to using some of his best men to round up the fainthearts who flooded to the rear whenever a battle started.

The enormously costly battle of the last half-year and constant retreat and defeat had reduced officers and men to a dangerous state of exhaustion. Many officers were nervous wrecks, others affected in health, others simply incompetent, while there was a dangerous shortage of junior officers. In the ranks strengths were unsatisfactory, replacements arriving at the front insufficiently trained, with no combat experience, in driblets, and, anyway, too late. They were accordingly no asset in action. Only where an intelligent commander had a full complement of experienced subalterns and a fair nucleus of elder men did units hold together.[20]

Kesselring's position was made more problematic by the refusal of Hitler to recognise that the defence of the Ruhr was a lost cause. A plan for Model to break out of the Allied encirclement, which would have saved a third of Kesselring's total fighting force, was rejected out of hand. Hitler wanted a Ruhr fortress; what he got was a closing-in by the Ninth and First Armies leading, on 18 April, to the capitulation of the last of the 300,000 men of Army Group B.

For Model it was the end of the line. Like Doenitz, he was one of the few who was prepared to stand up to Hitler and even occasionally to ignore orders that he judged impossible to carry out. His great talent was for improvisation. At the peak of his career, facing up to the advance of the Red Army, he had been dubbed 'the Fuehrer's fireman', the one who was first to be sent to whatever part of the front needing urgent bolstering. But in the Ruhr, there was nothing Model could do to stave off defeat. In mid-April when American troops were less than two miles from his headquarters, Model received, under flag of truce, an appeal from General Matthew Ridgway which the sender hoped would save further bloodshed.

It was Model's Chief of Staff who brought back the reply. The fighting would continue. Ridgway now gave the messenger a choice. 'He could go back under a flag of truce and take his chances ... or he could remain in our custody as a prisoner of war.'

He chose to stay.[21]

Model was more fatalistic. On the afternoon of 21 April, after a farewell handshake for each of his staff, he walked into the forest and killed himself with a single shot from his Walther pistol. In taking this way out he may have provided one last service to his Fuehrer. When he heard the news, Hitler's reaction was that if Model could find the courage to take his own life, so could he.

It seemed now that there could be no substantial military obstacle between the Allies and Berlin. But having once described Berlin as 'the main prize', Eisenhower had decided to concede the German capital to the Red Army, shifting the centre of the advance away from Montgomery's Twenty-First Army Group in favour of a central thrust by Bradley's Twelfth Army Group towards the River Elbe, there to meet up with the Russians.

The decision came as a huge shock to Montgomery who had already given orders that made Berlin the ultimate goal of his advance. Indeed it was probably this characteristically high-handed assumption by his British subordinate that brought Eisenhower to the point of resolution. Often accused by his confederates of being over-sensitive to British interests ('Ike is the best Goddamn general the British have got,' sneered Patton), Eisenhower had become increasingly exasperated with Montgomery, whose undoubted qualities of leadership did not include political sensitivities. If he had been so blessed he would have known that Eisenhower, at this late stage in the war, could not be seen to be paying deference to Montgomery at the cost of falling out with Bradley, not to mention the establishment in Washington. The worst possible scenario, and one that Eisenhower had every reason to fear, given the antipathy between Bradley and Montgomery, was a race between the Twelfth and Twenty-First Army Groups to be the first to fly the flag over the Brandenburg Gate. The likely consequences for Anglo-American relations, and for Eisenhower personally, were too catastrophic to think about. But if Berlin was taken out of the equation and Montgomery and Bradley were each given a task that matched pride with capability there was a good chance that the Atlantic alliance would emerge intact.

There were also sound strategic reasons for leaving Berlin to the Russians. For one thing they were closer, less than 40 miles from the city, with a million-strong force ready for the culminating attack across flat, open countryside. The nearest Anglo-American forces were still 250 miles off target. The rate of their advance was impressive but not so great as to guarantee coming in first. Even assuming that the 200 miles to the Elbe could be covered at Patton-like speed, the other 50 miles beyond was difficult terrain with lakes and rivers to hold up movement. Then there was the nightmare prospect of street fighting in Berlin with no means of distinguishing Russian friend from German foe.

Bradley calculated that a breakthrough from the Elbe would incur 100,000 casualties, 'a pretty stiff price to pay for a prestige objective'. The warning was not lost on Eisenhower, who was under pressure to conserve manpower against the then probability of the war with Japan outlasting the war in Europe by a year or more.

But it was politics rather than strategy that made the running. Roosevelt was keen to foster good relations with the Russians. However naïve this may have appeared once Stalin emerged in his true colours, it remains a fact that Washington was strongly motivated to treat the Russians as friends and most definitely not as prospective enemies.

Eisenhower knew very well that whatever means he chose to implement his policy, he had trouble ahead. There were too many contradictions to be reconciled, too many egos to be massaged, too many career considerations, not least his own, to be taken into account. To avoid a long and damaging debate he opted for a pre-emptive strike. Passing up the opportunity to discuss Berlin at a meeting with Churchill and Montgomery on 25 March, Eisenhower communicated directly with Stalin, proposing that his (Eisenhower's) forces, once they had secured the Ruhr 'in late April or even earlier', should focus their efforts on a centre thrust to the Leipzig-Dresden area, led by Bradley's Twelfth Army Group.

The logic of this was to allow Montgomery to concentrate on the Ruhr ('if the industrial heart stopped, the political heart would also die') before moving north to take Hamburg and the other North Sea ports. This would cut off the occupation forces in Norway, Germany's last major source of reserves, and frustrate any Russian designs on Denmark. Meanwhile, having reached the

Elbe, Bradley would also turn north, leaving the Russians to sweep up east of the river and, by clear inference, take Berlin.

The reaction from London was immediate and hostile. Eisenhower's initiative in going direct to Stalin instead of first consulting the Joint Chiefs of Staff smacked of a plot against Montgomery and a ruse to disappoint British expectations of being in at the kill. Churchill weighed in with a vigorous protest.

But simultaneously Churchill warned his advisers that the Americans would 'riposte heavily', as indeed they did. Eisenhower was riding high as a commander whose judgement could be trusted. When Roosevelt joined with his generals to deny that Eisenhower's plans involved any far-reaching changes from the agreed strategy, Churchill backed off, going soft on the issue until well after the war when hindsight enlivened his memoirs. Churchill was a realist. He knew above all else that he had to keep in with the Americans who held the whip hand. As Chief of Air Staff, Sir Charles Portal, observed of his boss, 'Churchill will fight to the last ditch, but not in it.'

One of the ironies of the war was that, in retrospect, Doenitz and the others of the German high command who feared Bolshevism above all else, must have been among those who wished most fervently that Eisenhower had decided to push on to Berlin and beyond. That way many thousands of German troops would have been spared Soviet captivity.

It was on 15 April, in anticipation of a new Soviet offensive, that Hitler faced up to the prospect of the Reich being split in two. His 'basic order' appointed two supreme commanders to defend the Reich. Kesselring was to be responsible for the south, Doenitz for the north. The assumption among Hitler's closest was that Kesselring was to be the prime mover in the continuation of the war since it was in his sector that the frequently mooted last stand could be made in the Bavarian Alps. On 22 April, Doenitz moved his headquarters to Ploen in Holstein, close to the border with occupied Denmark.

By then the Red Army was in easy reach of Berlin. The renewed Soviet attack had started a week earlier with an artillery barrage that gave the signal for more than a million Soviet troops under marshals Zhukov and Konev to advance from the line of the Oder and Neisse rivers. German defences held for just a few hours. By 20 April, Soviet tanks were in the outskirts of Berlin. Forty-two thousand artillery pieces and more than 6,000 tanks encircled the Reich capital. Opposing this military juggernaut were the fragments of an army: old men and boys in ragged uniforms, sick and exhausted Wehrmacht survivors from once-proud fighting units. The disaster had long been predicted by Hitler's Chief of General Staff, General Heinz Guderian. Having argued fruitlessly against a strategy that, in his view, made no concessions to reality, he now added his voice to demands for an armistice on the Western Front. For support he turned to the foreign minister, the duplicitous Joachim von Ribbentrop, who professed great surprise when Guderian asked him how he would feel if 'in three or four weeks the Russians are at the gates of Berlin?'

With every mark of horror Ribbentrop cried: 'Do you believe that that is even possible?' When I assured him that it was not only possible but, as a result of our leadership, certain, for a moment he lost his composure. Yet when I repeated my request that he accompany me to see Hitler he did not dare agree. All I managed to get out of him was a remark made just as I was leaving: 'Listen, we will keep this conversation to ourselves, won't we?' I assured him that I should do so.

But when Guderian appeared at Hitler's briefing that night, he found his Fuehrer in a state of great agitation.

> I must have been a little late, for as I entered the conference room I could already hear him talking in a loud and excited voice. He was insisting that his *Basic Order No. 1* – by which no one was allowed to discuss his work with any man who did not need such knowledge for his own official duties – be exactly obeyed. When he saw me he went on in an even louder voice: 'So when the Chief of the General Staff goes to see the Foreign Minister and informs him of the situation in the East with the object of securing an armistice in the West, he is doing neither more nor less than committing high treason!'[22]

So Ribbentrop had talked. Guderian experienced a sense of relief. Now, at last, he had got through to Hitler. But he reckoned without the Fuehrer's stubborn will. Guderian's dismissal, cloaked in an order that he should take six weeks' convalescence leave, was not long in coming. It was another measure of the confusion at Hitler's headquarters that Field Marshal Keitel suggested to Guderian that he should relax in Bad Liebenstein. 'It is very beautiful there.' Guderian had to remind him that the town was already in American hands.[23]

Nuremberg, 'the city of the Nazi movement', was under attack day and night from the beginning of April. Gauleiter Holz, who was to be killed in the final raid on the city, was determined to make Nuremberg a fortress, to be defended to the last man. Roadblocks were put up but 'it was clear to anyone with even the vaguest of military experience that these measures were inadequate'.[24] There were few fighters and even fewer weapons. 'German planes had long since become a fairy tale. Tanks were something we had only ever heard about and the few wornout flak guns didn't exactly cut the mustard either.'[25] Nonetheless, the city held out for more than two weeks.

Finding little in Nuremberg that was still standing except a few walls and the cathedral spires, Ed Murrow reflected on a nation committing suicide. With Nuremberg wiped out, most of Bayreuth had gone too.

> Wagner's piano is still there, but part of the house has been knocked down. Rare books and fine manuscripts are trampled underfoot. There is an empty champagne bottle on top of the piano. The young lieutenant in charge of Military Government has written a letter to the Army asking for permission to put a guard on the place.[26]

Murrow was bemused by the determination and sangfroid of the looters.

> A Russian walked down a street that was under small-arms fire. He carried a huge cheese – it must have weighed 70 pounds. He was interested in that cheese – not in the firing. As a new Burp gun opened up around the corner, an American corporal (in possession of a newly acquired Leica) said: 'Hey, Mack, do you know of any place around here where I can get some films developed?' There wasn't a building standing in the radius of a mile, but he was entirely serious.

From mid-April barely a day passed without the Allies notching up another German city. In the middle Ruhr, Wuppertal was one of the last industrial centres to submit to a change of regime. Goebbels condemned the city to *'pech und schwefel'* (fire and brimstone) when he heard of its surrender. Hannover and Brunswick fell to the US Ninth Army. In Hannover, less than a quarter of buildings were left standing.

> You could walk for miles without seeing a building left with a wall higher than your thigh. Electricity had been cut; the water supply wasn't working; there were no sewers. The city was a gigantic open sore – and crawling about in that sore were not a few thousand, or even a few scores of thousands of people, but a vast population of peoples of all lands and tongues and temperaments.

It was reckoned that there were over half a million people living on the breadline in Hannover – 250,000 Germans, 100,000 foreign workers and over 50,000 released British and Allied prisoners of war.

> They inhabited the ruins of this once prosperous city, and no Wild West town of the last century could compare with the lawlessness of the life they lived. It was a town of drunkenness and murder.[27]

In the third week of April the British Second Army was closing around the North Sea ports of Hamburg and Bremen, and the US First and Ninth Armies were up to and over the Elbe between Magdeburg and Halle. But the news everyone was waiting for was of the beginning of the Russian attack on Berlin. It came on 20 April, Hitler's 56th birthday, when the first shells began falling on the city centre. The distinctive rattle of the guns soon had a name.

Berliners called it 'Stalin's organ', which, once it started grinding, would continue its inharmonious tune for hours at a time.

Werner Girling was thirteen when his family abandoned their house to live in the cellar of an old people's home.

> 'They'll be coming over the Teltow Canal,' my father reckons. I can't help thinking about the Hitler Youth boys on the Kleinmachnower Weg. My friend Kurt and I had been there just three days before and found three or four anti-aircraft guns ready for ground battle on the footpath, 400 metres away from the canal. There was no cover on the marshland. We got talking to one of the operating crew and I remember his words quite clearly to this day. 'When Ivan gets here, it'll be the end of us – there'll be no one left!' Neither of us really knew what he meant at the time. But we realised when we returned, after the Russians had invaded. We could make out the barrels of the anti-aircraft guns jutting up towards the sky from quite a distance. Then we saw five, maybe more of the crew, lying dead beside them.[28]

Journalist Karl Brammer was equally pessimistic:

> The Russians are approaching Teltow and a German ground battalion comes out to defend Knesebeck Bridge. A sorry sight. The 'marchers' are taking a breather on the benches before they carry on, many have no weapons at all, most have grey hair. They haven't been fed for 12 hours and have no idea where they are going. They are marching because they have been ordered to march, but all are convinced of the futility of their actions. These last dregs of war don't

even have the energy to desert – entrusting them with the defence of Berlin is utter folly.[29]

Later, Brammer went to his local police station where guns were handed out.

> Ancient carbines, which none of us has ever used, and Greek ammunition. Great defence, but not for me. Without a word I stash the carbine in the bike shed, along with an ancient revolver. How many times have I told anyone who will listen? – I haven't the slightest intention of dying a hero's death for Adolf Hitler.[30]

Those who had no choice in the matter, the few regular soldiers and others more or less able-bodied, who were under orders, lived an unreal life. An anonymous diarist who was in barracks in Hohenzollerndamm found himself organising a concert to celebrate Hitler's birthday.

> The Berlin Philharmonic Orchestra was playing, conducted by Robert Heger. I was commissioned to pick up the conductor from the station and keep him amused in the casino until the commander arrived. We sat there, strangers drinking beer, talking of insignificant matters – that times were bad and the weather good ... Then the party began, with a calm introduction lacking in pathos, followed by a Clausewitz quote read by Paul Hartmann. At the end, Beethoven's Symphony in C Minor was played.[31]

It was a relief, admitted the diarist, to have something positive to do, however bizarre in the circumstances. His only other order of note was to deliver a message to the deputy Gauleiter, whose office was in the cellar of the Hotel Kaiserhof.

I rode my bike along Vosstrasse to Wilhelmplatz and entered the bunker. It was packed with top party functionaries and secretaries. All the doors were open, so one could easily see into the next room. Coffee cups and liqueur glasses littered the desks and the air was so thick with smoke that it stung my eyes. Telephones rang endlessly and everyone was working frantically. I had the impression that they were working to forget, to numb themselves.

I was given a bundle of special permits, which were to authorise me and my colleagues to enter off-limits areas. I had to make immediate use of them. The way back took me along Wilhelmstrasse and through the Brandenburg Gate. Unter den Linden was deserted. A sergeant stood at the main gateway of Gate B, wearing a Ritterkreuz (Knight's Cross) on his uniform. He checked my permit. He was a huge man, and seemed a decent sort of chap. I'd noticed that I had really been 'beside myself' the last few days – I wasn't myself anymore; I felt like I had a split personality. I somehow just got through it all calmly, but all the time felt as though I were watching everything from an observatory far away.[32]

The rumour factory was still churning out messages of hope. Ribbentrop was said to be on his way to London to negotiate a separate peace; freed from the battle in the West, reinforcements were on their way to save Berlin. Speaking in celebration of Hitler's birthday, Goebbels promised that 'Germany will rise again'. Even now the Fuehrer had great plans. If only the citizens of Berlin could hold out for a few more days.

On 25 April the Russian and American spearheads linked up at Torgau on the Elbe. The Americans were there first, much to the surprise of the Russians, who had assumed that the Western Allies would not get so far so fast. So the men of the First Army paused for two weeks, waiting at Torgau, some 30 miles from Leipzig, as one officer put it, 'for the Russians to climb over the nearest hills'.

Despite the urgings of Keitel and Jodl, Hitler refused to leave Berlin. There was to be no last stand in Bavaria. On 30 April he closed his door on the world. The rest was up to Doenitz.

CHAPTER SIX

Hitler was dead. Or was he? Doenitz could not be sure. He was named successor but without confirmation from Berlin it had yet to be made clear that he was, indeed, head of state. To assume too much too quickly was to invite retribution, as Goering had discovered. His response, therefore, had to be carefully worded. His first draft was short and to the point.

> My Fuehrer! I have received your charge. I will justify your confidence by doing my utmost to act for the good of the German people.

This had the virtue of leaving room for freedom of action. But Doenitz was persuaded, probably by Speer, to reaffirm his pledge of loyalty in the characteristically florid style of Party proclamations.

> My Fuehrer! My loyalty to you will be unconditional. I shall do everything possible to relieve you in Berlin. If Fate nevertheless compels me to rule the Reich as your appointed successor, I shall continue this war to an end worthy of the unique, heroic struggle of the German people.

His options were still wide open.

There was no immediate acknowledgement from the remaining occupants of the Fuehrerbunker. Holding back on the truth, Bormann and Goebbels wanted to leave an opening for one last try at coming to a deal with the Russians. At 3.30 a.m. on 1 May, General Hans Krebs, a Russian speaker who was on familiar ground with the Soviet military, crossed the lines to play a loser's hand with Colonel General Chikov. Not so much an offer as an appeal was made for an end to hostilities in Berlin 'to create a basis for peace negotiations'. The discussion, which went on for most of the night, was mostly small talk to postpone the inevitable. A high-sounding but meaningless concession to allow for putting together a German peace proposal was accompanied by a demand endorsed by Zhukov via Stalin for the unconditional surrender of Berlin. After a formal rejection was delivered in the early evening, the Russians resumed their attack on the Reich Chancellery.

Meanwhile, Bormann was again in communication with Doenitz:

Testament in force. I will come to you as soon as possible. Until then advise withhold publication.

So that was it. Hitler was no more.

There was still the question of how Hitler had died. Rejecting Bormann's advice, Doenitz decided to broadcast a tribute giving out that the people's Fuehrer had met a hero's death.

His life was a unique service for Germany. His war against the Bolshevist flood was fought for Europe and the whole civilised world.

Doenitz appealed for unity:

Give me your trust, for your path is also my path. Uphold order and discipline in the cities and provinces, everybody must do his duty at his post! Only in that way can we reduce the suffering which the days ahead are going to bring us all, and prevent the collapse. If we do everything in our power, the Lord God will not desert us after so much suffering and sacrifice.[1]

There is little doubt that Doenitz knew very well that he was fantasising Hitler's demise. He would have heard from Speer that Hitler had chosen to take his own life rather than risk capture by the Russians. If further evidence of suicide was needed, a message from Goebbels announcing 'Fuehrer deceased yesterday 3.30 p.m.' was revealing. If Hitler had indeed died fighting, 'killed in action' would have been the phrase to use.

Why, then, did Doenitz resort to fiction? To have done otherwise would have been to confess to the German people that the leader they had been taught to revere deserted them in their hour of greatest need. Chaos and social disintegration would have followed, so Doenitz believed. His purpose was to maintain order and discipline, the two cardinal virtues of his life.

Common sense decreed that the war was lost. The news on all fronts was of collapse or impending collapse of German defences. In central Germany the Americans were on the Elbe and had already linked up with the Russians at Torgau while Montgomery's forces were racing towards Hamburg and Luebeck.

On the Baltic, the Hela Peninsula and the narrow coastal strip of the Vistula were still in German hands but only just. To the north, the front in Kurland, 200,000 strong, was holding out but ammunition and fuel were almost exhausted and could not be replaced. Production of war materials had come to a stop and there were no reserves.

On the evening of 2 May, Kesselring reported the surrender of the Army Group in Italy, adding that while he had been taken by surprise when General von Vietinghoff decided unilaterally to end hostilities, he accepted full responsibility. The Balkan Army Group was now exposed and there was no hope of salvaging it. Berlin was in its death throes. In military terms, the Reich was reduced to East Friesland and Schleswig-Holstein. Denmark, Norway and Holland were still under occupation but all were vulnerable.

Hitler's testament was a clarion call for Doenitz to continue the war 'by all possible means'. There was part of Doenitz that responded to this command from beyond. Often, he had voiced a wish to die in battle. But when the moment came, he rejected the futile gesture. His friend and close colleague, Admiral Godt, recalled his immediate response to the news of his succession: 'An end to it, we have fought enough heroic struggles, save the people, no more unnecessary bloody sacrifices.' He told his adjutant, 'As head of state, there is nothing left for me to do but end the war as quickly as possible.'[2]

But this begged several questions. Capitulation, immediate and all-embracing, raised nightmare visions. The future, not just of the military but of Germany itself, was at stake. German propaganda made much of the Morgenthau Plan, the brainchild of Henry Morgenthau, US Secretary of the Treasury, which had been put before Roosevelt in September 1944. Morgenthau blamed German industry for the war. German industrialists had brought Hitler to power, financed the Nazi Party and manufactured the weapons that made aggression possible. It followed that 'To Prevent Germany Starting World War Three' (the subtitle of the Morgenthau Plan) its industry must be eradicated. The post-war economy would be based on agriculture; Germany was to be reduced to a nation of farmers.

Reaction against Morgenthau was fast and furious. US Secretary for War Henry Stimson was not the only one to point out that the political castration of Germany would damage the economy of the whole of Europe. As Churchill observed, it would leave 'England chained to a dead body'.

But while Morgenthau was dismissed as a fantasist, the Allied demand for 'unconditional surrender' implied the end of the Reich. Germany in defeat could not expect to survive in any recognisable form. This was confirmed when the Big Three – Roosevelt, Stalin and Churchill – met at Yalta in January 1945. Having approved the post-war carving up of Germany into occupation zones, every encouragement was given to the press to promote, as a war aim, the quelling of the German spirit and to destroy, as Doenitz put it, every element of self-respect.

However, all was not lost. While Doenitz gave no credence to the Nazi mantra of the imminent collapse of the American–British–Soviet alliance, he did have in mind exploiting the divisions in the enemy ranks to secure surrender terms that stopped short of total, unconditional surrender.

It did not take sophisticated military intelligence to know that the façade of Allied unity was held together with sticky tape. Differences between America and Britain sprang largely from Britain's sensitivity at being cast as the junior partner. It was no secret that the military did not get on. Each side saw the other as arrogant and patronising – and invariably wrong. Patton and Montgomery could hardly bear to be in the same room together. Both were walking parodies of national prejudice and both came close to being sacked by Eisenhower for their pig-headedness. It was much to the credit of the Supreme Commander that he managed to keep the whole show on the road.

But more significant, and more hopeful for Doenitz, was the

division between East and West. Both America and Britain had cause to distrust the Soviet Union. For public consumption Stalin was the amiable and amenable Uncle Joe who had committed his country to an unprecedented sacrifice for the Allied resolve to exterminate Nazism. But behind diplomatic doors, the talk was of a fractious relationship once victory had been achieved. Churchill had embraced the USSR on the principle that any enemy of Germany was a friend of his. But he needed no persuading that Stalin's territorial demands were liable to take over where Hitler had left off. He was not alone. There were even Soviet sympathisers who feared that in the forthcoming peace settlement 'the power of principle would have far less consideration than the principle of power'.[3] The evidence was in Russian propaganda against any imagined slight from 'reactionary' or 'sub-Fascist' critics of heavy-handed Soviet policy in captured territory now claimed for communism.

Roosevelt would have none of this. Having served his political apprenticeship in the Great War, he was inbred with the idealism of Woodrow Wilson. The failure of the League of Nations, Wilson's creation, only made Roosevelt more determined to crown his presidency with a new start in international affairs – the US and USSR, as the leading world powers, working in partnership to support a United Nations framework for peace. Convinced that Stalin's notions of 'democracy' and 'anti-imperialism' were in line with American values, Roosevelt allowed himself to be 'brutally frank' with his friend the British prime minister, telling him, 'I can handle Stalin better than either you or your Foreign Office'.[4]

But Roosevelt died on 12 April. His successor, Harry S. Truman, was more hard-headed. While Doenitz knew very well that anti-Soviet rhetoric washed off Roosevelt, he had high hopes that with Truman some of it would stick. If there was a deal to be had on the surrender, it would only come with nods from Washington and London. It therefore made sense to look to the West while continuing the struggle to the East.

There was another consideration. Operation Hannibal still had a long way to go. Hundreds of thousands of German troops and refugees were still waiting to be lifted across the Baltic. To allow the rescue to continue, Doenitz had to play for time, which meant fighting off the Russian embraces.

To be taken seriously at home and abroad, Doenitz needed at least a semblance of a government. His first choice for deputy, one with sufficient stature to be taken seriously on the international scene, was Konstantin von Neurath who had been known to him since the early part of the Great War. Neurath was a diplomat turned politician who had served as foreign minister in the last days of the Weimar Republic and had continued in office under Hitler until his outspoken opposition to war plans led to his replacement by the more malleable Ribbentrop. The problem was that no one seemed to know where Neurath could be contacted.

Doenitz's adjutant had the not-so-bright idea of asking Ribbentrop if he knew of his predecessor's whereabouts. That brought Ribbentrop hotfoot to Ploen to inform Doenitz that it was his, Ribbentrop's, legal right to remain foreign minister and that, anyway, he was the only man for the job since the British knew him and had always been pleased to deal with him. Doenitz having a low opinion of Hitler's lapdog ('He is really too stupid to be borne'), the offer was rejected.

Failing to reach Neurath, Doenitz turned his thoughts to Graf (Count) Schwerin von Krosigk. A low-profile but astute member of Hitler's outer circle, Krosigk had risen from assistant in the Finance Ministry to become head of department responsible for the national budget. Since neither Hitler nor his immediate

entourage were in the least interested in economics or budget-
ary control – they just wanted things done – Krosigk survived by
juggling the figures to create a semblance of financial orthodoxy.
Having witnessed, against his own expectations, the revival of
Germany as a leading power, he was able to persuade himself
that a Nazi dictatorship, surely a temporary phenomenon, was
justified by results.

When the magic wore off he stayed at his post, 'at first from
a sense of duty, later to check injustices and hardships within his
sphere of responsibility and finally because it seemed to him cow-
ardly to leave the sinking ship'.[5] It was a familiar story. With Berlin
in ruins and the 'political gambler', as Krosigk called Hitler, having run out of tricks, he had sided with Speer 'to bring about the
inevitable end as soon as possible and with the minimum casualties
and damage'.[6]

Pliant he may have been but Krosigk was no fool. Encouraged
by Speer, Doenitz caught on to Krosigk as one who could balance
the military influence in what was already known as the Northern
Cabinet. With his knowledge of English (he was a Rhodes scholar
at Oriel College, Oxford for eighteen months) and his aristocratic
lineage, Krosigk was thought to understand the Anglo-Saxon
mind. Impressed by his 'clear and wise appreciation' of the issues,
Doenitz named him foreign minister. He quickly settled in as
Doenitz's right-hand man while describing himself deprecatingly
as a 'minister foreign to foreign affairs'.

The only other high-flyer from the old regime that Doenitz
had much time for was Speer, who had gained credit for revital-
ising the construction of U-boats and for having the courage to
defy Hitler openly after orders were given on 15 March for the
destruction of all military and economic assets. Speer and Doenitz
were as one in bringing an end to the war. On the understanding

that the appointment was temporary (who would have thought otherwise?), Speer took the role of minister of economics and production.

Doenitz readily agreed to Speer's suggestions for a general order rescinding Hitler's scorched earth decree. Reconstruction rather than destruction was now the official policy. Thereupon, Speer drafted a radio speech calling on the German people to take courage and to avoid anything that might further damage their welfare. In particular, demolition charges on bridges were to be rendered harmless. On Krosigk's advice, Speer added a few lines about the rescue of troops and civilians stranded in the Eastern battle zones. The broadcast was made on 3 May. Krosigk also took to the airwaves. This was, he said, 'Germany's darkest hour'.

The world still hears the sounds of war, German men are still dying in the last battles to defend the German homeland. Along the highways of German territory as yet unoccupied, a stream of desperate, starving people hunted by fighter-bombers heads westwards, fleeing from an unspeakable terror, from murder and rape. In the East the Iron Curtain is advancing and behind it, hidden from the eyes of the world, the work of exterminating those who have fallen into Bolshevik hands goes on.

But this time there was a twist.

In San Francisco talks are being held to debate the organisation of a new world order to indemnify humanity against a new war. The world knows that a Third World War would not mean just the destruction of one nation, but the end of the human race. The terrible weapons not used in this war would appear in a Third World War, bringing death and destruction to the whole world.

Germany welcomed a new world order to prevent future wars but it could not be created 'if the Red arsonists also sit in judgement in peacetime'.[7] What, then, was Krosigk proposing? A triple alliance against the Soviet Union? He did not spell it out but the implication was clear. The message was to be drummed out incessantly over the following weeks.

While Doenitz was thinking about what jobs he wanted filled and by whom, there came a final message from Goebbels. It now appeared that in naming Doenitz as his successor, Hitler had also decided who should serve under him. The list of appointments gave Goebbels the title of Reich Chancellor with Bormann as Party Minister. There were fifteen more names attached, each with specified responsibilities.

With a touch of dry humour, Krosigk pointed out the contradiction in putting someone at the head of an authoritarian regime while at the same time choosing his ministers for him. He and Doenitz suspected a plot by Goebbels and Bormann to hold on to power. It was decided that should Hitler's front men turn up at Ploen, they would be arrested. The contingency did not arise. Goebbels and his family took poison while Bormann, having failed in an attempted breakout from Berlin, committed suicide on a bridge near what is now Central Station.

Settling on a clean sweep of the hangovers from Hitler's administration, Doenitz told former ministers who were hanging about Ploen to settle their affairs and hand themselves over to the Allies. The casualties included Walter Funk (economics), Wilhelm Ohnesurge (post and communications), Hans Lammers (head of Reich Chancellery) and Leonardo Conti (health). There were those who did not go quietly. Dr Bernhard Rust, minister for education and science, infamous for ordering students and teachers to start the day with the Nazi salute and who rejected Einstein's genius as 'Jewish physics', committed suicide in hospital, while Ribbentrop adopted a false name and went to ground in Hamburg where he was soon recognised and arrested.

The downfall of Alfred Rosenberg, former Reich minister for the occupied Eastern territories, turned into farce. Having been thrown out of Doenitz's headquarters when he arrived drunk, he was dispatched to a military hospital in Muerwick with a sprained ankle. There he managed to get a medical certificate to show that he was 'confined to bed with severe bleeding as a result of torn joint ligaments'. This he sent with a covering letter to Montgomery. He remained at liberty until 18 May when British troops surrounded the hospital and he was led away bleating about the unfairness of it all.

With most of the old guard disposed of, Doenitz pressed ahead with his own list of appointments. There was no shortage of candidates. In the second half of April, a bevy of middle-ranking ministers had already left Berlin to seek relative security at Eutin, which happened to be within easy driving distance of Ploen. Most were backroom functionaries who could be counted as apolitical though all, in varying degree, were undeniably part of the Nazi regime. Doenitz was subsequently blamed for not doing more to disassociate himself from Hitler's retinue but, as the occupying powers soon discovered, it was not as if one could simply walk out into the byways to find capable advisers untainted by Nazism.

Then again, even on the safe assumption that Doenitz was having second thoughts about a career devoted to a leader who had snatched defeat from the jaws of victory, it was impossible for him to make a clean break with the past without undermining his own authority. Doenitz was a pragmatist, doing the best he could with the available resources.

His biggest mistake was to select Dr Wilhelm Stuckart as his minister for the interior. A rabid anti-Semite and an early proponent of the Nazi sterilisation programme, Stuckart was a thoroughly unsavoury character who damaged the credibility of the Doenitz government. Why he was chosen remains a mystery, though it can be said in his favour that he did little except prepare a few legal documents and that at least he was more acceptable than his predecessor as interior minister, Heinrich Himmler.

On 28 April, two days before his accession, Doenitz had an unplanned meeting with Himmler. When the conversation turned to life after Hitler, the critical question was put by Himmler. If control of the state should pass to him, would Doenitz be prepared to serve? It was a nasty moment. Doenitz disliked Himmler and distrusted him. But a flat refusal was liable to put him into open conflict with the most powerful member of Hitler's inner circle, a conflict that he was bound to lose. His reply was therefore suitably ambivalent. He told Himmler that 'the only thing that now mattered was to prevent a reign of chaos which would inevitably lead to further bloodshed'. He was therefore 'prepared to serve under any legally constituted government'.[8]

This has often been held against Doenitz as a tacit admission that if circumstances demanded he would have backed Himmler as the new fuehrer. It is hard to believe. Rather, while there remained so many uncertainties, Doenitz was being his usual cautious self. He must surely have known that, whatever their feelings about Hitler, few senior commanders would transfer their oath of loyalty to a military incompetent who was also a hate figure for the Allies. But, whatever he wished, it was impossible for Doenitz to hold his distance from Himmler.

Early on the morning of 30 April, a message came through from the Chancellery in Berlin:

Fresh treachery afoot. According to enemy broadcast Himmler has made offer to surrender via Sweden. Fuehrer expects you to take instant and ruthless action against traitors. – Bormann.

This might have been taken as welcome news in that it freed Doenitz from any assumed obligations to Himmler. But action against him? With what? The Reichsfuehrer had the SS and the police behind him. Doenitz had a few naval ratings. 'To use force was therefore impossible.' But equally the order could not be ignored. He decided to set up another meeting with Himmler. It took place at the police barracks in Luebeck.

Himmler kept me waiting. He seemed already to regard himself as head of the state. I asked him whether the report was true that he had sought contact with the Allies through the medium of Count Bernadotte. He asserted that it was not true, and that in his opinion it was essential, in these last days of the war, that discord among ourselves should not be allowed to create further chaos in the country. We parted amicably.[9]

Returning to Ploen that evening, Doenitz was handed the signal that gave him the leading role in bringing the Reich to its end. As far as Himmler was concerned this left Doenitz in a quandary. There was no way of knowing how Himmler would react to Hitler's rebuff. But it had to be assumed that he would use his power base to assert his claim. Doenitz decided to take the initiative.

I told my ADC [Luedde-Neurath] to telephone Himmler and ask him to come to Ploen forthwith. To my ADC he retorted with a blunt refusal, but when I myself spoke to him and told him that his presence was essential, he eventually consented to come.[10]

Himmler turned up at midnight in a fleet of open Volkswagens with a six-strong bodyguard led by Heinz Macher, his head of security. Luedde-Neurath was waiting to accompany Himmler to the meeting room. As they moved forward Macher spotted armed men crouching behind trees. He thought it all a bit of a comedy turn but for Himmler it was a sign that he was being taken seriously. The welcome from Doenitz was polite and formal.

When the two were alone, Doenitz produced a transcript of the radio message confirming his appointment. Anticipating a violent confrontation, he had taken the precaution of placing under some papers a pistol with the safety catch off. He waited while Himmler absorbed the news. There are various accounts of what happened next. According to Doenitz,

As he read, an expression of astonishment, indeed, of consternation spread over his face. All hope seemed to collapse within him. He went very pale. Finally he stood up and bowed. 'Allow me,' he said, 'to become the second man in your state.' I replied that that was out of the question and that there was no way in which I could make any use of his services.[11]

A crushed Himmler then departed, trailed by his bodyguard. But Himmler was not so easily put down. A more likely version of events has Doenitz pressing the case for non-political leadership while assuring Himmler that he would have a vital role to play as police chief responsible for maintaining law and order. Meanwhile, would Himmler please absent himself from the seat of government?

Luedde-Neurath and Krosigk knew that Himmler was anything but deflated. He held to the conviction that he and the SS would have a role in the post-war order. He may even have retained a vestige of hope that, getting the edge on Doenitz, he would be called upon to lead the peace talks. When Krosigk paid a visit to Himmler at his command post between Eutin and Ploen, he found him in the best of spirits, referring to himself as 'an indispensible factor for law and order'. It was only a matter of time before Eisenhower called on him to lead the fight against Bolshevism. And there, for the moment, the matter rested.

For military advice, Doenitz looked first to his own immediate staff, notably Admiral Godt, who had worked alongside him throughout the war, and Admiral von Friedeburg, who had succeeded Doenitz as chief of the submarine fleet and finally as Commander-in-Chief of the Kriegsmarine. Acknowledging his ignorance of the land war, Doenitz hoped to enlist the services of Field Marshal von Manstein, a noted strategist who, having fallen out with Hitler over his direction of the war, had been without a command for the best part of a year. But attempts to contact Manstein failed. There was a rumour that he had been captured by the British, though, in the event, he remained at liberty for three months after the surrender. Other likely prospects had been captured or were otherwise out of reach. Doenitz had to fall back on Field Marshal Keitel and General Jodl.

Keitel has been described as 'painfully conscientious, the typical obsequious, pliable subordinate' whose chief virtue was his 'incredible industry and conciliatory manner'.[12] Head of the

Wehrmacht Office since 1935, Keitel was valued by Hitler as a good organiser who kept his ideas to himself. It was only after Hitler's death that he began to think independently. Doenitz was to find him a useful ally.[13] Jodl was a tougher proposition. Head of the OKW (Oberkommando der Wehrmacht) Operations Staff from 1939, he pushed hard but failed to achieve a centralised military command. Hitler preferred to divide and rule. For most of the war, Jodl confined himself to tactical problems while, like Keitel, skirting political matters as unnecessary distractions. Under Doenitz he emerged as a stronger personality.

After leaving Berlin, Keitel and Jodl had set up temporary headquarters at Neu-Roofen, north of Berlin and then, as gunfire came uncomfortably close, had moved to Himmler's former operational headquarters at Mecklenburg. Taking heart from news filtering through that the American advance had stopped at the Elbe and that a regrouping of German forces had reduced the chances of a Russian encirclement of Berlin from the south, Keitel busied himself with visits to the front to give irresolute commanders a hard time. With the breakdown of telephone links, contact with Berlin was by wireless aerial attached to a balloon. This ended when the balloon was burst by a Russian fighter. On 1 May, braving machine gun and cannon fire from the RAF, Keitel decided to make direct contact with Doenitz at Ploen. It was there that he learned of the change at the top. Accepting that the finale in Berlin would come at any moment, Keitel returned to his base, now at Neustadt, only to be summoned for another meeting with Doenitz. This time he was shown the message from Goebbels with Hitler's list of members for the new Reich cabinet. Keitel pledged his support for Doenitz. Keitel recalled:

The afternoon was spent on composing proclamations to the German people and the armed forces. In a situation like this it was clearly impractical to swear-in the whole of the armed forces afresh: I proposed as a formula that the oaths of allegiance sworn to the Fuehrer automatically transferred their validity to Doenitz as the new Head of State.

It emerged later that this was ignored by most of the top brass.[14]

As soon as the proclamations were ready to be broadcast, I left Doenitz's headquarters and drove back to Neustadt with the intention of reporting to Doenitz again early next day, 3rd May. On my arrival, I analysed the new position with Jodl; both of us had only one thought now – to bring the war rapidly to an end as soon as the evacuation of East Prussia and the operations designed to salvage our armies on the eastern front permitted. We decided to go over these points with Doenitz next day.[15]

Doenitz had to bring into line others of the senior military who were ready to fight on whatever the cost. Field Marshal Busch, who was holding the Northern Front none too successfully against the British, told Doenitz to his face that he was not 'acting in Hitler's spirit'. Busch wanted approval for realigning scattered forces for a major counter-attack. He did not get it.[16] Troops still in action were to limit themselves to delaying tactics.

But what was to be the next move? If there was general agreement on trying to secure an armistice in the West while holding the front to the East, there were differences on how best to meet the objective. The strategy favoured by Keitel and Jodl was for any units to surrender piecemeal. In this way they hoped to avoid the stringent conditions that might be imposed if negotiations were conducted at the highest level. The opposing view was put by Speer and Krosigk who argued that to drag out the process carried the risk of a continuation of Allied bombing and further destruction.

Doenitz favoured a middle way, a regional surrender roughly on an army group basis but under his central direction. In this way he aimed to keep open a 'gate', an escape route extending from Lauenburg on the northern bank of the Elbe to Hamburg that would allow for German troops caught on the wrong side of the Elbe to cross over to the Anglo-American zone.

Central to Doenitz's blueprint for ending the war was to hold open the Hanseatic ports for German refugee ships crossing the Baltic. But in this he was to be disappointed. As soon as he had been designated supreme commander in northern Germany, he had made it his mission to prevent what he called a 'premature' surrender of Hamburg, at the mouth of the Elbe, and Luebeck on the river Trave. Ironically, his failure to do so was largely a result of Eisenhower trying to put the brake on Soviet territorial ambition, a cause that Doenitz might have been expected to support.

Eisenhower was learning from his mistakes. Having agreed to pull back 90 miles from the Elbe to the boundary of the proposed Soviet zone of occupation he was sceptical, and rightly so, that the Russians would stick by the rules in Austria and Czechoslovakia. If the Red Army was allowed to take the Hanseatic ports it would then be a short step to liberating, and subsequently occupying, Denmark. That prospect was as unappealing to Eisenhower as it was to Doenitz.

The prizes were directly in front of the British Twenty-First Army with Montgomery at its head. Eisenhower urged him to get a move on. But before Montgomery could get close there was a formidable obstacle to overcome. On the River Weser was the port of Bremen, one of the last of Hitler's fortresses to put up a fight to the finish. Looking back on the last week of April, a *News of the World* war reporter remembered Bremen as being 'different from all the other German cities we have captured. Its death agony was more convulsive. It was determined to resist its fate.' The SS were busy rounding up teenagers to fight with whatever they could lay hands on. The older people huddled in air raid bunkers without fresh water or sanitation. Venturing out for scraps of food they were regaled with loudspeakers. 'The German Volk is determined to fight to the last breath.'

By 21 April most of Bremen was in ruins and British forces were closing in. But still there was no surrender. 'A handful of madmen are in charge,' wrote one disillusioned citizen as he surveyed the wreckage that was once a street of fine houses. 'Everything is covered in a chalky layer of greyish red ... the road is strewn with tree branches and rubble.' But now the end was near. Irmgard Hagemeyer saw it all through the eyes of a twelve-year-old.

My father hid his home-brewed potato schnapps, which was an excellent medium of exchange. Everything was in a state of collapse, but the newspapers and radio gave orders to fight to the very last. On the walls of the houses posters were stuck up saying 'Weser-Ems will not give in' and was supposed to spur on the population to hang in there and fight. But most Bremeners yearned for surrender. Their constant hunger, fears for husbands and sons at the front, sleepless nights in the bunker and despair at burned houses had exhausted the population.[17]

As a measure of the disorganisation that now ruled, a British intelligence officer in Bierden, a village which had been vacated by German troops 24 hours earlier, picked up the telephone to find himself speaking to a German staff officer. The caller wanted to know how close the British were. Replying in German, the intelligence officer assured him that the village was secure. The delighted officer promised an early visit, bringing with him his commanding general. The subsequent ambush bagged not only two senior officers but also a fine Mercedes.

Hagemeyer went on:

In the city itself the last line of defence was left to the young and frightened. I went into the street and saw boys my age (around 13–15 years old) had gathered on a street corner to go to war. Of course they had no uniform and no equipment. There was one gun for around ten children. They were ordered to march to Brinkum to hold up and chase out the English army. However, the 'leaders' of these children's corps preferred to stay in Bremen. When they reached the front line in Brinkum, the English soldiers came, disarmed them and sent them home.[18]

Bremen surrendered on 26 April.

Despite an emotional appeal from Doenitz, Hamburg's gauleiter was disinclined to follow Bremen's example. In early April Karl Kaufmann had refused Hitler's demand to turn his city into a fortress. With over 40,000 citizens killed and more than 50 per cent of homes and factories destroyed by blanket bombing, Kaufmann was intent on handing over the entire North Sea coastal region to the Western Allies.

His refusal to respond to Doenitz was reinforced by his personal antipathy to the Grand Admiral. When Doenitz had taken command of the northern sector, his authority had extended to all merchant as well as naval shipping. This stripped Kaufmann of his powers as

Reich Commissioner of Shipping, a job he held in addition to that of Hamburg gauleiter. As he saw it, he owed Doenitz no favours. When, on 23 April, Doenitz invited the gauleiters of Mecklenburg, Schleswig-Holstein and Hamburg to Ploen to put together a coordinated plan, Kaufmann failed to appear. It soon became clear that he was in contact with the British via the Danish resistance with every intention of capitulating. Doenitz sent a final appeal to Kaufmann to support his efforts 'to save German territory and German people from Bolshevism'. The door to the West had to be kept open.

The decisive theatre of operations is on the eastern front. On the military side, everything possible is being done to put an end to the Russian advance into Mecklenburg, or at least to hold it up for as long as possible, to enable the maximum number of Germans to leave the province.

This evacuation is practicable only as long as a door through the zonal demarcation line agreed at Yalta remains open. If the Elbe-Trave canal is closed by the British, we shall be handing over seven million Germans to the mercy of the Russians.

It is therefore absolutely vital to defend the Elbe position against the west with the utmost tenacity. Demolition of the property necessitated by these operations will be justified a thousand times over by the number of German lives that will thereby be saved in our eastern provinces.

By supporting these vital military operations without reservation you and the town of Hamburg will be making the best contribution that it is in your power to make to the cause of our nation.[19]

He held out the prospect of an eventual relief.

Once the task of transporting refugees by sea from the east and accommodating them in Schleswig-Holstein had been completed, the situation as far as Hamburg was concerned, would be entirely altered, and once that had been accomplished I had no intention whatever of insisting upon further and futile defence. But at the moment it was still vital to hold the Elbe front against the British, so that the reception area behind it could be retained in our hands. Above all it was essential that the bridges over the Elbe in Hamburg should not fall into British hands. It was also highly desirable that the line defending them should be sited as far to the south-west as possible in order to save the town and its inhabitants from becoming involved in the subsequent battle.[20]

But Kaufmann was not listening. A positive response did come from General Wolz, the commander of the Hamburg garrison, who put together an anti-tank battalion consisting of land-locked submariners, grounded air crews and police, which carried out several daring commando raids. It could hardly be described as a counter-attack but it slowed the British advance by a few days.

On 2 May British and Canadian spearheads reached the Baltic to take Wismar and Luebeck. Doenitz heard the news by an indirect route. While Jodl was telling him that Busch was confident of holding the front, Luedde-Neurath was on the telephone to a contact in Luebeck.

I was surprised when the person at the other end began shouting into the instrument, and upon my request that he should lower his voice he shouted back: 'I can't understand a word you're saying, there's such a racket in the streets, one tank after another is rolling past … yes, all British – do you want to listen?' and turned the receiver towards the street so that I could hear the clanking of the tracks more clearly.[21]

Except for a pocket west of Bremen, there was no longer any real opposition on the Twenty-First Army front. Reconnaissance flights showed white flags flying from houses 50 miles behind the enemy line. That night, two German divisions surrendered. Doenitz accepted the inevitable. Hamburg was handed over to the British Seventh Armoured Division. An order was sent by Jodl:

1. Hamburg is not to be defended. The troops are to be moved out of the city into the area north of Hamburg, and, to avoid the threatened bombardment of the city, this fact is to be reported to the enemy by an officer with a flag of truce.

2. In order to gain time, the battle is to be continued throughout the whole area of C.-in-C., North-West. A surprise break-through on and over the Kaiser Wilhelm Canal must be prevented, so as to give the German Government sufficient time to negotiate with Montgomery over North-West Germany …

As Hamburg succumbed, the Eleventh Armoured Division prepared to enter Neumuenster to the north of the city, only 30 miles from the naval base of Kiel. A few hours later, British troops of the Sixth Airborne Division linked up with the Russians near Wismar, while two of the German armies that had opposed Marshal Rokossovsky's Second Belorussian Army north of Berlin declared their readiness to surrender.

That day, 2 May, also marked the end of effective resistance in the south of Germany where the US Third Army had shot off in three directions, driving into eastern Germany, into Czechoslovakia and into the Austrian Alps to take Salzburg. By now nobody worried about the Southern Redoubt where, supposedly, the leaders of the Reich with the SS elite would hole themselves up in a mountain stronghold with the purpose of waging guerrilla warfare. The only discovery of note was the whereabouts of Hermann Goering who gave himself up to American captivity. One of his last official acts was to write to Doenitz suggesting that he, Goering, should negotiate with Eisenhower, 'Marshal to Marshal'. The suggestion was ignored.

That evening Montgomery reported to Field Marshal Alan Brooke, Chief of Imperial General Staff.

There is no doubt that the very rapid movement from the ELBE bridgeheads northwards to the BALTIC was a very fine performance on the part of the troops concerned. There is also no doubt that we only just beat the Russians by about 12 hours. Alls [*sic*] well that ends well and the whole of the SCHLESWIG peninsula and DENMARK is now effectively sealed off and we shall keep it so.

The flood of German troops and civilians fleeing from the approaching Russians is a spectacle that can seldom have been seen before and it will be interesting to see how it sorts itself out tomorrow.

He added that General Blumentritt, commanding 'the forces facing us between the Baltic and the Weser river' was coming the following day to discuss surrender. 'It may well be that he is plenipotentiary for some bigger commander.' In fact, Blumentritt was acting on his own initiative. He was not an isolated example. Signs of Wehrmacht disintegration were everywhere apparent. The

Karl Doenitz in 1939 when he was commander-in-chief of submarines.

(*above*) Hitler wit▸
Doenitz and navy chie▸
Grand Admiral Raeder i▸
September 193◖

(*left*) Admiral Doenitz awards
the Iron Cross to one of his
U-boat commanders.

(*above*) U-boats outside their reinforced concrete 'pens' built to protect them from air attack.

(*right*) A German U-boat at sea. Like all submarines, they spent much of their time on the surface, diving only for torpedo action or to avoid detection.

U-boat interior, showing the minimal space crews had in which to perform their duties.

The *Wilhelm Gustloff*, one of the large ships used in the Hannibal evacuations. Over 9,000 refugees died when she was sunk by a Russian submarine.

Allied forces advance through Aachen.

American and Soviet troops meet at the Elbe.

The German delegation arrives at Lueneburg Heath to meet with Montgomery.

Jodl signs the German surrender at Rheims. Friedeburg is on the right.

(*left*) Doenitz announces the German capitulation.

(*below*) The arrest of Speer, Doenitz and Jodl at Flensburg.

Doenitz takes the oath at the Nuremberg trial.

(*below*) Doenitz, shortly after his release from Spandau, on his way to Duesseldorf to spend time with his lawyer, Otto Kranzbuehler.

challenge for Doenitz was to keep track of the ever-accelerating turn of events.

It fell to Admiral Friedeburg, next in naval seniority to Doenitz, to head a delegation to Montgomery's headquarters. For his briefing, Friedeburg met with Doenitz on the Levensau bridge over the Kiel Canal, the choice of venue fitting in with Doenitz's decision to move his headquarters from Ploen (only an hour from Luebeck by tank) to Flensburg, closer to the Danish border.

Breaking his journey to Flensburg, Doenitz was kept waiting, Friedeburg having been held up by British fighters diving in to machine gun his car. His instructions were short and to the point.

Attempt to save the maximum number of German soldiers and Europeans from Bolshevism and enslavement. Army Group Vistula therefore to withdraw into the Anglo-Saxon zone. Rescue from destruction and starvation of the men concentrated in the Schleswig-Holstein area. Medical supplies for this area. Prevention of destruction of major localities by bombing. In addition attempt to discover an arrangement to save Central and Northern Europe from further chaos.[22]

Friedeburg was to make first for the HQ of the British Second Army where he would witness General Wolz's signature to the surrender of Hamburg. He was then to drive on to Lueneburg Heath.

Accompanied by Admiral Wagner from Doenitz's staff, General Kinzel, Chief of Staff to Field Marshal Busch, and Major Friedel as adjutant, Friedeburg crossed the British lines on the morning of 3 May.

The opening scene of the final act of a long-running drama was about to begin.

CHAPTER SEVEN

B ack on the road to Flensburg, Doenitz and his companions, Krosigk and Luedde-Neurath, were the target for British fighters. Their vehicle, an armoured Mercedes, a gift from Hitler, was designed to frustrate attempts at assassination but was no protection at all from air attacks. The telltale drone of an approaching aircraft was the signal for an emergency stop and a dive for cover. So frequent were the interruptions to their journey that it was not until 3 a.m. that they arrived at Muerwik, just outside Flensburg.

A naval school, vacated by its cadets, was put at the disposal of Krosigk and other office holders along with their staff. Quarters for Doenitz and his staff had been made ready on the *Patria*, a former passenger ship, no longer seaworthy but moored permanently in the harbour. Luedde-Neurath was not happy with the arrangements.

In contrast to Ploen, the appointments were meagre and by no means self-contained. The barrack huts were only partially equipped and the signals hopelessly inadequate.'[1]

Doubtless knowing what was coming, the base commander volunteered to move out from his own, better appointed, lodgings. As the newcomers settled in all the talk was of Friedeburg on his way to Lueneburg Heath and of the prospects for a successful outcome of his meeting with Montgomery.

Warned of the imminent arrival of Friedeburg and his party, Montgomery prepared the ground. The German delegation was to be lined up under a Union Jack facing the caravan that Montgomery used as his office. No British soldiers were to be in evidence, just three of Montgomery's staff: Lieutenant Colonel Trumbull Warren, Colonel C.P. Dawnay and, as interpreter, Colonel Joe Ewart, who was to die a few weeks later when his jeep hit a land mine. Apart from these supporting actors, Montgomery wanted the stage to himself.

The lasting image of the encounter was of contrast, the meeting of opposites. The German officers were dressed impeccably, all in greatcoats, the navy favouring black leather, the army light grey. Though Friedeburg was quite short and slightly built, his companions looked to be sturdy characters. General Kinzel was well over six foot, very erect, in his late forties. With his monocle in place, no one could mistake him for anything but a Prussian officer. The youngest, at 28, was Major Friedl. Also over six foot, he had, according to Trumbull Warren, 'the cruellest face of any man I have ever seen'.[2] For about five minutes no one moved. Then:

> Quietly the door of the centre caravan opened and there stood a rather short Anglo-Irishman, wearing khaki trousers and battle dress, a black beret (which he was not entitled to wear) with two badges, one of the Royal Tank Regiment and the other a hat badge of a general; his hands behind his back.[3]

Every military leader has to be a performer. To put together a dedicated fighting force requires a personality of a high order while presentation is the key to maximising gains and minimising losses. Montgomery was good on inspiring confidence in his troops; less good on explaining away his mistakes (in his view, he never made any). In celebrating victory, he inclined towards ham acting.

> The minute they saw him, they saluted ... In the German Army the Junior Officer's hand comes up and his arm remains there until the Senior Officer has completed his salute – and it just so happened that Montgomery took a hell of a long time to complete his salute! With his hands behind his back he walked very slowly down the five steps to the ground and then the 25 feet so that he was directly in front of the Germans and all the time they remained at the salute. He then very casually put his right hand to his beret in a most slovenly manner and they dropped their arms.[4]

Walking slowly down the line, Montgomery started with von Friedeburg. 'Who are you?' The question came as a shout. Friedeburg told him. Montgomery was not impressed. 'I have never heard of you. What do you want?' Without waiting for an answer, he turned to Friedl. 'A major!' It was a bellow of assumed outrage. 'How dare you bring a major into my headquarters.' Friedeburg was allowed to speak.

> At first the Admiral tried to get our Commander-in-Chief to accept, within the Anglo-American lines, the soldiers and civilians who were retiring in front of the Russian advance from the east. Montgomery refused to discuss this, saying that since they were fighting the Russians, they must surrender to them.
>
> He then asked the Germans whether they would like

to discuss the surrender of their forces facing us. At first Friedeburg said 'No,' and went on to enquire whether we would agree to an arrangement whereby the German forces could withdraw by stages in front of us with our troops following up.

Montgomery said 'No.' He then said that to him the issue was quite clear and simple. Would they surrender on a tactical basis the troops on 21st Army Group's front and in Denmark? If they would do so, then he would be prepared to discuss the best way of carrying out the surrender. If they would not discuss it, then he would be delighted to continue fighting.[5]

Warren glanced towards Dawnay: 'The Chief is putting on a pretty good act.' Dawnay shrugged: 'He's been rehearsing this for six years.' After a few more words, Montgomery left his visitors standing while he turned to Dawnay and Warren. 'He told us to put on the best possible lunch in the Visitors' Mess and to supply them with all the drinks they wanted.' Then:

At his rather more spartan meal, Montgomery planned the afternoon session. He told us to put our two Mess tables together, to cover them with army blankets and to put one chair, that he would sit at, at one end and four chairs as close as they could be put at the other end; to put two maps on the table, one marked in red, which was to be our front line, and one marked in blue, which was to be their front line. He told Dawnay and me to sit at a table to the side and that we should be armed but to be sure our revolvers were not noticeable; the interpreter [Colonel Ewart] was to stand behind him. The rest was to be left to him.[6]

When the meeting resumed, Montgomery was in full uniform showing his field marshal's rank and decorations. He wasted no time in getting to three points. As Montgomery telegraphed to Brooke:

First. They must surrender to me unconditionally all forces on my western and northern flanks (including forces in west Holland, Friesland and Heligoland and in Schleswig-Holstein and Denmark).

Second. Once they did this I would discuss with them the best way of occupying the areas and dealing with civilians and so on.

Third. If they refused to agree as above then I would go on fighting and a great many German soldiers and civilians would be killed. I then showed them a map of the situation of the western front.

The delegation was invited to study the war maps. They showed overwhelming strength on the ground, a gross exaggeration since Montgomery knew that his request for reinforcements had been rejected. More realistically, he posed the threat of further devastation by air. 'They had no idea of this situation,' Montgomery cabled Brooke, 'and when they saw the map they at once gave in.'

This gave little credit to Friedeburg's sagacity. Well aware of Allied military superiority, he followed Doenitz's instructions to play for time. When he pressed Montgomery on his policy towards German troops approaching his lines, he noted the encouraging reply that Montgomery would 'naturally take prisoner all German soldiers who came into my area with their hands up', adding that while civilian refugees were no concern of his, 'I am no monster'.

Friedeburg asked for 48 hours (he got 24) to report back to

Doenitz for the final say as to whether a wider surrender than that originally proposed was acceptable. Colonel Warren accompanied von Friedeburg and company back to the German lines.

We started out immediately. We had their car, with their driver, and an orderly. In front of this I had my own jeep with my driver and two British Provosts. Behind their car I had another jeep with four British Provosts. We put a small flag pole on each windshield with a white bed sheet which would be visible for some miles and we set out …

We then drove through Hamburg … There was hardly a building left standing. We had to go down back alleys and the like to get around the debris on the main streets and we were driving quite slowly hoping, of course, nobody would take a shot at us. It took us well over an hour to go through Hamburg … and in that whole period we never saw one living thing – not even a cat.

After we had gone about 12 miles north of Hamburg we turned a corner and drove right into the muzzles of two guns mounted on two German tanks. A young-looking officer, with one arm, was standing by the side of the road in command of these tanks and when he saw the German vehicle he gave the Heil Hitler sign. Major Friedl got out, spoke to him in German, got in the car and left with great speed. I was left facing this officer and I said out loud to my men 'Get in your jeeps, turn around, and let's get the hell out of here as quickly as we can.'[7]

They returned safely.

While Friedeburg was sitting uncomfortably across a table from Montgomery, Doenitz was turning his mind to the territories still under German occupation. The most contentious in terms of relations with the Western powers was that part of the Netherlands bypassed in the Allied invasion. This covered the heavily populated sector including Amsterdam, Rotterdam, Utrecht and The Hague. Not wanting to be diverted from the main objective which was to make all possible haste for the German border, the Allies had been content to leave Holland to its own devices under what was hoped to be a relatively benign German rule. That this was not to be was chiefly as a result of the tragic fiasco at Arnhem. The humiliating setback for the Allies had boosted German confidence.

Reichskommissar Dr Arthur Seyss Inquart, a National Socialist loyalist with myopic political vision, was encouraged to crack down on signs of dissent. This he did by holding back on food supplies. By the end of 1944, the daily ration for urban dwellers was a third below subsistence level. In Amsterdam, hitherto one of the world's cleanest cities, there was fear of epidemic as doctors and hospitals ran out of basic medicines. Dutch politicians in exile pleaded for relief for their countrymen, only to be told that there were food shortages everywhere and warned that precipitate Allied action might well lead to Seyss Inquart giving the order to destroy the flood barriers. There was no need for a reminder that nearly all the occupied territory was under sea level. And so the Dutch had to endure what became known as the Hunger Winter.

By the spring of 1945 it was clear, even to Seyss Inquart, that some sort of accommodation with the Allies had to be made. His proposal was to let the Allies bring in food supplies on condition that they held their advance into western Holland at the Grebbe Line, a barricade of blockhouses and trenches east of Utrecht. Eisenhower was attracted to the idea. A deal would release troops to join Montgomery's push through to northern Germany while removing the threat of wide-scale flooding. Moscow had to approve what might have been construed as a U-turn on unconditional surrender. But on this occasion Stalin was amenable. His agreement was signalled on 24 April.

While BBC radio gave notice of an imminent air drop of food, a negotiating team led by General de Guingand, Montgomery's Chief of Staff, flew to Nijmegen. From there they were driven to a village school, the selected rendezvous just across from the German lines.

> There was an atmosphere of subdued excitement around us, for it was obvious to everyone that something of great moment was taking place. It had been arranged that the enemy delegates should be blindfolded when leaving the German lines and that they should be driven in jeeps by a very roundabout way to the meeting place. Eventually the convoy arrived with white flags flying on each car and a rather miserable and cold-looking collection of Germans got out who were then led into the school.[8]

On the German side it was Ernst Schwebel, Seyss Inquart's deputy, who led the negotiations. He listened without interruption while de Guingand made the offer of help on condition of assurances that the food would reach the Dutch and not be taken by the Germans. Schwebel, 'a plump, sweating German who possessed the largest red nose I have ever seen, the end of which was like several ripe strawberries sewn together', agreed in principle but would make no definite commitment until he had reported back to Seyss Inquart. But de Guingand had something else on his mind. The second part of the brief was to sound out the prospects for an early surrender of German forces in Holland. When the meeting broke up he took Schwebel aside. Guessing what the conversation was to be about, Schwebel insisted on having the representative of his army staff alongside. De Guingand spoke of reports from the Dutch resistance that suggested the German high command in Holland was well aware of the hopelessness of its position, isolated as it was from any possible outside assistance.

I pointed out how difficult the feeding of the Dutch would be if hostilities continued. ... Schwebel, looking rather uncomfortable and glancing repeatedly at the soldier next to him, said he was not empowered to discuss such matters. He agreed, however, to convey my remarks to his chief.[9]

The next Allied–German meeting took place on 30 April. This time General Walter Bedell Smith, Eisenhower's Chief of Staff, and Prince Bernhard, Commander-in-Chief of the Dutch military, joined the Allied team, while the Germans were led by Seyss Inquart with General Blaskowitz's Chief of Staff in tow. Prince Bernhard arrived in a Mercedes with the licence plate RK-1. It was the car that Seyss Inquart had used until it had been captured by the Dutch resistance. After detailed talks about the relief plan, Bedell Smith turned the discussion to that of a general truce, arguing that it was only weeks, possibly days, before Germany capitulated, so why not give up now and so avoid unnecessary bloodshed and suffering. To the amazement of the Allied negotiators, Seyss Inquart accepted the inevitability of defeat but added that he had no orders which would allow him to surrender and in any case it was for the Commander-in-Chief, General Blaskowitz, to make the decision.

To this, Bedell Smith said, 'But surely, Reich Kommissar, it is the politician who dictates the policy to the soldier, and in any case our information points to the fact that no real Supreme Headquarters exists any longer in Germany today.' The German rather avoided answering the question and merely said, 'But what would future generations of Germans say about me if I complied with your suggestion – what would history say about my conduct?' It was then that Bedell Smith got really tough. 'Now, look here, General Eisenhower has instructed me to say that he will hold you directly responsible for any further useless bloodshed. You have lost the war and you know it. And if, through pighead-edness, you cause more loss of life to Allied troops or Dutch civilians, you will have to pay the penalty. And,' continued the Chief of Staff, 'you know what that will mean – the wall and the firing squad!' Seyss Inquart slowly turned his watery eyes towards us and said rather quietly and slowly, 'I am not afraid – I am a German.' That ended the meeting.[10]

Doenitz first heard of these talks on 2 May when Seyss Inquart asked for instructions. Seyss Inquart was invited to Flensburg and advised to inform his Allied contacts of his movements. The conference with Doenitz and Krosigk took place the following day.

Doenitz was wary of confronting one of Hitler's favourites. Conscious that if Hitler had had his way it would have been Seyss Inquart instead of Krosigk managing foreign affairs, he was polite but firm. Though Seyss Inquart doubted that a limited surrender would be acceptable to the Allies he agreed to wait on events at Lueneburg Heath.

Also on parade at Flensburg were the Wehrmacht commanders-in-chief for Norway and Denmark, Generals Boehme and Lindemann together with their political confederates, Josef Terboven, Reichskommissar for Norway and Dr Werner Best,

Plenipotentiary for Denmark. While Seyss Inquart seemed reconciled to his fate, the spokesmen for Norway were in bullish mood. German forces in Norway were among the best. Numbering close on 420,000 at the end of 1944, they owed their relatively easy life to Hitler's long-standing fear of a British invasion. Their only active service was in the north where Norwegian and Finnish patrols made occasional forays against German positions. Taking over command in Norway in January 1945, General Franz Boehme was a brutal ideologue who, post-war, was to be convicted of massacring thousands of Serbian civilians. He was intent on persuading Doenitz to mount a death-defying last stand.

Terboven was another hardliner, as too was Heinz Fehlis, his Gestapo chief. 'In Norway we can face any battle,' Terboven told Doenitz. The resistance movement, though 'formidably armed' was an irritant, said Boehme, but was easily containable and would be swept aside in any major operation. Against this, his troops were without battle experience. He and Terboven were eager to correct that omission.

It was while Norway was under discussion that Himmler turned up, uninvited. He had with him his closest associate, Gruppenfuehrer Schellenberg. Invited to say his piece, Schellenberg held forth on his plan to surrender the German army in Norway, not to the Allies but to Sweden. Doenitz was incredulous. Even assuming that Sweden was prepared to cooperate, a very long shot indeed, who was to say that this benefactor would not subsequently bow to pressure to hand over its prisoners to the Russians? Post-war experience of Swedish susceptibility to Soviet bullying rather proved his point.

Denmark too had an occupation force of around 230,000 but few of them were of fighting calibre. Leaving aside the 10 per cent who were non-Germans – mostly Hungarians with a few

Russian and Polish volunteers – the rest were too old or too inexperienced to put up much of a fight. As in Norway, the resistance in Denmark had gathered strength as the war had turned against Germany. This had counted against Dr Best, who had started out on his job with a soft approach to winning Danish support for the German war effort. By early 1945 he was having to defer to the Gestapo chief, Guenther Pancke, and his deputy, Regierungsrate Hoffman, described by the Swedish newspaper, *Expressen*, as 'the Gestapo's strongest brain and weakest backbone'.[11] Hoffman, a graduate of Cambridge University who came on like an English gentleman in all but his purposeful brutality, was a heavy-handed exponent of martial law. Despite the military weaknesses General Georg Lindemann went along with the Gestapo policy of holding out to the end.

Having led the Eighteenth Army on the Eastern Front until Hitler had decreed that he was 'too old and too weak' to give more than token service, Lindemann was eager to prove himself by going out in a blaze of glory. 'We shall make the last brave stand of the war,' he told Krosigk, who interrupted him: 'But what for, Herr General?'

When Doenitz opened up the discussion, Speer and Krosigk came out strongly against any continuation of the war in the Nordic strongholds. They were supported by Best. Enemy strength was overwhelming. It was not only the Americans and British who might get involved. Having regained all their northernmost territories, the Soviets were close to the Norwegian border and into Finmark, home to the nomadic Lapps. Then there was Sweden to consider. Best had reliable sources who told him that the Swedish government would intervene to prevent a 'frivolous' struggle. Armed brigades, young Danes and Norwegians who had spent the war years in Sweden, were eager for the chance to help drive the invaders from their homelands.

But the prime consideration for Doenitz was the future of the German refugees from across the Baltic. With the closing off of the Hanseatic ports, Denmark was the only haven left to those rescued by Operation Hannibal. The best estimate was of over 230,000 refugees living hand-to-mouth in Denmark, most of them arriving in the first three months of 1945. In the event of a last-stand fight, the Danes, already feeling overwhelmed by strangers who accounted for 5 per cent of their population, would turn against all Germans whether military or civilian. The risk of Operation Hannibal becoming the disaster it had sought to prevent was all too real. A fruitless attempt to salvage German pride by engaging in a suicidal battle for Scandinavia was to be avoided at all costs.

Terboven listened but was not persuaded. Doenitz decided on sending Godt to Norway, ostensibly on a mission to prepare for a possible evacuation of the Northern Government to Oslo should the Allies move in to Schleswig-Holstein. His real task, however, was to try to keep Terboven on a tight leash. A supplementary idea of moving the government to Oslo was soon dropped when it was pointed out to Doenitz that by prolonging its life on foreign territory, it would lose any legitimate claim to represent Germany.

Doenitz also found time to hear Karl Frank, Protector for Bohemia and Moravia, parts of Czechoslovakia hijacked by the Reich, indulge in the fantasy of Czech politicians persuading the Americans to occupy their country ahead of the Russians. Doenitz thought it a hopeless proposition but gave credit to Frank for returning to Prague to take his chances. His words of sympathy for this cold-blooded autocrat were ill-advised, though he might be excused for counting any enemy of the Soviet Union as a useful ally. Nothing more was heard from Frank, who was executed a year later.

Another brief relationship was with Field Marshal Schoener, Hitler's favourite commander, whose Central Army Group was defending Czechoslovakia against the Red Army. On 2 May he was reported to be fighting his way west to surrender his army to the Americans but when, a day later, his representative turned up at Flensburg, it was to tell Doenitz that his army group would disintegrate if it gave up on its heavily fortified positions in Sudetenland. Doenitz ordered him to 'take all necessary steps to ensure an immediate withdrawal of the whole army group'.

The order was ignored, which was unfortunate for the troops swept up in the Soviet advance. Schoener himself escaped by plane to Austria where he was later arrested and charged with war crimes. It must have crossed his mind that Hitler would have had him shot for desertion.

Throughout these deliberations, Doenitz had an overriding thought: had Friedeburg succeeded in his mission? With no communication from Montgomery's headquarters, the only hopeful sign was the silence overhead. There had been no air raids during the day.

It was not until shortly before midnight that Friedeburg was able to report to Doenitz. Montgomery had appeared tough and uncompromising but Friedeburg had gone away from the encounter much heartened. True, the terms set by Montgomery were beyond Friedeburg's immediate power to concede but the Field Marshal had not pushed for unconditional surrender on all fronts and had not ruled out a continuation of Operation Hannibal or indeed, the continuation of the war in the East.

Though Jodl warned against giving up 'trump cards', neither Doenitz nor Krosigk could see any serious objection to including the Netherlands and Denmark in the surrender. They were only too pleased, as Doenitz put it, to 'get these countries off our hands'. There was a question mark over landing refugees at Danish ports but it seemed likely that ships already at sea or setting off from the last German enclaves on the Baltic would be allowed to continue their journey westwards. Then again, some advantage could be seen in opening Denmark to the Allies who would then, he assumed wrongly, have to share responsibility for providing essential supplies to the refugee population.

Keitel and Jodl jibbed at Montgomery's demand for the simultaneous surrender of all war and merchant shipping. They reminded Doenitz that handing over the fleet, albeit much diminished, was contrary to a naval tradition shared by all the combatants. But strongly supported by Krosigk, Doenitz was not about to lose everything on a point of honour.

> If I refused … the separate surrender would not go through. The air-raids on north Germany would start afresh and cause yet more loss of life. … Accordingly I remained firm in my decision to accept this stipulation as well. The reproach has since been levelled at me [he later wrote] that we should still have had time to destroy weapons and sink warships before the surrender came into force. To that I can only retort that such an action would have been against the spirit of our undertakings. Nor must the fact be forgotten that on May 3, as soon as he heard of our intention to surrender, Montgomery had ordered an immediate cessation of air-raids, although the surrender had not yet been implemented.[12]

At his morning conference on 4 May, Doenitz gave orders that no weapons were to be destroyed. At the same time he cancelled *Regenbogen* (Rainbow) the code name for the scuttling of warships and U-boats. He had a personal message for his submarine force.

My U-boat men, six years of U-boat warfare lie behind us. You have fought like lions. A crushing superiority has compressed us into a very narrow area. The continuation of the struggle is impossible from the bases which remain. U-boat men, unbroken in your warlike courage, you are laying down your arms after a heroic fight which knows no equal. In reverent memory we think of our comrades who have sealed their loyalty to the Fuehrer and the Fatherland with their death. Comrades, maintain in the future your U-boat spirit with which you have fought at sea, bravely and unflinchingly, during the long years for the welfare of our Fatherland. Long live Germany. – Your Grand Admiral.

There were several U-boat commanders who could not bring themselves to believe that Doenitz was acting otherwise than under duress. They set charges and sank their boats.

There was some surprise that the scuttling of the U-boats was not picked up by the Allies as a contravention of the surrender terms. Later it was acknowledged that the destruction came as a relief to the Americans and British who were keen for the new super submarines not to fall into Russian hands. In the event, none did.[13]

Two of the older U-boats made it to Argentina. On the voyage south *U-977*, commanded by Heinz Schaeffer, a 25-year-old with little combat experience, along with his volunteer crew, remained submerged for an incredible 66 days.

Food, clothing, woodwork, even the painted metal surfaces of the interior, began to sprout a soft, green covering. Even the men, it seemed, were mouldering. As the long days underwater passed, they grew paler and more listless. Skin rashes and fungal infections multiplied.[14]

After surfacing and clearing Madeira, *U-977* cruised steadily towards the south-west. On 14 July the islands of Cape Verde came into sight. The equator was crossed on 23 July. A week later, a news report revealed that another German submarine, *U-530*, had also made a run for Argentina but on reaching the coast had been handed over to the US Navy. Having reached the limit of international waters, three miles off Mar del Plata, Schaeffer and his crew accepted that their hopes of asylum were to be disappointed. They were interned and, after interrogation, repatriated. They had been at sea for 107 days.

Of the German U-boat strength at the surrender, 226 were scuttled and 156 fell to the Allies. One hundred and twenty of the advanced type XXI were ready or close to ready for service. The large XVIIs, capable of speed up to 25 knots underwater, were in the final stages of construction when the war ended.

U-2511, the first of the new XXIs, had been at sea for five days when the order came through to cease hostilities and return to base. For Commander Schnee, one of the most experienced submarine commanders, the feeling of anticlimax could not have been greater. *U-2511* had more than lived up to her promise. Soon after leaving Norwegian coastal waters to begin what was intended to be a record-breaking underwater voyage, the U-boat had been spotted by a British naval patrol. Schnee had easily evaded action diving to 20 fathoms and then deeper still while putting on speed, a combined action that would not have been possible with earlier models.

With the ceasefire order of 4 May, *U-2511* turned back to make for Bergen. A few hours later, Schnee came upon a British cruiser flanked by three destroyers. This was precisely the sort of target that the XXI was designed to take on. Such was the capability of *U-2511* that Schnee was able to get close to the target, even passing under one of the destroyers, without detection. Six torpedoes were ready for firing and another six ready for quick loading. But the cruiser and her escort were allowed to go on their way unhindered. Schnee had to be satisfied with the sure knowledge that, in what had become no more than a war game, he had emerged the undisputed victor.

This was made clear two days later in Bergen when *U-2511* was handed over to the British. Schnee was asked to give an account of his last voyage; had he come across any prospective targets? His response was unequivocal. 'I encountered the cruiser on which we are now standing.' His interrogators judged that to be impossible. If Schnee really had succeeded in getting as close to the enemy as he claimed, he would surely had been identified. But the U-boat's log book proved otherwise. At the time shown, two days earlier, the British squadron had, indeed, been at the very point in the North Sea where Schnee claimed to have made contact. The telltale sounds of a U-boat closing in were no longer a factor. The *U-2511* could move so quietly that even in the boat itself there was virtually no sound of the engine.

U-3008 was another of the XXIs to have set out on an operational sortie in the last days of the war. The British warships that crossed her sights, sitting targets for the most part, were allowed to go on their way.[15]

★

On the morning of 4 May, Friedeburg was given full authority to accept Montgomery's conditions.

The programme was set to begin with Colonel Warren picking

up Friedeburg at the point where he had dropped him the day before. At the appointed time, Warren was in place but there was no sign of Friedeburg. Warren's instructions were to wait for two hours but no longer. It got to the point where he was nervously anticipating returning to Montgomery empty-handed when the German delegation drove up. They had with them an officer Warren had not so far encountered. This was Colonel Pollok of Wehrmacht intelligence who carried with him in his briefcase all the German army and navy wireless codes along with the locations of German minefields in the North Sea, Frisian Islands, Heligoland Bight and the Baltic.

It was abundantly clear that the Germans were ready to do business. Montgomery had no need to be told. Early in the day his staff had been in consultation with General Kinzel who had stayed over at Montgomery's HQ. Kinzel had declared that the forces to be surrendered would total over a million. This was all very satisfying except that it landed Montgomery with formidable logistical problems. Accommodating such a large number of demoralised troops was challenging enough but Kinzel had made the score card look even more forbidding with the addition of around 400,000 Russian prisoners of war and 2 million refugees from the East, all crowded into Schleswig-Holstein. The best guess on essential supplies was that the food would run out in ten days. Montgomery reported to Brooke, 'You can well imagine … there are some nice problems to solve'.

Friedeburg and his party were delivered at Lueneburg Heath at just after 5 p.m. It was raining. A full contingent of war correspondents was already gathered. 'They served us tea from a YMCA truck and refined paste sandwiches,' recalled Leonard Mosley. For the benefit of the only woman journalist, 'a latrine had been dug fifty yards away and a large sign with LADIES painted on it stuck beside the canvas'.[16] In smart battledress with five rows of decorations, Montgomery took his time giving the press a briefing on the events leading up to this, the culmination of his military career.

Montgomery kept the German delegates waiting, standing miserably about in the rain. … With their backs towards us, Von Friedeburg and his three companions stood there, on the spot where all of them must, at some time in their careers, have watched German armies manoeuvring on the plain below in the exercises of pre-War days, and where now unending convoys of British troops were moving. Montgomery kept them standing there, letting them watch and think, letting the rain splash over them, until he judged the moment right; and then he sent Colonel Ewart clattering down the steps to round the Nazi generals up and shepherd them to the tiny army tent on the lip of Lueneburg tor, where the Klieg lights were ready, and the microphones, for photographs to be taken and records made of the signing ceremony.[17]

An Australian war reporter had a glimpse of what went on inside the tent. The Germans were seated at a plain trestle table covered by an army blanket.

There were no frills over the ceremony – ordinary unpainted Post Office pens were used for the signatures – but Montgomery had worked with Movietone's Paul Wyand until the cramped stuffy tent was 'lighted like a Hollywood film set'. Like any good cameraman, Wyand exulted in the unrehearsed performance of Admiral Hans von Friedeburg, the principal signatory – 'absolute misery and abysmal despair ... superb picture material' – an effect dispelled when a photoflood bulb slipped from its socket and exploded with a bang on the Admiral's bald head.[18]

Montgomery dominated the proceedings 'rather like a schoolmaster taking an oral examination', noted Alan Moorehead. There was one departure from the script. Having read the terms of the surrender in English (there were copies in German) Montgomery had intended to put the question, 'Do you accept?' But this formality was dropped. Instead:

'You will now sign,' he said, and meekly, one by one, they came. The Post Office pen scraped on the paper; the delegates sat down again, expressionless, and waited. There was a moment, while the last photographs were being taken, when Von Friedeburg turned his full face into the lights, an expression of tremendous anguish in his eyes as he posed for the pictures, and then the flap of the tent dropped and it was over.[19]

But not for Friedeburg. He signalled Doenitz, 'Conditions signed – Ceasefire [will come into effect] 8 a.m. 5 May – leaving tomorrow by air for higher authority'. The 'higher authority' was the Supreme Commander of Allied forces in the West.

It was early evening on 4 May before Eisenhower heard from Montgomery. He was on the point of leaving his headquarters when Lieutenant Kay Summersby, his personal secretary, suggested he gave it five more minutes. At 7 p.m. the call came. Eisenhower was laconic. 'Fine. Fine. That's just fine Monty.' If the plenipotentiaries had authority from Doenitz to stop all fighting, then they were to come to Reims. Montgomery thought they had full powers but wanted more time. A follow up call from Bedell Smith confirmed that the Germans would be flown in the following morning, weather permitting.[20]

Montgomery was misinformed. The 'full powers' Eisenhower expected were for an unconditional German surrender on all fronts. This was not within Friedeburg's brief. What he hoped to negotiate was the surrender of all German forces in the West. Those facing the Russians were to fight on.

After confirmation of the surrender on Montgomery's front, Doenitz was in touch with Army Groups Centre, South and South-East to tell them that by continuing the struggle they were defending 'many millions of German men, women and children still to the east of the American zone'. He called for 'iron discipline ... for the fulfilment of your great task'. The morning of 5 May found the Friedeburg delegation along with two British officers boarding an aircraft bound for Reims.

CHAPTER EIGHT

Friedeburg's journey to Reims was protracted by bad weather. After his plane took off from Brussels, it did not get far. The pilot was Flight Lieutenant Albert Ricketts.

> As we got closer to Reims the cloud base became lower and lower until eventually I was forced to fly above the cloud. As my radio was not performing I had no alternative but to return to our main base at Brussels.[1]

There was talk of sending Eisenhower's personal train to a point where the weather was clear enough for a landing. While Friedeburg paced up and down outside the airport buildings the decision came through from Reims. It would be quicker by car.

Eisenhower and Montgomery did not have much in common; indeed, they heartily disliked each other. But on one thing they agreed: neither was attracted to the high life generally favoured by the military elite. When Eisenhower moved his headquarters to Reims, the champagne capital in northern France, it was to a former technical school alongside a railway. Meetings were accompanied by the rumble of freight trains arriving or departing from a station a mile down the line. What he called 'home' for the duration was a small chateau which visitors found to be gloomy and spartan.

Eisenhower was kept aware of the need to keep the Russians onside. Washington had left him in no doubt that Stalin had to be pacified. The Soviet leader's angry reaction to what he had seen as a surrender exclusively to Western forces in Italy was not to be repeated. On hearing of Friedeburg's imminent arrival, therefore, Eisenhower's first move was to inform the Russian High Command. General Ivan Susloparov, head of the Russian Mission to France, was invited as an observer. He came with an interpreter, Colonel Ivan Zenkovitch, noted for his 'shiny bald head without a hair on it'.

Realising that if he fronted the negotiations it would appear to the Russians as an act of one-upmanship, Eisenhower delegated the job to his Chief of Staff, General Bedell Smith, supported by General Kenneth Strong who spoke fluent German. It was Smith who took the lead. A self-made general who had never been part of the West Point 'old boy' network, Smith was something of a bully, quick to criticise others but dreading criticism from his superiors. He took pride in being known as a 'number one square-wheeled SOB'.[2] Eisenhower made allowance for Smith's 'Prussian' personality while having cause to regret his rough handling of close colleagues and his tendency to act as if he was the sole authority in all things relating to SHAEF.*

A case in point was the confusion caused by Smith in the preparation of surrender documents. A three-power and, after France joined, four-power European Advisory Commission had been labouring over draft surrender documents for nineteen months. These Smith chose to ignore, largely because he thought them

---

* Supreme Headquarters Allied Expeditionary Force.

too long for immediate purposes. This high-handed decision put Eisenhower in difficulty. He had to make sure that the Russians would accept his 'shorter version' hastily compiled by his team of post-hostilities planners.

They were asked to approve two documents. The first, the 'Act of Military Surrender' provided for the unconditional surrender of German armed forces on all fronts. The second was an 'Undertaking Given by Certain Emissaries to the Allied High Command' to send representatives of the High Command to 'formally ratify the military surrender at a location and place decided upon by SHAEF and the Soviet government'. After some delay, these were accepted in principle, though, as it turned out, the devil was in the detail.

Friedeburg arrived in Reims at about 5 p.m. His sallow complexion and sunken cheeks were an indication of the strain he was under. He asked for time to put on a fresh collar. Strong saw him as a 'friendly and pleasant officer, little suited to the fanaticism of the Third Reich'.[3] Smith quickly got down to business.

> Discussions … were in German [recalled Strong]. I did the interpreting but von Friedeburg knew enough English to be able to follow what Bedell Smith said. We had prepared a map showing Allied dispositions, thinking it would be the easiest way of conveying to our visitors the hopelessness of their situation and the strength of the Allied position. It was left lying face upwards on Bedell Smith's desk so that von Friedeburg could see it on entering the room. For good measure we added two large arrows indicating entirely imaginary attacks, one an advance from our own front and the other from the Russian, both converging to cut off the remaining German forces.[4]

Also on display was a large swastika from which sprouted a graphic thermometer showing the number of Germans (over 4 million) taken prisoner by Allied forces.

Though Smith claimed otherwise, Friedeburg was not taken in by the imaginative content of the visual display. When it came to giving a false impression with oversized arrows on war maps, he knew that the same trick had been pulled on Hitler often enough – though on those occasions the intention had been to give an exaggerated impression of German strength. But even allowing for their ruse to be easily penetrated, it came as a surprise to Strong to find Friedeburg in bullish mood, bargaining, as he seemed to suggest, from a position of strength. It was surely inconceivable that the Admiral had been so poorly briefed.

The realisation soon dawned that Friedeburg was intent on dragging out the negotiations to allow maximum time for German troops and civilians to escape from the East. His opening proposal to Smith was for a purely local surrender of all the remaining German forces on the Western Front. That, he claimed, was his best offer. He had no authority to decide the future of German troops facing the Russians.

With no resolution in sight, the talks were adjourned while Smith rethought his strategy. Later he claimed to have been well in control, even to the extent of sympathising with Friedeburg: 'It was a terrible thing for a man to see himself as completely help-less.'[5] Maybe, but he had sufficient respect for his adversary to bring in some heavyweight support including America's air force chief, General Carl Spaatz. The meeting resumed in a second-floor conference room with Friedeburg and three aides facing Smith and four other Allied officers. Friedeburg continued to insist that surrender to the Russians was 'unthinkable'. He was disinclined to accept Smith's assurances that if the Germans surrendered promptly on all fronts they would be treated 'with the normal dictates of humanity'. Smith made more impact with his threat to resume hostilities and to close the front to refugees.

The circular argument was broken eventually when Smith told Friedeburg bluntly to sign the surrender or to defer to someone with wider powers. Accepting the inevitable, Friedeburg appealed to Doenitz for instructions on the next move. There being no code or agreed radio frequency with Flensburg, his message was sent by code from SHAEF to 21st Army Group where it was decoded and then taken to Flensburg by General Kinzel. He arrived on the morning of 6 May.

Doenitz may have retained a faint hope that Eisenhower would accept surrender on the same terms as those agreed with Montgomery. But he had no need to be reminded that Eisenhower, as supreme commander, had to take account of the wider picture. The regional surrender acceptable to Montgomery was made possible by it leading on to a general surrender at Reims. The only realistic prospect for Doenitz – and he knew this very well whatever protests he made for general consumption – was to persuade Eisenhower to agree to a surrender on all fronts to be implemented in two stages. It fell to Jodl to fly to Reims to support Friedeburg in presenting this latest proposal to Eisenhower:

> During the first phase all hostilities will have ceased, but the German troops will still be allowed liberty of movement. During the second phase this liberty will be withheld.

Jodl was told to:

> try and make the period elapsing before the introduction of phase two as long as possible and if you can, get

Eisenhower to agree that individual German soldiers will in any case be allowed to surrender to the Americans. The greater your success in these directions, the greater will be the numbers of German soldiers and refugees who will find salvation in the west.[6]

The best that Doenitz and Krosigk reckoned they could expect was for Jodl to secure a four-day gap between the two phases. Jodl was authorised to sign a general capitulation but only after confirmation from Doenitz.

Shortly before Jodl arrived in Reims, Eisenhower was given to understand that Moscow had granted approval, for which he had been waiting over the Easter weekend, for Susloparov to agree the instrument of surrender. This was encouraging just as long as there was a surrender to be signed. Jodl and Friedeburg were taken to Smith's office at 6.15 p.m. on 6 May. With Strong as interpreter, Jodl was allowed to make his presentation.

> He told us frankly and with deep conviction that we would soon find ourselves fighting Russia and that, if Germany were given time to evacuate as many troops and civilians as possible to the West, there would then be large resources available to help the Allies in their struggle against the Russians.[7]

Jodl agreed to a general surrender but with a suitable delay for the transmission of orders. Doenitz had wanted four days, Jodl was prepared to settle for two. Eisenhower, when the proposal was put to him, refused to consider any delay at all. But Smith and Strong pointed out that there really were problems with communications to German field commands. Allied intercepts gave support to Jodl's claims. Could not a ceasefire be permitted before the surrender came into force? Eisenhower agreed but the surrender had to be signed immediately. It would then come into force 24 hours later, at midnight on 7 May.

On the way back to Smith's office, Strong suggested that it might expedite matters if he, Smith, had a private soldier-to-soldier talk with Jodl. Given that Smith had been on nodding acquaintance with Jodl in his days in Berlin before the war and respected him, albeit grudgingly, as a fellow professional, the idea had substance. If Smith is to be believed, the discussion concentrated on finding the best way to preserve the honour and prestige of the German armed forces: 'The world would be grateful to them for putting a quick end to the fighting.' Strong maintained that it was a 'good, long speech showing a fine understanding of German mentality'.[8] This may indeed have been so, but was anything more said to bring Jodl onside? From all that happened subsequently it seems likely that Smith encouraged the belief that more would be done to support German efforts to escape the Bear's embrace.

Jodl asked for time to think over all that Smith had said. After an hour closeted with Friedeburg, he emerged to announce that he was ready to settle. In fact, he had already drafted a message to Doenitz. This caused a flurry of concern when Smith realised that his comments favourable to the German High Command had been extensively quoted as a way of reassuring Doenitz that fair play would be observed. He ordered all copies of the draft to be destroyed.

But, supported by Strong, he did urge Eisenhower to agree to a further delay on the grounds that an over-hasty implementation of the surrender would lead to a total breakdown in communications. Reluctantly, because he knew that Soviet suspicions would be aroused, Eisenhower agreed to a delay of two days between the signing of the surrender at 2.41 a.m. on 7 May and its coming into effect.

Jodl radioed Doenitz:

Eisenhower insists that we sign today. If not, the Allied fronts will be closed to persons seeking to surrender individually, and all negotiations will be broken off. I see no alternative – chaos or signature. I ask you to confirm to me immediately by radio that I have full powers to sign capitulation. Capitulation will then come into effect. Hostilities will then cease at midnight, German summer time, on May 9th.

Though he described Eisenhower's demands as 'extortion', Doenitz was forced to acknowledge that there was nothing more he could do to win concessions. Less than an hour after hearing from Jodl, Doenitz authorised him to sign.

The general relief in the Allied camp was not shared by Susloparov. He had authority to participate in the surrender but, despite requests to Moscow, he was short of a direct order from Stalin to sign the surrender document. This put him in a quandary. If he refused to sign it could be made to look as if the Soviet Union was intent on continuing the war. But if he fell in with the Western Allies before receiving a clear directive from Moscow, his own future would be in doubt. In the end, Susloparov took his lead from Eisenhower who reaffirmed his commitment to a follow-up ceremony in which the Soviet Union would play the dominant role. He agreed to sign.

Kept waiting in a side room for six hours, eighteen hand-picked war reporters had been selected to witness the big moment. Among them was the Australian correspondent, Osmar White.

L'Ecole Professionelle, Reims, was a drab, commonplace French school crouching in a drab, grey twilight through which a light rain drifted.

On the wall of the anteroom … hung a large-scale map of Europe. The coloured flags with which it once was sprigged had been taken out and arranged in a V at the bottom right-hand corner.

When the waiting was over White and his colleagues were taken up a flight of stone stairs, down a narrow corridor and into a classroom that Eisenhower's staff had used for briefings.

A long table stood in front of a flagged map of the battlefronts. The top of the table had been painted black and about it were set fifteen yellow deal chairs with unpadded seats. The table was furnished with thirteen pads of white notepaper, thirteen yellow pencils and six white inkpots. Nothing else.

We lined up against one wall behind a chalk line beyond which we were forbidden to walk until the signatories to the Act of Surrender were seated.

Black cables of sound recording gear and cinecameras coiled over the shabby, patterned carpet that covered most of the floor. A calendar on the wall behind the table read:

MONDAY

MAY 7

1945

Camera crews and sound technicians raced about, bent double, checking and re-checking their equipment. Staff officers paced up and down, glancing every few seconds at their wristwatches.

At 2.19 a British colonel walked in and said in a brisk voice: 'Get ready, gentlemen, they're coming.'

There was an echo of footsteps as the Allied delegation led by Admiral Sir Harold Burrough came in. The floodlights were switched on.

Burrough's high-boned face was ruddy and gleaming. Susloparov, a huge-shouldered giant of a man, filled his tight-waisted Russian jacket and striped whipcord breeches with a sort of bounding physical defiance of the room's weighted tensions. His gold teeth gleamed as he made casual asides to his aide. All the others had violet shadows under their eyes and their faces were pallid and slack.

Five minutes later, General François Sevez, the French representative, hurried in, bowed to the table and shook hands nervously with his nearest neighbour. Then came Bedell Smith. He was never a robust-looking man but under the glare of the Kliegs he looked ghastly, ill and exhausted.

All stood a little stiffly behind the chairs awaiting the Germans. The heat from the lights mounted steadily and we began to sweat.

At 2.39 a.m. Jodl and Friedeburg were ushered in. At the table they stood to attention until Smith nodded to them to take the seats opposite him. Smith asked if they understood the terms of the documents to be signed. The question was put again in German. They murmured assent. The papers were handed round.

Each was in quadruplicate, and every copy was signed by the naval, land and air authorities of the signatory Powers.

The film cameras made a low, whirring sound and dozens of small flash-globes popped as the official photographers, still bent double, scuttled from point to point, ripping black papers from film packs and adjusting lenses. Every gesture, every muscle twitch was recorded. Pen nibs moved swiftly as aides passed copy after copy.

Air Marshal Robb, the RAF delegate, was the only man at the table who did not watch every movement of the signing. He appeared distracted, studying maps on the wall. The Russians were the only ones upon whose coun-tenances could be discerned the faintest expression of satisfaction. They sat absolutely motionless and upright, chests out. Their slightly slanted eyes were narrowed and fixed unwinkingly on the Germans' hands.[9]

Jodl signed with a gold pen which Eisenhower later presented to President Truman. After Generals Smith, Susloparov and Sevez had signed both documents, Jodl stood and, addressing himself to Smith, said, in English, 'I want to say a word'. Then, in German:

General! With this signature the German people and German armed forces are for better or worse delivered into the victor's hands. In this war, which has lasted more than five years, both have achieved and suffered more than perhaps any other people in the world. In this hour I can only express the hope that the victor will treat them with generosity.

The official time of the signatures on the surrender documents was

2.41 a.m. local time, 7 May. Jodl also had to sign a declaration guaranteeing formal confirmation before the Commander-in-Chief of the Allied Forces and Soviet High Command. Jodl and Friedeburg were then taken to see Eisenhower. He asked them if they fully understood the terms and were prepared to execute them. Strong interpreted. Jodl answered 'Ja'.

Eisenhower then said, 'You will officially and personally be held responsible if the terms of the surrender are violated including its provisions for German commanders to appear in Berlin at the moment set by the Russian High Command to accomplish a formal surrender to that Government. That is all.' Jodl and Friedeburg saluted, bowed stiffly and left the room.

Before Jodl signalled Doenitz, he asked for a clarification. The 48 hours allowed for implementation of the surrender were presumably to run from 2.41 a.m. 'No way,' declared Eisenhower. The clock had started ticking from midnight.

When, much later, military leaders were collecting together their memories and impressions, Montgomery criticised Eisenhower for allowing the Germans to get away with two days' grace. It did not seem to occur to him that the greater lengthening of the surrender timetable was the result of Eisenhower granting the Field Marshal his moment of glory at Lueneburg Heath. The Supreme Commander would have been well within his rights to insist on Montgomery refusing to meet with Friedeburg and his party but instead to send them directly to Reims. Fortunately for Anglo-American relations, Eisenhower's political antennae were more sensitive than Montgomery's.

Having sent a one-line confirmation of the surrender to the Combined Chiefs, Eisenhower posed for the crowd of photographers, holding up the two pens used for the signing to make a V for victory. He spent the next hour on the telephone. His call to

London tells us something of the problem of communication, even at the highest level, in the pre-digital age.

General Hastings ('Pug') Ismay, Churchill's Chief of Staff, was sound asleep when the Supreme Commander put through his call.

About 3 a.m. that morning, I was awakened by my telephone bell, and told that the Supreme Commander was on the line. These nocturnal calls had never brought good news and I was afraid that something had gone wrong. But my mind was soon put at rest. 'Is that you, Pug?' 'Yes, Ike. What has happened?' 'They have signed on the dotted line. It's all over.' My wife heard what had been said, and her eyes filled with tears. I too felt a lump in my throat, and could scarcely voice my congratulations. I had got back into bed before it occurred to me that Eisenhower may have intended me to pass the news to the Prime Minister. To be on the safe side, I rang No. 10, but the operators had evidently failed to disconnect me from Reims and my telephone was dead. There was nothing for it but to collect some coppers, put on a dressing gown, and go to the public call-box a hundred yards down the road. I had no difficulty in making contact with No. 10, only to be told by the best switchboard in London that Mr Churchill had already heard the glad news and gone to bed.[10]

Eisenhower's relief that it was all over did not last long. A signal from Moscow revealed that Stalin was not happy. The Soviet Union having, in his view, and with some justification, contributed most to the winning of the war, it was humiliating for his country to be relegated, as it were, to the second division in the formalities at Reims. Moreover, the Germans showed no signs of giving up on the Eastern Front. Stalin strongly suspected that the Western Allies were stitching up a 'shady deal' with the enemy. A little too late in the day, he ordered Susloparov to sign nothing.

Stalin was on firm ground when he claimed that the Germans were still fighting on in the East. Even while Jodl was assuring Eisenhower that he was very clear on the terms of the surrender, Keitel was ordering troops 'facing the Eastern enemy ... to withdraw westwards with the greatest urgency, fighting through the Russians if necessary'. His interpretation of Eisenhower's agreement for two days of transition was that hostilities could continue up to 1 a.m. on 9 May. This was furiously disputed by SHAEF but there was little Eisenhower could do to counter the excuse of a 'poor communication network' which somehow still allowed Doenitz to talk directly with field commanders. From his headquarters in the southern zone Kesselring reported 'whole formations still on the march and fighting against the Soviets'.

Stalin's anger was fuelled by a letter from the head of the American military mission in Moscow asking him to coordinate the Soviet declaration of the German surrender with the Americans and British before the final ceremony agreed by Eisenhower and now planned to take place on 8 May in Berlin. What looked to be yet another attempt to downgrade the Soviet Union to a secondary role had a simple (though for Stalin unsatisfactory) explanation. It had to do with a mishandling of the news media.

When the reporters gathered at Reims, they were warned that the announcement of the surrender would first be made by the Allied heads of government. After the signing, orders from 'a high political level' decreed that the news could not be released until the following day at 8 p.m. when it would be announced simultaneously in Paris, London, Moscow and Washington. There were objections. The news agency men, the most fiercely competitive of the press corps, doubted that an embargo would hold that long. But they protested in vain. The best news story they were ever likely to have was to be kept under wraps.

Edward Kennedy, head of the Associated Press Paris bureau, described as 'a hardnosed wire service correspondent', on this occasion refused to bend the knee to the censor. Using a military telephone link the authority had overlooked, he put through a brief report to the AP office in London. Since the British censors had no special instructions on surrender stories, they allowed the report to be relayed to New York. Less than ten minutes later, the story was around the world.[11]

At this point bureaucratic inanity took collective hold. Insisting that the embargo stay in place, SHAEF bullied Kennedy's colleagues into denying the story. Confusion was total. While Germany's collapse was widely believed to be only hours away, the fact that AP had once before got it wrong – on 28 April an AP bulletin had said that Germany had accepted unconditional surrender – gave credence to the official version of events. But this did not deter the celebrations which were soon in boisterous evidence, particularly so in London.

Churchill was quickly on his 'secret line' to the White House asking that the official announcement be brought forward. The response was unhelpful. Truman would refuse to act 'without the approval of Uncle Joe'. Churchill blustered his objections. 'What is the use of me and the President looking to be the only two people in the world who don't know what is going on ... It is an idiotic position.'[12] Telegrams had already been sent to Moscow; now Churchill sent another appeal for cooperation. An hour later he was back in touch with Admiral Leahy, Truman's Chief of Staff. There had been no reply from Stalin. 'I feel I can delay no longer,' said Churchill. Leahy said he understood but could not give the go-ahead for an official announcement 'unless Stalin approves'. Knowing that Stalin was playing power games, Churchill did not feel similarly restrained. Shortly after ending his conversation with Leahy, he wired the Pentagon:

> British Ministry of Information announced that to-morrow, Tuesday, May 8, will be V.E. Day, and a holiday throughout England. The Prime Minister will make a statement at 3 p.m. The King will broadcast at 9 p.m., and Wednesday, May 9 will also be a holiday in England.

Truman continued to hold on for word from Moscow. It came shortly after midnight, Washington time, on 7 May. Stalin wanted the announcement to be postponed until he had given further consideration to the surrender terms. At this, even Truman's patience ran out. Early the following day he held a news conference to announce the German surrender on all fronts to Anglo-American-Soviet forces.

Up to 30,000 revellers gathered in Times Square and, though disappointed not to hear Truman's victory proclamation (nobody had thought to have it relayed over loudspeakers), they did hear sirens and whistle blasts from the tugs and cargo boats on the Hudson and East River, a refrain taken up by cabbies and other motorists hooting their delight.

> Then the great paper and cloth throwing orgy began. Paper in every possible form and description cascaded from a hundred thousand windows – scrap paper, ledgers, playing cards, torn telephone books, fragments, stationery, streamers, ticker-tape … [garment trade workers] threw bale upon bale of textiles into the street: rayon, silk, woollens, prints,

foulards, every conceivable remnant in every possible shade and hue turned and squirmed in the thin morning sunlight ... Within the hour, Sixth, Seventh and Eighth Avenues and Broadway were eight to ten inches deep in multi-coloured fabrics. Thrifty passers-by forgot their delirium long enough to salvage some of the larger remnants. Passing trucks, pleasure cars and cabs were draped in the material. It clung to ledges, sills and cornices and the wind played with it and tore at it. Men and women in the streets tore it from their hats and shoulders ... Opposite Macy's women hung from windows waving bottles of liquor and screaming 'Hey soldiers, hey sailors, come on up and get a drink!'[13]

Partying in Britain was slower to get under way. VE Day had a damp start with the rain falling steadily from the early hours. Those who had been out the night before had searched in vain for the bright lights that would signal that the war was well and truly over. Except for a belt five miles inland from the coast where the lights-out rule after dark stayed in force until 10 May, the blackout had officially ended on 24 April. But street lights had been extinguished for so long, few of them were working. The same could be said of shop signs and illuminated advertisements. Some householders kept their curtains pulled back to let their living room lights shine out of the windows but it was hardly a festive display. The flag wavers did better. There were Union Jacks everywhere, on poles jutting out from windows, strung across streets and between lampposts and fluttering from the rooftops of every official building. BBC Radio helped to get the national party under way with spirited tunes like 'Victory Parade' and 'Keep Your Sunny Side Up', which in some places were relayed to the streets through loudspeakers. A more common sound was of church bells rung enthusiastically, if not always in harmony.

In London the crowds gathered early, encouraged by a change in the weather from storm clouds to warm sunshine. By lunchtime it was almost impossible for traffic to get through the masses milling back and forth between Buckingham Palace, Trafalgar Square and Piccadilly Circus. 'This is it – and we are all going nuts,' exulted a *Daily Mirror* reporter.

> There are thousands of us in Piccadilly Circus. The police say more than 10,000 – and that's a conservative estimate.
>
> We are dancing the Conga and the jig and 'Knees Up Mother Brown', and we are singing and whistling and blowing paper trumpets.
>
> The idea is to make a noise. We are. Even above the roar of the motors of low-flying bombers …

Then at dusk:

> We are dancing around Eros in the black-out, but there is a glow from a bonfire up Shaftesbury Avenue and a newsreel cinema has lit its canopy lights for the first time in getting on for six years.
>
> A huge V sign glares down over Leicester Square and gangs of girls and soldiers are waving rattles and shouting and climbing lampposts and swarming over cars that have become bogged down in this struggling, swirling mass of celebrating Londoners.[14]

Churchill's secretary, Elizabeth Layton, was standing a little behind the prime minister when he and members of the war cabinet appeared on a balcony overlooking Parliament Square.

> Flags and bunting had been put up, and floodlights were directed upon the balcony. A crowd which some estimated at 20,000 stood below, the roar of their cheering seemed almost to lift one off one's feet. It was just a sea of faces and waving arms. As Mr Churchill emerged, the noise increased almost to deafening point. Microphones were ready. He knew so well what to say. He congratulated the Londoners on their fortitude, saying 'I always said "London can take it." Were we downhearted?' The response was overwhelming. He mentioned Japan, and the crowd booed happily. Then he began the first few words of 'Land of Hope and Glory', and the multitude took it up with a will.[15]

For Edward Kennedy there was a less happy ending to the story. In a senseless fit of pique, SHAEF suspended AP facilities throughout Europe and withdrew Kennedy's accreditation. Reviewing his case, AP offered to let Kennedy stay with the agency as long as he admitted he had been wrong. He refused and was fired. So much for the war reporters' proud boast that they told it as it happened.

To add insult to Kennedy's injury, the story would, in any case, have got out since Krosigk announced the capitulation on Flensburg radio. In the first draft of his speech he referred to the 'armistice'. Doenitz insisted that he changed this to 'unconditional surrender'.

The following day (8 May), Doenitz spoke on the radio. For the first time he resisted the urge to indulge in high-flown rhetoric. His message was matter of fact and to the immediate point.

I have promised the German people that, in the coming time of need, I will strive, so far as it lies in my power, to create tolerable conditions of life for our brave men, women and children. Whether, in these hard times, I can make some contribution, I do not know. We must look facts in the face. The foundations upon which the German Reich was constructed have been shattered. Unity of State and Party no longer exists. The Party has disappeared from the arena of its activity. With occupation authority lies in the hands of the occupying powers. Whether I and the government I have appointed can act or not, depends on them. If in my official position I can serve and help our Fatherland, I will remain in office, until the will of the German people can be expressed in the nomination of a new Head of State or until the occupying powers make the continued exercise of my office impossible. Only my love of Germany and my sense of duty keep me in this onerous office. Without regard for my own person, I will remain not a moment longer than I feel is required by the respect which I owe to the Reich, of which I am the highest representative ...[16]

There were no illusions left.

*

The scene shifts to Berlin. A two-storey building, once the mess for the German military engineering school, had been chosen for the last formal act of capitulation. Eisenhower decided not to attend. It was pointed out to him that he would lose face since Marshal Zhukov, the Soviet Commander-in-Chief in Germany and Moscow's representative at the signing, was junior to Eisenhower. So it was that his deputy, Air Chief Marshal Tedder, went in his place along with

General Spaatz and, for the French, General de Lattre de Tassigny, who was to travel separately. The cavalcade eventually set off for Berlin in two American aircraft escorted by Russian fighters.

> We devoutly hoped that warning of our journey had been given to the Russian air defences which were known to be extremely trigger-happy and we were relieved when, after circling the city several times, we landed at Tempelhof Airfield. Here we were received by a Russian guard of honour of three companies, carrying the national flags of Britain, America and Russia – there was no French flag. The national anthems of the three countries were played by a large military band. All of us were surprised by the extensive and careful preparations the Russians had made for our reception. It seemed to me that they must have always expected the surrender to take place in Berlin and that they had been making ready for it for some considerable time.
>
> The streets to Karlshorst Military Engineering College, which was about ten miles from the city centre, were policed by Russian women in uniform who used little red and yellow flags to direct the traffic. The rubble had been partially cleared and every effort had been made to avoid delaying our journey through the ruined city. It was warm but Berlin was covered in haze and yellowish smoke which made it difficult for the sun to break through. Many buildings were smouldering from the battle and those which were still standing were burned and blackened. Crazily canted structures threatened to collapse at any moment. Bomb craters were filled with water. Unexploded bombs were marked with prominent notices. It was a scene of incredible destruction.[17]

There were no Germans to be seen on the route. They had been told to keep clear.

De Tassigny almost didn't make his appointment with history. An American Dakota had been promised for the journey from Mengen to Berlin. It was an hour late in taking off and then, for some mysterious reason, landed at Magdeburg, 62 miles short of Berlin. There it was explained that a fighter plane escort had been arranged to take the Allied representative on to their venue but that, unfortunately, the escort had already departed with the American and British representatives. No one seemed to care.

> I had to remind [the Russians] of the object of my presence. Then two cars came up to take us to Marshal Zhukov's command post. With a Soviet colonel to escort us, our drivers went off at top speed and plunged towards the ruins of what had been the German capital ... I saw masses of still smoking and tragically similar ruins, where demining squads were handling their long metal rods and in the midst of which were wretched lines of dazed women, children and old men who had left their cellars and, provided with the most varied receptacles, queued up interminably for a little water at the public fountains and fire hydrants.
>
> At all the crossroads – the only bright feature – young Russian girls, stocky, impeccably neat in their simple uniforms, with bare knees above high boots, were controlling the traffic with great seriousness. They handled their little yellow and red flags with surprising dexterity and cleared the way – then they smartly tucked the flags under their left arms in order to salute our cars.[18]

At the end of a tiring journey de Tassigny was welcomed into the band of Allied brothers. But there remained obstacles to French participation in the surrender ceremony. First there was a problem over who should sign the surrender document. Zhukov had been happy to accept an additional signature, though up to the point of de Tassigny's appearance he was unaware that the French were involved. However, instructions from Moscow ruled that if de Tassigny signed, one of the other participants had to step down. The obvious choice was Spaatz since Tedder was signing on behalf of Eisenhower and his own government. Spaatz was not having that. De Tassigny made an emotional appeal to Tedder: 'If I return to France without having fulfilled my mission, that is to say, having allowed my country to be excluded from signing the capitulation of the Reich, I deserve to be hanged. Think of me ... !'

Tedder went back to Zhukov. A compromise was hammered out. Zhukov and Tedder were to sign as contracting parties, Spaatz and de Lattre as witnesses. But first of all the protocols had to be retyped. And there was still another matter to sort out. In the room where the signing was to take place the sole decorations were three flags upon the end wall: the Red Flag, the Union Jack and the Stars and Stripes. The French colours were nowhere to be seen. De Tassigny declared that France could not be represented at the ceremony without her flag alongside those of her Allies. But where could a French flag be found?

The Russians decided to make one, with a piece of red stuff taken from a former Hitlerite banner, a white sheet and a piece of blue serge cut out of an engineer's overalls. Alas! our tricolour was less familiar to the young Russian girls than the red flag to many French girls, for when a jeep brought along the flag that had been run up in this way we found a magnificent Dutch flag: the blue, white and red had been sewn not one beside the other but one above the other! It had to be all begun again but the blue was this time too short to go round the staff. Everybody worked with a will. At last, at 20.00, our national emblem was placed between those of Great Britain and the United States in a cluster, surmounted by the Soviet flag.[19]

Keitel, Friedeburg and General Hans-Juergen Stumpff for the Luftwaffe were flown by a British transport plane to Tempelhof.

A Russian guard of honour had been drawn up for the British and American parties, with a military band; from our landing area we were able to watch the ceremony from afar. A Russian officer had been detailed to accompany me – I was told he was General Zhukov's chief quartermaster – and he drove me in one car while the rest of my party followed in other cars.

We drove across Belle-Alliance-Platz through the outskirts of the city to Karlshorst, where we were put down at a small empty villa not far from the Pioneer and Engineer School's barracks. It was about one o'clock in the afternoon. We were left absolutely to ourselves. Presently a reporter came and took some photographs, and after a while a Russian interpreter came: he was unable to tell me at what time the signing of the Instrument of Surrender was to take place.[20]

In the event, it was approaching midnight before the now-furious Keitel was escorted to the mess hall of the barracks.

Every corner of the hall was packed, and brilliantly lit by spotlights. Three rows of chairs running the length of the hall and one across it were crowded with officers; General Zhukov took the chair with the plenipotentiaries of Britain and America on either side of him.[21]

At ten minutes past midnight Keitel was brought forward, blinking in the glare of the newsreel lights. He clicked his heels and saluted with his marshal's baton. With the baton still raised he took in the scene. His eye fell on the French flag and then on de Tassigny. 'Ach,' he growled. 'The French are here too. It only wanted that.'

Witnesses saw what they wanted to see. For some, the Germans were 'arrogant and dignified'. Others thought that Keitel had to struggle to maintain his dignity. His face was blotchy and red; his hand shook. As he walked to the table to sign the surrender his monocle dropped from his eye and dangled by its cord. But General Strong, an acute observer, concluded that 'if the Germans wanted to have a majestic figurehead on this day of capitulation, they could not have chosen anybody more self-possessed or confident'.[22]

Notable by his absence was General Susloparov who had signed the surrender at Reims on behalf of the Russian High Command. He was part of the Allied contingent that flew to Berlin but 'from the moment he stepped out of the aeroplane at Tempelhof we never saw him again; any enquiries we made about him were received with blank faces'.[23] In fact Susloparov did not disappear entirely. After the war he surfaced as an instructor at Moscow Military Academy where he trained military attachés and intelligence officers.

In Susloparov's place was Andrey Vyshinsky, Soviet Deputy Foreign Minister and Stalin's legal frontman in the 1930s Moscow show trials. Soon to be sitting in judgement over German war crimes at Nuremberg, Vyshinsky himself was, by any standards of common decency, guilty of crimes against humanity. Zhukov gave him the respect due to a superior in the Soviet pecking order.

Keitel, Friedeburg and Stumpff sat at a small table at right angles to the main table. Their staff stood behind them. After a brief pause, Zhukov asked if they were prepared to sign. Tedder then rose to ask if they accepted the terms of the surrender as written in the document he was holding up. Keitel replied with a loud 'Ja'. Having signed the three copies put in front of him, Friedeburg and Stumpff added their signatures. Zhukov and Tedder then signed as principals for the Allies, followed by Spaatz and de Tassigny as witnesses. The crowd of reporters and photographers pressed in on them. When a Russian newsreel man, carrying a heavy camera, barged his way through to the front, punches were thrown.

While the signing was taking place in Berlin, Doenitz sat at a desk writing his farewell to the officer corps.

Comrades. … We have been set back for a thousand years in our history. Land that was German for a thousand years has now fallen into Russian hands. Therefore the political line we must follow is very plain. It is clear that we have to go along with the Western Powers and work with them in the occupied territories in the west, for it is only through working with them that we can have hopes of later retrieving our land from the Russians …

Despite today's complete military breakdown, our people are unlike the Germany of 1918. They have not yet been split asunder. Whether we want to create another form of National Socialism, or whether we conform to the life imposed upon us by the enemy, we should make sure that the unity given to us by National Socialism is maintained under all circumstances.

The personal fate of each of us is uncertain. That,

however, is unimportant. What is important is that we maintain at the highest level the comradeship amongst us that was created through the bombing attacks on our country. Only through this unity will it be possible for us to master the coming difficult times, and only in this manner can we be sure that the German people will not die …

There was no one to receive his declaration. Instead, he locked it away in his desk drawer.

★

After Zhukov declared the capitulation ceremony to be at an end, Keitel raised his field marshal's baton in salute, turned on his heel and led the way out of the hall. Strong recalled:

This was the second time I had taken an active part in capitulation ceremonies. Both brought home to me the futility and tragedy of war. Both I hated intensely. After the waste of the past years I felt that they were curiously degrading to the victors, as well as to the vanquished.[24]

An all-night banquet with apparently inexhaustible supplies of the best food and wine was punctuated by a succession of toasts starting with a fulsome dedication to Stalin, closely followed by an equally extravagant tribute to Eisenhower, 'the greatest military strategist of our time', according to Zhukov. The celebrations ended at 6 a.m. with a tour of Berlin, as described by Strong:

A fleet of cars – some German, some Russian, some captured French – were placed at our disposal. We drove past the Opera House, down Unter den Linden, past the

Reichstag, and finally stopped at Hitler's Chancellery. Its smoke-stained walls were still standing but much of the roof had gone. We walked through and I pictured it as I had last seen it in 1939. It was then a magnificent building with marble floors and beautiful walls, an edifice designed to impress. Passing through the Chancellery we came to the entrance to the underground bunker which had been Hitler's headquarters. We asked Sokolovsky what had happened to him but he professed complete ignorance. I seem to recollect, however, that he pointed to a small area of ground outside the bunker where something had been burned, but at the time we did not connect this with Hitler's death.

Although I had known Berlin intimately, I found it quite impossible to recognise any of the usual landmarks. Heaps of rubble and burned buildings concealed the outlines of roads and turnings. Cattle were roaming in the streets and in the Tiergarten, and the place appeared entirely devoid of humanity, except for small groups of Russian soldiers. ... We passed the spot where the Kroll Opera House had stood; Hitler had made many of his speeches there and I had lived opposite. Not only was there no Opera House but there were no houses or buildings or even streets of any description; I found it impossible to locate the spot where my own house, In den Zelten, No. 11, had stood.[25]

A few days later, General Ismay came over from London to view the scene.

A party of us visited Berlin one afternoon. It was a depressing experience. The only Germans to be seen were a few old men and women pushing wheelbarrows, perambulators and hand-carts piled up with their pathetic possessions aimlessly about the streets. The part of Berlin that we visited was a shambles with scarcely a house that was habitable. There was a smell of death and decay, and one wondered how many corpses still lay in the ruins. The only building that I entered was the Chancellery. It was smashed to smithereens and the Russians had made no attempt to clear up the mess. Perhaps they had left it on purpose, as an awful warning. In Hitler's study a huge marble-topped table had been blasted into a thousand pieces ...

I hurried out of the study in disgust, but an adjacent room was almost equally obscene – Iron Crosses and medal ribbons strewn all over the floor in hopeless confusion. Decorations that would have brought pride to brave men seemed in that setting to be a symbol of utter defeat and degradation. I was sorry that I had gone sightseeing, and when, some months later, I was given an opportunity of visiting the Nuremberg Trials, I refused without a moment's hesitation. My first act on returning to Babelsberg was to plunge into a hot bath with a great deal of disinfectant in it; my second was to take a very strong drink to try to get the taste out of my mouth.[26]

CHAPTER NINE

There were those who refused to accept that the war was really over. In the West, pockets of German resistance held out in the unlikeliest places. One of these was Dunkirk, the setting for Britain's 1940 mini version of Operation Hannibal. Bypassed by the Canadian First Army sweep into Belgium, the German occupiers had settled in for the duration and now showed no inclination to submit to the Czech, British and French troops laying siege to the town. As a fledgling war reporter eager to make his reputation, Tom Pocock decided to investigate. He was provided with an army staff car and a driver.

The countryside was dead and deserted, the fields flooded, or grey with mud where the floods had receded. The road was empty and potholed and the houses we passed deserted and often wrecked. Then suddenly a group of men sprang from a ditch, aimed Sten sub-machine-guns at us as an order to stop. They were Frenchmen of the *Maquis* ... We showed them our papers and they told us that, whatever might or might not have happened elsewhere, no Allied forces had approached Dunkirk by this road. If we wished to continue, that was up to us.

We did so and soon there were signs of activity. Down the

road half a dozen men lounged on plush and gilt chairs out-side a seaside villa, machine guns on the grass beside them. They were German soldiers. As we passed, they sprang to their feet and saluted. Farther on, we passed more, who either saluted or stared, and, either side of the road, tangles of barbed wire and black-and-white notices on which were stencilled the skull-and-crossbones symbol and the words *Achtung Minen!* Soon the road was crowded with Germans: non-commissioned officers in high-crowned caps; soldiers cleaning vehicles and equipment; military police, with their Nazi gorgets across their chests, directing traffic. Their uni-forms were often patched – they had been under siege for eight months – but they were clean and smart and did not look like a defeated army.

The sights seen, the pressmen were directed out of Dunkirk towards Allied lines. It was all perfectly friendly; perhaps too friendly.

There was something ominous about that empty road and our driver, who had been with the 2nd Army since Normandy days and had highly-tuned instincts for survival, opened the door of the staff car and ordered the German to climb in beside him. The sergeant demurred until the driver reached for his Sten. With our hostage aboard, we started down the road until he threw up his hands, crying, '*Nein, nein, nach links!*' Presumably, as our driver had anticipated, the road down which we had been directed was mined.[1]

Dunkirk was taken back into Allied hands on 9 May. The German garrisons at St Nazaire and Lorient on the Atlantic coast were even tardier. It was not until the following day that American troops finally took possession.

In Amsterdam there was a post-surrender shootout in Dam Square where crowds had gathered to celebrate their city's liberation. The firing came from the Groote Club, a popular watering hole for German officers. Commander Overoff of the Internal Forces, the senior Dutch officer at the scene, set off on his motorcycle to find someone from the German military police capable of restoring discipline. He returned with a Captain Bergmann. Forcing their way into the Groote Club they found all four floors of the building and the roof occupied by marines with rifles and machine guns; 'men firing and ready to fire'. Shots were being returned from the streets around the Dam where now three German army vehicles began taking up position to join the action. Bergmann ordered the marines out on to the street. As recalled by Overoff,

When all was quiet, we walked back to the Dam to collect our motorcycle. We rode back past the Dam again and onto the Damrak. This, too, was deserted; all the civilians stood in the side-streets and alleyways. The Dam itself was a tragic scene. The dead were lying in front of the Nieuwe Kerk and in and around the entrance to the Nieuwendijk. All had been hit by German fire … Continuing towards Central Station we heard heavy rifle fire and as we reached the corner by the Victoria Hotel, the motorcycle rider was hit by a fatal shot. He died instantly and slid sideways off the saddle. Since the last thing he did was to put the motorcycle into neutral, I was able to bring the vehicle to a standstill.[2]

But these were isolated examples. Where clashes were anticipated, the handover to Allied forces proceeded with only minor setbacks. In Norway, General Boehme gave an early indication of living up to his reputation as a diehard. On 5 May, he made it known to Doenitz that his forces were ready to handle any assignment 'within the limits of our strength'. Refusing all communications with the Allies, it was only when he heard of the surrender at Reims that he announced over Oslo Radio that all military operations were to cease. A British brigadier, representing SHAEF, confronted Boehme at his headquarters at Lillehammer, 80 miles north of Oslo. Even at this stage Boehme pressed for concessions and when these were not forthcoming complained to anyone who would listen that the capitulation terms were 'unbearably severe'. His chief complaint seems to have been that while his men were confined to barracks, Russian slave labourers who were herded together in camps built for half their number were treated with 'incomprehensible esteem'.

Unfinished business did not take long to complete. Josef Terboven followed the example of his erstwhile Fuehrer, though rather more messily: he blew himself up by detonating a pack of dynamite. The Gestapo chief Heinz Fehlis and the senior SS officer Wilhelm Redless chose to go by bullet. Five months later, Vidkun Quisling, Norway's token prime minister, faced the firing squad.

The first Allied officer to arrive in Copenhagen was Major John Ray, who had been stationed in Stockholm as SHAEF liaison officer for the 17,000-strong armed force of young Danish and Norwegian expatriates who had been waiting for the call to battle. To their great disappointment, it never came. It was Ray's task to persuade them to stand down.

A SHAEF mission landed in Copenhagen on 7 May while armoured units of the Royal Dragoons crossed the border from Germany. Then next day a company of the South Lancashire parachute battalion flew in from Hamburg to administer the surrender. The senior British officers were Major General Dewing and Rear Admiral Holt, who found the Germans only too happy to comply with their instructions. Montgomery arrived to take Copenhagen's salute on 12 May.

The only trouble spot was the island of Bornholm. Fifty-seven miles from Denmark and 22 miles from Sweden, Bornholm was a preserve of the Kriegsmarine. Its significance at the end of the war was that it happened to fall on the Russian side of the agreed demarcation between Allied spheres of interest. The SHAEF expectation was that since Bornholm was undeniably Danish and that Denmark was to return to independence courtesy of the Western Allies, the Soviet presence would be short-lived.

As the senior German officer on Bornholm, Commander Kamptz was working to a different game plan. From April, he began building up defences against a possible Russian attack. With 20,000 fully armed troops at his disposal, many of them with first-hand experience of fighting the Red Army, a pitched battle was in prospect. Russian reconnaissance planes were met by anti-aircraft fire. On 6 May, two days after the German capitulation in Denmark, Kamptz was still defiant. But meeting with Peter Stemann, the chief Danish administrator on the island, and other Danish representatives, he gave some ground. He was prepared to put up his hands but only to the British. A lone officer landing on Bornholm would suffice.[3] Stemann made an urgent appeal to Copenhagen only to be told that the British military was not prepared to risk a diplomatic incident by intruding on what was purely a Russian affair.

On 7 May the tension was raised when Russian aircraft bombed the towns of Roenne and Noxoe, killing nine civilians. A few hours later more planes appeared to drop leaflets urging surrender. The offer to the German commander was to send negotiators, under promise of safe conduct to Kolberg. When Kamptz failed to comply more bombs were dropped. It was only when Doenitz gave the order for all troops to stand down that Kamptz bowed to the inevitable. In the days that followed, 5,000 Russian troops landed on Bornholm. They stayed for the best part of a year. In April 1946, the island was formally handed over to Denmark.

As part of the surrender in the West Doenitz accepted that all ships in the northern capitulation should be handed over to the Allies. But if he had anything to do with it, that would take time. On 5 May an order went out from OKW.

Hostilities against English and Americans to cease immediately.

All minesweepers, torpedo-boats, despatch-vessels, as well as the steamers *Linz*, *Ceuta*, *Pompeii*, at present lying in Copenhagen to start immediately for the east to assist in evacuation; also the auxiliary-cruiser *Hansa*. Report to Eastern Naval Command; port of destination to be announced by radio.

For Hela, Libau, Windau and Bornholm: as from 5 May, 08.00 hours, German summer time, armistice in regard to troops of Field-Marshal Montgomery. Transports at sea to continue on their way, navy's task to rescue Germans from the east. Engage in no destructive activity, sinking of ships or other demonstration. Ensure safety of stores.

After the signing in Reims, Doenitz signalled all shipping in the Baltic.

In consequence of the capitulation all naval and security forces, as well as commercial vessels, must have left the ports of Courland and Hela by midnight 8 May. Transport of German population from the east must be executed with all possible speed. Supreme Naval Command.

Operation Hannibal went into overdrive.

Across the Baltic every ship moving east carried supplies; every ship moving west carried people. Engelhardt commandeered anything that could float. His big ships were no longer fit for purpose or had simply run out of fuel. This is what happened to the *Sachsenwald*, a new steamer launched as recently as early 1945. On 3 May she was off the Hela Peninsula braving artillery fire and air attacks to take on board 5,000 military and civilian refugees. As she prepared to sail, there were cries of despair from those still waiting to be rescued. One of the crew, leaning over the ship's rail, shouted as hard as he could, 'We will be back'.

It was a promise the *Sachsenwald* was unable to keep. Arriving safely in Copenhagen she was out of coal. Since there was no more to be had, Copenhagen was where she remained.

Of the smaller cargo ships able to make the crossing, the biggest was the 10,000-ton *Hansa*. She was joined by an armada notable for its weird and wide diversity ranging from whaleboats, icebreakers, tugs and barges to family-owned motor coasters. There was even a floating harbour crane and a four-masted schooner.

Though precise figures are impossible to come by, well over 1,000 ships took part in the Baltic evacuation. They rescued between 2 and 2.5 million soldiers and civilians, the latter around 75 per cent of the total. Some 250 vessels were lost. Over 33,000 passengers were drowned, tragic enough but only a tiny percentage of the number saved. Thousands more died on the beaches and windswept dunes, victims of hunger, disease and indiscriminate air and artillery attacks.

Of the Kriegsmarine's big ships, only *Prinz Eugen* and *Nuernberg* were operational at the end of the war. The *Leipzig* survived but it was unfit for anything except dry dock. Of the others, British bombers sank *Admiral Scheer* in Kiel on 9 April and her sister ship *Luetzow* at Swinemuende on the 16th. Settling on an even keel with her guns still above water, *Luetzow* kept firing until she had to be blown up.[4]

Hipper and *Emden*, at Kiel, were both bombed out of action while the old battleships *Schleswig-Holstein* and *Schlesien* were scuttled. Handed over to the Allies, *Prinz Eugen*, taken by the US, ended its days in the Bikini atom bomb test of 1946. *Nuernberg* fell to the USSR and was renamed *Admiral Makarov*.

On 5 May, led by four destroyers and five torpedo boats, a patchwork convoy left Copenhagen for Hela. They loaded up that night and headed back the next day. Thereafter, any semblance of organised evacuation was abandoned. It was every vessel for itself. Hela is a 30-mile long, narrow wooded peninsula east of the Bay of Danzig. At Hela's eastern tip was a fishing harbour of the same name, the focal point of the evacuation, and except for Kurland the last German rallying point in the East.

After the fall of Gotenhafen, Russian batteries positioned on the opposite shore were able to fire across at Hela. Soviet fighters and fighter-bombers were constantly on the hunt for the small craft which, night after night, ventured over Danzig Bay on a rescue mission to what was left of the German front on the Vistula flats and on the sandspit. Thousands were waiting for them in the shallow water. The wounded and old were carried to the boats. The start of a long journey took them to the tip of the Hela Peninsula where they waited for the Baltic crossing. Many waited in vain. From his makeshift headquarters, Admiral Thiele looked out on what he reckoned to be some 200,000 refugees, all terrified that the Russians were about to catch up with them.

From Kurland, described by Goebbels as the Reich's 'last reservoir' of fighting men, the evacuation had been in progress since early December 1944. By the following May, well over half the army strength had been shipped out. Incredibly, the front held. But the Red Army was closing in. On 6 May 175 small ships left Windau and Libau. They carried 25,000 troops. Apart from two straggling trawlers that were forced back, the rest of the convoy succeeded in running the Soviet gauntlet.

By then, Doenitz had sent his personal representative, Colonel de Maizière, to explain his policy of a phased surrender and to win the cooperation of the Kurland Commander-in-Chief, General Carl Hilbert. Orders were confused by political developments when Hilbert reported that an attempt was being made to set up a Latvian National Committee as an anti-Soviet provisional government. It was a pipe dream, as Hilbert soon realised, but he did win approval from Doenitz to negotiate with Russian commanders to try to minimise casualties.

On 7 May Hilbert was told that all ships had to leave the Kurland ports by midnight the following day. Priority went to the sick and wounded and to soldiers with children in Germany. Loading continued throughout the afternoon and evening of the 8th. It was reported back to Doenitz by de Maizière that discipline remained strong and that the mood of the troops was 'sober' and 'composed'.[5]

In the last hours 65 ships carrying 14,400 troops left Libau in four convoys. Two convoys sailed from Windau carrying 11,300 men on 61 ships. They were accompanied by Soviet gunfire. As the last vessels prepared to leave, the Russians marched in. There was a frantic rush to board the remaining boats.

'Another twenty men!' shouted the skipper of a ferry. 'More than that and we'd go down.'

Twenty crowded on board. The twenty-first was an elderly man. He stood there, his arms hanging limply by his sides. One of the lucky ones who got on board – a young soldier – all at once noticed him, and just as the ferry was casting off her lines, he jumped back to land and urged the older man to take his place. However, whether it was that the latter hesitated or refused outright to accept such a sacrifice, the ferry had already started and in a few seconds even the best of jumpers could not have reached it. So both were left behind.

Suddenly the rescue vessel with the officer in charge of operations on board was once more fussing alongside. This last had been watching the loading of the boats from some distance away.

'Hurry up, come over, you two!' he yelled. 'And another two with you. But get a move on!'

The four of them beamed at their comrades as they were helped on board the little boat. They were the last to be embarked from Libau. As even this boat was danger-ously overloaded some twenty soldiers were left behind. At another point a group of fifty stared blankly at the rapidly disappearing boats as they managed to escape from the har-bour canal without let or hindrance.

A few moments later the Russians were there.[6]

Those left on the dockside made desperate attempts to com-mandeer anything that would float. Some managed to cross the Baltic to find temporary refuge in Sweden but many more were drowned. For the rest, 200,000 men from Army Group Kurland were led by General Hilbert into Soviet captivity.

At dawn on 9 May, the small boats that had left Hela the night before were making slow headway across the Baltic. Those on deck, packed shoulder to shoulder, had spent a cold, sleepless night. As the wind freshened, vessels that were never intended for the open sea were bounced on the swell. No one needed to be told that they were easy targets for roving Soviet aircraft. But for the moment, the elements posed the greatest risk. The least seaworthy boats were soon in trouble. Many had to be abandoned or taken in tow, an operation that made the convoy more vulnerable. Passing the island of Bornholm, 130 miles east of Copenhagen, raised a cheer. It meant that they had passed the halfway mark. There would have been less optimism had it been known that the island was under Russian occupation. And whatever bright hopes there were soon faded when the lookout on the *Rugard*, an old holiday steamer, reported the telltale bow waves of fast-approaching patrol boats. They had to be Russian. It soon turned out that they were motor torpedo boats, three of them, and they were intent on sending the convoy back to its starting point.

In response to a burst of machine-gun fire across her bows, *Rugard* hove to. Uncomfortably aware that his only means of defence was a French-built 25mm gun, the captain radioed naval headquarters for orders. He was told to sail on. By now one of the MTBs was alongside, her torpedoes and guns in full view. The *Rugard* had a plain choice, either return to Hela or make a fight of it. The order was given: full ahead. Zig-zagging as she went, she dodged two Soviet torpedoes. The *Rugard* proved to have the more accurate fire power. Suffering a hit, the lead MTB exploded and sank. The other two gave up the chase. So ended, almost a day after the capitulation, the last naval battle of the war. *Rugard* and her convoy made Kiel the next day.

For at least a week after the surrender, boats of all shapes and sizes drifted into harbours on the north German and Scandinavian coastlines. Many relied on navigation by the stars and the sun. A naval report of 18 May estimates that over the previous eight days, 116,000 troops including 6,000 wounded and 5,000 civilians were carried safely across the Baltic. On 6 May alone, 43,000 people were shipped from Hela. Setting some sort of record, a submarine, *U-721*, managed to accommodate 100 civilians and wounded soldiers for the Baltic journey. The last recorded arrival from Hela, after six days at sea, was an unnamed trawler towing a barge. It carried 135 passengers including 75 injured.

In East Prussia and in Kurland sporadic fighting continued. It was not until 14 May that the last surviving units of the Wehrmacht finally laid down their weapons. On top of his other worries, Doenitz was obsessed by the fear of a breakdown in naval discipline. There was no risk of a repeat of the collapse of morale in 1918 when the navy was the focal point for the revolution that brought down the monarchy. Nonetheless, his officers were under orders to stamp hard on any sign of insubordination. The hard-line policy led to a terrible injustice. On 9 May the crew of the minesweeper *M612* anchored off the Danish harbour of Sonderborg, having been told that they had done their time and could now go home, were ordered to embark on one more highly risky rescue trip to Hela. They refused. It was hardly a mutiny in any proper sense of the word but after a hastily convened court martial in which twenty accused were defended by a legally inexperienced NCO, eleven men were sentenced to death. They were shot by firing squad.

Doenitz could be confident that his U-boat officers and crews would put honour and discipline before all else. Among Allied forces, it fell to Corporal Dai Evans of the Royal Welch Fusiliers, who spoke German, to discover that a U-boat officer was out of the normal run of commissioned ranks.

He was about 24 years-old; tall, beautifully uniformed and full of courage. He seemed the personification of the *Herrenvolk* ideals of Hitler and the Nazis. He obviously loathed the idea of surrender, wished to deal only with an officer above the rank of Major and, at first, refused to give any details about himself. Under the circumstances this was ridiculous and I told him so. He made no effort to assist us so I said, 'Smudger, look in his breast pocket, see if there's any identification papers, paybook, passes or suchlike there.'

Smudger put his hand to open the officer's breast pocket. This wasn't to the officer's liking and he thrust the hand away with a fierce gesture. He'd picked the wrong man as Smudger simply backed off a pace, then clouted him on the jaw. The German reacted immediately by backing away and adopting a fighting posture, ready to defend himself.

'This won't do,' I thought, so, cocking my Sten with an ostentatious gesture, I pointed it at his chest. He had enough presence of mind to realise the odds stacked against him and, with an ill grace, put down his hands and submitted to being searched.

Dai Evans found that he could only admire the man.

There, surrounded by six of us, he maintained defiance even in the face of a possible beating-up. He was the type any country loves to have on their side. His medals proved his valour, won in a desperate and claustrophobic calling.[7]

Operation Hannibal was a massive achievement for which Doenitz and the Kriegsmarine have received too little credit. But success was marred by a tragedy that brought shame on Germany and Britain. It happened in Neustadt Bay near Kiel where the *Cap Arcona*, along with the *Thielbek* and the *Deutschland*, lay at anchor a mile and a half offshore. The *Cap Arcona* had been the largest of the refugee ships. Built to carry fewer than 1,500 passengers, she trebled this number in three crossings to Danzig. By mid-April, barely seaworthy for lack of maintenance, she was in dry dock in Copenhagen for essential repairs. With the work only half-finished, Captain Bertram was ordered back across the Baltic where he learned that he was to take on board thousands of prisoners from German concentration camps in Poland. Captain Jacobsen of the *Thielbek*, a freighter which had never carried passengers, and Captain Steincke of the *Deutschland* were given the same order. They all protested vigorously. To run a prison ship was the last thing they expected or wanted. They were supported by Engelhardt who argued, as if it was not blazingly obvious, that the ships were ill-equipped for any sort of active duty. The SS thought otherwise. The order was allowed to stand.

The first inmates, many in desperate physical shape, were marched into Neustadt on 19 April. Bertram made one last protest. There was an alternative, he was told. He could choose to stand before a firing squad. He wrote later, 'I had a wife and two children. That was the only reason I complied with this insane order.'

As the holds filled with human cargo, deaths were routine. On 24 April Captain Jacobsen wrote to his wife:

> The dead are removed every morning. We had five this morning. But because [the number of corpses] increases so rapidly, they are being picked up [by boats, to be taken ashore] … prisoners of all ages from 14 to 70 and from ministers, professors, doctors, captains, to workers – all

are represented. Germans, Hungarians, Poles, French, etc. represent the nationalities. The foreigners are forced to remain in the [holds]; they are not allowed on deck. They are crammed like sardines.[8]

The point of it all was a mystery. It was ludicrous to imagine the SS was planning to send the prisoners to Denmark for their own safety. Another possibility was that Himmler had ideas of handing over this human cargo to Count Bernadotte and the Swedish Red Cross as a sign of good intentions. But given the insidious mentality of the SS, there was a likelier reason for turning derelict ships into floating concentration camps. Set on destroying evidence of their barbarity, Himmler and his cohorts may have planned for a disaster at sea. For them, the sinking of the evacuation ships with all on board was just another form of mass execution. If this was indeed their reasoning, they had their wish.

When the *Cap Arcona* eventually weighed anchor, there were around 5,500 on board. They had little food and water. Sanitation was non-existent. It was as bad on the *Deutschland* and *Thielbek*, which together carried around 4,000 prisoners. All three ships soon came within easy spotting by RAF 184 Squadron of Typhoon fighter-bombers based at Hunstedt, just short of 100 miles from Neustadt.

The *Deutschland* was the first to be hit. Of the 32 rockets fired by four Typhoons, three found their mark, causing fires which the crew were unable to extinguish. To try to ward off a second attack, white bedsheets were strung between the two funnels and a single red cross painted on the forward funnel. It was to no avail. The *Cap Arcona* offered a bigger target. The first rockets struck home in the early afternoon of 3 May. Benjamin Jacobs was asleep on the steel floor of a storeroom, his brother Josef beside him.

I woke up to a violent *boom!* as a tremendous concussion shook the ship. The storeroom rocked back and forth ... I struggled to my feet, the floor tilting beneath me, everyone around me also trying to stand up. Hands grabbed at coats and arms. People lost their balance, or got shoved, and fell back down.

As the fire spread across the promenade deck it set off more explosions, probably in the oil tanks, which blew a hole in the ship's side. The water poured in. While the *Cap Arcona* struggled to stay afloat, the *Thielbek* was hit below the waterline. Walter Felgner was one of the 50 survivors:

> Captain Jacobsen, First Officer Andresen, First Engineer Lau, Third Officer Shotmann, and I were standing on the boat-deck. ... The ship was listing nearly 50 degrees. We were afraid to go into the water, because the prisoners who could not swim were holding on to anything they could grab. Then Captain Jacobsen said to us, 'Go now. The ship is about to capsize.'

Felgner and Shotmann leapt into the water. As the ship slowly turned over, the cargo on deck broke loose. Huge crates slid from the high side to the low side, crushing prisoners and crew members. Bursting into flames, the *Thielbek* sank to the bottom. With her went Jacobsen, Andresen, Lau, eleven crew, 200 guards, and 2,300 prisoners.[9]

In all, the RAF sank 23 ships in Neustadt Bay on 3–4 May. Those who took to the air had no idea who they were killing. To the best of their knowledge, their targets were high-ranking Nazis and their staff intent on escaping to Norway to continue the war. Yet intelligence sources were better informed. It was simply that the officers concerned failed to give a proper briefing. A catastrophe to rank high in the annals of military incompetence has never been adequately explained. Relevant documents have either been destroyed or remain closed to historians.

In the last phase of Operation Hannibal, one of the biggest challenges was to find a landing place where ships could offload their passengers. With the British military in control in Denmark, Admiral Holt, one of the two senior officers representing SHAEF, declared that the port of Copenhagen, overwhelmed by refugees, could not allow any more ships to enter the harbour. Moreover, by the terms of the surrender, no German ship would be allowed to leave Danish territorial waters. But rules were made to be circumvented. The apparent stalemate was first on the list for discussion when Admiral Kreisch, the last commander of the German Baltic fleet, arrived at Holt's improvised headquarters in the Hotel Angleterre. They came to a deal. The log jam in Copenhagen could be eased if the ships waiting for orders beyond the three-mile limit were allowed to sail close to the coast to land their refugees opposite Flensburg. They would then still be in Danish territorial waters. Of course, once there, as Holt very well knew, there would be nothing to stop them sailing on to German ports and from there back across the Baltic. And that was what happened. After their meeting, Holt took his German counterpart aside. Their conversation had been conducted by an attractive woman interpreter. Next time, he told Kreisch, bring a male interpreter. Then, smiling, 'It is so hard to say "no" to a lady.'[10]

For the last of those who took their chances on the Baltic crossing, their vision of Denmark was of a Shangri-la, a peace-loving society relatively untouched by the war, blessed with liberal antecedents and a reputation for tolerance. But five years of occupation had hardened Danish hearts. To be German, even one too old or too young to have fought in the war, was to be an object of hate. Even those who were sympathetic to the plight of their reluctant guests shared a fear of their country being overwhelmed by the influx of strangers.

The reality was born in on Guy Sajer and his companions who were lifted off the Hela Peninsula and delivered to Denmark in their grubby uniforms at the beginning of April.

We saw things we had almost forgotten, like pastry shops, which we devoured with enormous eyes, forgetting our filthy faces ravaged by misery. We scarcely noticed the looks of mistrust fixed on us by the shopkeepers, who couldn't understand us. We had no money, and the wares on display were not free. For a moment we even thought of our machine guns.

Hals could not resist temptation. He held out his big hands, which looked like dead wood, and begged for charity. The shopkeeper tried to pretend that he hadn't noticed, but Hals persisted. Finally, the baker put a stale cake into those filthy hands. Hals divided it into four pieces and we tasted a substance which had become unknown to us. We thanked the man, and tried to smile, but the rotting teeth in our grey faces must have produced an effect of grotesque grimace, and made the baker think we were mocking him. He turned on his heel, and disappeared into the back of his shop.[11]

The great majority of refugees were women and children. There were at least 100,000 youngsters under the age of eighteen, of whom 10,000 were without any family. They were herded into 1,000 camps strung out along the Danish coast. The largest, Oksbøl, on the west coast of Jutland, held 37,000 refugees. Originally a military training area, it had barracks and stables that had been converted to basic accommodation but as numbers increased, huts were built with wood from the surrounding forest. The camp was fenced with barbed wire and guarded by Danish troops. Fraternisation between Germans and Danes was forbidden. While American and Swedish charities were allowed to give aid, there was no help from the Danish Red Cross, which refused to get involved in supervising or inspecting the camps. Much of this is just about understandable given the stressed conditions of the time. What is less easy to accept was the widespread malnutrition in the camps and the failure of the Danish government and the British army to provide medical aid of any kind, even the most basic. This when the British press was confidently reporting on the Danish recovery:

> Denmark is fully prepared to send agricultural products immediately to other countries, as her production machinery is largely intact, indeed to a much greater extent than it was after the last war.[12]

In June, more than 15,000 tons of food were shipped to Britain alone. But not willingly. Allied authorities made clear that further assistance to Denmark would depend on cooperation in meeting the food needs of other countries less well provided. The Danish government was compelled to reduce consumption at home to comply with Allied demands.[13]

The Baltic refugees fell even further down the list of administrative priorities. There were other factors at work. The Danish Medical Association led a campaign of non-cooperation as a protest against the brutality of the Gestapo who had executed ten of their number. Anger was stoked by fanciful stories of 'paradise' conditions in the camps. Schools in Copenhagen refused to open their doors. Donations of food, toys and clothing were turned away. When a delegation of priests spoke out for humane treatment, the press was uniformly hostile. 'We despise the Germans as much as we did in wartime,' said *Information*. 'We want them to be treated harshly as they will only behave when they are given orders.' 'They are all parasites,' declared *Free Denmark*.

While those stranded in the camps did much to help themselves (at Oksbøl there was even a theatre organised by Walter Warndorf, former director of the Danziger Staatstheater), the lack of medicines, particularly for infants, exacted a high death toll. Of the 13,000 refugees who died in Denmark in 1945, 7,000 were children under the age of five. The great majority of these died before their first birthday. A typical family story recently came to light.

On 20 March 1945, the heavily pregnant German citizen Erna Perlmann arrived exhausted and weakened in Aalborg. Together with 3,600 wounded German soldiers and 4,000 civilian refugees, she had crossed the Baltic on the *Potsdam*, sailing from Danzig to Copenhagen Freeport, where she was kept on board an extra week by the authorities. She was eventually accommodated at Kjellerupgade School, which like many schools had been temporarily redesigned as a makeshift refugee camp. Here she gave birth on 26 March to two boys. One died immediately and the other a few hours later. Three days later she died.[14]

The repatriation to Germany, where conditions were rarely any better, started in 1946. By the end of the year, the number of camps was down to 465 and the official count of the inmates was put at 196,518. Most of the refugees went to the British and French occupation zones. Fortunately, since few wanted to go East, the Russians refused to take their share. Only a third of the 100,000 marked out for the Russian zone were eventually dispatched to East Germany. The last refugees left for Germany on 15 February 1949, four years after their arrival in Denmark.[15] Eight hundred emigrated to Sweden.

Contrasting treatment was meted out to refugees who could show that they had no German connections. Split by nationality, for the most part they had their own camps where conditions were reasonable. There were around 31,000 non-German refugees, a third of whom were Poles. Many of these remained in Denmark for most of their lives. Others migrated to Sweden, France and Britain. Very few returned to Poland. Less fortunate was the Russian contingent. They were sent back to the Soviet Union, whether they wished it or not.

There was a parallel situation in Sweden, though the number of deportees was much smaller and, strictly speaking, they were not Russians but Latvians and Estonians, many of whom had been drafted into the Wehrmacht. For public consumption, the distinction was academic. The word from Moscow, assiduously promoted by the Scandinavian communist parties and picked up by the popular press, was that anyone from the Baltic states was bound to be a Nazi camp follower. Whatever support was going for the dispossessed was reserved for those with Nordic credentials, chiefly evacuees from occupied Norway and Denmark.

By the end of 1944, of the 170,000 refugees in Sweden, around 30,000 had crossed the Baltic. Fears of harbouring fascist sympathisers were given added force by the familiar prejudices against immigrants – that they expected something for nothing and, when they did work, they were taking bread out of the mouths of Swedish workers.

In the week following the capitulation, 3,200 German troops arrived from Bornholm. They were put into a camp at Elssjo in the south of the country, a short distance away from the civilian refugees. In the early days relations with their Swedish military guardians, most of whom spoke basic German, were easy going. But this changed when hostility broke out between those who held to the Nazi creed and a minority of social democrats. Taking the side of the conservatives, the authorities made clumsy efforts to re-establish camp discipline. The disaffection soon spread to the Balt camps. If the Swedish government was not prepared to stand up for its principles against a Nazi rearguard, what chance was there of it resisting Soviet demands for repatriation of the Latvians, Lithuanians and Estonians? The answer was, not much.

Rumours of an impending extradition started circulating in the late summer but it was not until November that matters came to a head when a Soviet ship, *Beloostrov*, docked at Trelleborg. While there was never any question that the German contingent should be packed off, a fierce public debate centred on the Baltic citizens who, with some justification, assumed Swedish protection. There were just 167 of them, mostly Latvians who had been drafted into the Wehrmacht and had escaped from Kurland. Moscow designated them Soviet citizens.

Having recognised Soviet rule over the Baltic states, a compliance refused by the US and UK, the Swedish government was in a quandary. While there were no legal grounds for automatic extradition, the political establishment, egged on by Soviet sympathisers on the far left and fearful of retaliation, submitted to Moscow's demands. The reaction in the Elssjo camp was a hunger strike, many self-mutilations and threats of suicide. To an orchestrated chorus of anti-Swedish propaganda in the Soviet press, the deportations started on 30 November. Within a week it was all over, except, of course, for the victims. Thirty-five of them were known to have ended up in labour camps. There is no record of what happened to the others.

CHAPTER TEN

Those who fled across the Baltic were outnumbered by the troops and civilians desperate to escape the Red Army as it swept forward on a broad front across eastern Germany. Ever since mid-April getting to and across the Elbe had been the primary objective of a mass migration. General Omar Bradley had little sympathy for the dispossessed streaming 'tearfully' towards the US lines. 'We turned them back,' he recorded drily.[1] But it was never as simple as that. After a long and arduous trek, the getaways were not liable to be deterred by a mere river, however wide and deep. Many drowned.

But those that made it were docile and happy to be in the hands of the Americans. I was one of the three men guarding thousands of prisoners. I was sitting on a roof of a little barn of a farmhouse ... just sitting there with a rifle next to me. I really didn't need it because there was nothing but happiness on the part of the people who had come over. Most of them looked pretty beat up after a long, hard war but the officers were beautifully turned out, well uniformed, and almost every one of them with his female companion ... It certainly [was] an astonishing sight.[2]

A cursory effort was made to identify members of the SS and others who might qualify as war criminals but for the most part those in uniform were simply put into trucks to be sent off to POW camps spread over western Germany.

> The trucks were loaded with as many discharged German soldiers as they could carry, standing like cord wood in the back. The German driver and an assistant driver (mechanic), who were not discharged, had the responsibility of getting the trucks back to the camps. One armed GI was assigned to each truck, to be sure that it, and the drivers, returned. I acted as a truck guard for two different trips returning the Germans to areas close to their homes. There were no complaints among the returnees, even with their cramped conditions. They were going home, after many years of war. I took one truck to Nuremberg, and another to Munich. It was a bit scary on these trips, being the only GI among some 40 to 60 ex-enemies. The trips took two days, with a stay at a hotel over night.[3]

Captain C.T. Cross ran one of the many reception camps set up to receive German prisoners and, as it turned out, anyone else who happened along.

> Here the soldiers are searched for arms, organised into bodies of 200 approx. and marched off. Many are wounded, many have marched so far that they can go no further. Their own medical services have to be organised to cope with these, transport arranged for them and so on. We are miles ahead of supporting troops so we have no facilities for feeding the blighters. Furthermore we have civilians to cope

with. So at all costs we have to keep them moving back. Yesterday I had something like 10,000 through my place. By the end of the evening I had no voice left at all, having been shouting orders in German at them all day. This I did mainly from the back of a horse![4]

Where the choice was between surrender to the Red Army or to Anglo-American forces, no German commander had to be told where his best interests lay. Despite Eisenhower's aversion to being seen to approve piecemeal bargaining, many a local deal was struck. On 2 May General Kurt von Tippelskirch, commander of the German 21st Army in Brandenburg and Mecklenburg, knew that it was only a matter of hours before his forces were overwhelmed by the Red Army. A meeting was set up with General James Gavin of the American 82nd Airborne. Tippelskirch feared a bloodbath. There was no way, he argued, that his men would meekly surrender to the Red Army. Aware of what would happen to them once they were in Russian hands, they would choose to stand, fight and die. What then did he propose? Tippelskirch's offer was for his forces to continue fighting the Russians while contriving an orderly retreat to the West. 'I will order my men not to fire against you and to lay down their weapons as soon as they reach your lines.'[5]

Appealing as it was for Gavin to take the surrender of an entire army, he knew that his superiors would refuse any deal that gave support to the continuation of German military action on the Eastern Front. But what if the two generals agreed a simple formula allowing for the 21st Army to stage a withdrawal which put them in line to be captured by Anglo-American forces? This was agreed. That same day, an entire army, some 150,000-strong, surrendered to a division of just over 10,000 men.[6]

Other partial surrenders enabled what was left of General Busse's army in Silesia, General Wenck's army in Brandenburg and General Heinrici's army group in Pomerania to be brought across the Elbe along with large contingents of Army Groups Centre and South who fought their way through to the West. Even so, the majority of Army Group Centre went into Soviet captivity. Some 220,000 soldiers were taken prisoner by the Red Army between 1 and 8 May and as many as 1.6 million after the capitulation. Against this around 450,000 crossed over Western lines.[7]

The numbers were overwhelming. Attempts to keep count of those in need of food and medicine were reduced to wild guesses. Bradley was not alone in fearing a total breakdown of the overburdened supply lines. When the 11th Panzer Division in Czechoslovakia sent word that it wanted to surrender to US forces, Bradley told them to come in 'but only if you bring your own kitchens and can take care of yourselves'.[8]

The civilian refugees followed. As an eyewitness recalled,

They rode in Wehrmacht trucks, trailers, tracked vehicles and automobiles. Many others rode in wagons, resting on bundles of hay for their horses. The convoy moved on anything with wheels, bicycles, charcoal-burning and gasoline civilian autos, all manner of carts – ox-drawn, hand-drawn, tractor-drawn … Many walked until they could walk no further, then flung themselves along the roadside until they recovered strength to push on.[9]

Allied troops caught in the waves of pitiable humanity did the best they could.

I've read of the Great Trek, and I've seen films about

covered-wagon trains. But never did I conceive anything like this. Nose to tail all day there has been an unending stream of wagons, each pulled by two or three horses. We cannot let them go further because they would clog completely the lines of supply. So we have to arrange camps for them in the woods. We have appointed little fuhrers to see that latrines are dug and so on. We have to provide water carts for them. They have no food apart from the potato they have brought with them, and there are too many thousands for us to feed. German Red Cross and WAAFs, etc. have been organised to set up some sort of medical facilities. But disease is there, and the people are in poor condition to withstand it. Thank God they are out of doors anyway! Better that a few old ones should die of pneumonia, than a lot of others from typhus, etc. Mixed up with them are batches of Polish and other liberated workers, who have begun to commit 'News of the World' offences! Tomorrow we have to start to disperse them a bit, and thus reduce the disease danger and ease the water supplies.[10]

Charlotte Zettler, a student nurse in Bavaria and, as she put it, 'quartermistress' of a refugee camp, tried to be positive.

I have a room full of refugees to take care of in a school, more children than adults, who are either quartered in the area or being sent ahead. You can imagine what these people have to go through, often it exceeds human capacity. Many of them traded in their last worldly goods at the station in Dresden or Chemnitz, have been travelling for weeks, squeezed into freight trains with no food or sleep or the necessary hygienic conditions. And the poor children almost all have a temperature, colds, stomach problems, cry all the time, are deathly pale and terribly nervous.[11]

The strongest sympathy among the Allies was for liberated prisoners of war who simply wanted to go home. For those who were left to their own devices, the challenge was to find a safe way of crossing the Elbe where Soviet vigilance was light, since there were powerful rumours and some evidence to suggest that troops of the Western Allies caught on the wrong side of the river were liable to encounter rough treatment. For W.A. Lewis of the Royal Artillery and his two companions, the best chance of escape was a pontoon used by the Russian armour. Watching a convoy of tanks approaching the bridge, Lewis had a bright idea.

> Why don't each of us walk between two tanks? Then when reaching the bridge hide behind the side of the tank opposite the bridge sentry. Without much more ado we each selected a tank – to our utter astonishment the ruse worked. We were now over the bridge in the town of Torgau – another obstacle safely negotiated.[12]

Others made for the wrecked bridges, scrambling over twisted girders to a welcoming committee on the west bank. James Witte made a precarious crossing by a damaged railway bridge.

> The brick piers only supported badly buckled railway lines which were so distorted that they were arched into 'S' and 'U' shapes. We had to crawl along the sleepers with the water some 75 feet below. One false step and we would have plunged into the river. When we got across at last we

saw that the water couldn't have been all that deep in parts as the Americans were making German prisoners-of-war wade through it up to their necks.[13]

Still others preferred to bargain with the Russians – not always with satisfying results.

We wandered along the banks of the Elbe looking for a crossing point. We heard the grenades exploding before we saw the Ruskies [sic] fishing the stunned fish out of the water. We spoke to them in sign language, indicating that we wanted to cross. They seemed quite amiable and allowed us to get into a rowing boat with one oar which a German had nearby. Then they got a bit awkward and wanted to see our papers. We showed them various items of pay books and letters which seemed to mystify them to the extent that they looked at them upside down. Then they intimated that we could go. We stepped into the boat and the swift flowing Elbe carried us downstream with the one oar and a branch of a tree. Suddenly for no apparent reason, one of the Ruskies started firing his revolver at us, so we had to crouch in the bottom of the boat until we eventually grounded on the other side of the river.[14]

★

While countless human dramas were being played out across Germany, Doenitz and his fledgling administration waited and wondered. What was the next move? Doenitz struggled but failed to come up with a convincing answer. With hindsight, it was Speer who had the clearest understanding of what was happening. On 7 May, as soon as he heard that Jodl had put his name to the surrender in Reims, he told Doenitz 'the sovereign rights of the German people have ceased to exist'. The formalities in Berlin confirmed him in his view that 'a Reich government possessing freedom of action no longer exists'. Henceforth, he declared, 'the fate of the German people will be decided exclusively by the enemy'.

For Krosigk, this was unjustified defeatism. Doenitz had a sacred duty to preserve the continuity and sovereignty of the Reich. If not the Northern Cabinet, who else would take final responsibility for the maintenance of good order, the distribution of food and the restoration of essential services? Doenitz prevaricated. His instinct, having achieved his objective of bringing the war to an end, was to go quietly. But would the Allies allow him to do so? Might not retirement be regarded by both sides as an act of cowardice? Eventually, he settled for a compromise that constituted the worst of all possible worlds. His administration would keep a close watch on events, acting where desirable and possible, and resigning 'when the time was right'.

Some encouragement for holding on came with Churchill's victory speech on 8 May when the prime minister referred to Doenitz as the 'designated head of the German state'. But it was naïve to assume that the representatives of SHAEF based in Flensburg would treat Doenitz and his ministers as equals. The illusion was blown apart by the Allied reaction to an order – more a proclamation – made public over Radio Flensburg on 11 May by Field Marshal Busch, who Montgomery had made responsible for ensuring that German forces in the north behaved themselves and cooperated in providing relief for the civil population. With the absence of tact for which he was notorious, Busch announced:

> In accordance with the Grand Admiral's orders and in agreement with the British occupation authorities I have

assumed command in Schleswig-Holstein and the area to be occupied by Field Marshal Montgomery's forces. I have been charged with the maintenance of law, order and discipline, supply of the troops and the civil population in all sectors of public life. To carry out this task all military and civilian authorities in my area have been subordinated to me. They will receive directives from me or from the military and civil authorities represented in the Supply Section North. Executive instructions will be issued separately. I expect unquestioning obedience and devotion to duty in respect of all orders, and willing collaboration on the part of every individual in fulfilment of the tasks laid upon me.

Montgomery exploded. Busch was summoned for a dressing down. His value was in implementing the surrender, no more, no less.

If he did not carry out his orders promptly and efficiently, I would remove him from his command and find some other senior German officer to do the job. In the last resort the British Army would do the job themselves; but this method would result in delay, which could only cause further hardship to the German civil population, and this I was anxious to avoid. He was to understand that the German Army had been utterly defeated in the field and must now accept the consequences of that defeat.[15]

Doenitz tried for a more balanced approach, advising those in uniform to remain where they were and await further orders. The timing of carrying out demobilisation was solely at the discretion of the occupying powers.

Until then it is the bounded duty of every German soldier to show himself worthy of his uniform by his manner and bearing, and to obey his superiors as hitherto. By his manner he must show firm determination to continue to serve our people and his own family as a useful member of society. His bearing should be military and saluting discipline will be maintained.

Meanwhile,

In contacts with our Anglo-American ex-enemies we should behave with dignity and pride. We have nothing to be ashamed of. Over these six years the achievements of the German Wehrmacht in battle and the endurance of the German people have been unique in history and in the world. Never has there been such heroism. We soldiers stand without a stain on our honour. It would therefore be undignified now to go rushing to our ex-enemies. It is right that we should wait for them to come to us, but then meet them with propriety and courtesy.[16]

German liaison staff were appointed to Eisenhower's and Montgomery's headquarters. At Lueneburg Heath, orders to the German military were channelled via General Kinzel. Montgomery's Chief of Staff said of him:

He was undoubtedly a most efficient staff officer, and one could not help being impressed by his attitude and quickness as he sat there opposite me dressed in a magnificent field grey great-coat with scarlet lapels. He wore an eyeglass and was in every respect the typical Prussian General Staff

Officer. If he had lived he might have made a fortune in Hollywood.[17]

De Guingand felt partly responsible for shortening Kinzel's life.

Shortly after he set up his small headquarters close to Main Army Group he asked me whether he could carry his pistol. As he was head of the German party and had executive authority over his people, I rather weakly said he could.

Some of our liaison officers who had visited Busch's Headquarters had reported seeing a beautiful blonde who worked in the German Field-Marshal's office.

Well, one day Kinzel asked whether he could have a P.A. (Personal Assistant) on his establishment, as he found the work rather heavy. I agreed to this, but shortly afterwards had to cancel the permission when I received information which showed that the beautiful blonde was the P.A. concerned.

It was not long after I had left 21st Army Group that Kinzel, whilst on a visit to his old headquarters, shot his girl friend and then himself. And so we lost a rather unpleasant but very efficient enemy staff officer. We survived the shock.[18]

The SHAEF representatives at Flensburg were led by General Lowell W. Rooks for the Americans and Brigadier Foord for the British. Having decided to install themselves on the *Patria*, Doenitz's staff were moved to the Murwik Cadet School.

The first meeting with the SHAEF Control Party started badly when the OKW representative turned up late. He had a good excuse, having been involved in a car accident, but Foord, who was keen to assert his authority, made an issue of it. His mood was not improved when, in compiling the list of German notables in the Flensburg district, it emerged that no effort had been made to arrest suspected war criminals. Of particular interest was the whereabouts of Himmler. Doenitz had dismissed him from all his offices on 6 May but had let him go free. Jodl had advised Himmler to join the main body of SS troops in the south, but he claimed not to know if his suggestion had been taken up.

There was a little more to it than that. Widely known, and a subject of bemused gossip, was Himmler's final appearance before his staff at Flensburg on 5 May. His rallying speech was notable for its unconscious humour. Even the most hardened of SS officers found it hard to stifle a laugh, or a yawn, when Himmler held forth on his plan to set up a 'reformed' Nazi administration in Schleswig-Holstein that would be recognised by the Western powers as an independent entity. All it needed for the pieces to fall into place was for the Reichsfuehrer to have a face-to-face talk with Montgomery. Himmler remained an embarrassment, with his frequent appearances at meetings to which he had not been invited.

Two weeks after the surrender, he adopted a clumsy disguise to join a wandering party of soldiers and civilians who were hoping for nothing more than anonymity. Inevitably, they were picked up by a British patrol and brought in to an interrogation camp near Lueneburg where three of the prisoners complained of being kept waiting. The duty officer was intrigued. In ordinary circumstances those brought before him were only too pleased to be left alone. The three prisoners were brought in.

A fairly short, ill-looking man in shabby civilian clothing entered his office, followed closely by two taller men of distinctly military bearing dressed half in civilian, half in

military clothing. All three were under suspicion of belong-
ing to the Secret Field Police. Selvester sent the two taller
men out again in order to take a closer look at the shorter
one, who was clearly in charge. The man removed a black
patch covering his right eye, put on a pair of horn-rimmed
spectacles, and introduced himself calmly as the person
his outward appearance unmistakably indicated: Heinrich
Himmler, the former Reichsfuehrer-SS and Chief of the
German Police, Commander of the Reserve Army of the
German Wehrmacht, and Reich Minister of the Interior.[19]

The prisoner was searched. According to a paybook found on him
he was Sergeant Heinrich Hitzinger. Hidden in his clothing were
two suicide capsules. During several hours of interrogation the
assumption of his captors was of another poison capsule, probably
lodged in his teeth. Around midnight, Himmler was taken to the
headquarters of the Second British Army in Lueneburg. There he
was subjected to a full medical examination during which the doc-
tor discovered a blue-tipped object in his mouth. When an attempt
was made to remove it, Himmler jerked his head to one side, bit
into the cyanide capsule and collapsed. Efforts to revive him failed.
Within minutes he was dead. Three days later Himmler's body was
buried. Only a British officer and the three sergeants who had dug
the grave were present. The grave was unmarked.

At midday on 13 May Doenitz had his first meeting with Rooks.
It appeared that he could no longer rely on Keitel. On orders from
Eisenhower, the Field Marshal was to be relieved of his post and
was now a prisoner of war. Jodl was designated as temporary head
of the OKW. In the discussion that followed, Doenitz urged a central agency, with himself at its head, to deal with urgent problems
in cooperation with the Allies. He came away with the impression

that Rooks had accepted his arguments. It was not how Rooks saw it. In his version, he stressed the primary role of Allied military government with Doenitz providing the backup. Rooks was a polite man. It is likely that Doenitz gave too much credence to ordinary courtesies.

Keitel having been dispatched to Reims (Kesselring followed him into captivity on 15 May), Jodl emerged from his shell to become not quite a rival to Doenitz, but one who held firm views on the independent role of the OKW. There can be little doubt that he saw himself as the embodiment of the German spirit, in contrast to Doenitz who had sullied his authority by engaging in grubby politics. Germany and the Wehrmacht were as one. Jodl's staff engaged in a frantic output of across-the-board recommendations for correcting shortages and the misallocation of resources. Constant reference to the 'armistice' rather than the 'surrender' was a source of Allied irritation, as was Jodl's lobbying for a strengthening of OKW. After the arrival of the Russian Control Party headed by General Truskov on 17 May, Jodl took pains to be cooperative while snatching at every opportunity to point up Allied differences.

Much time was devoted to the wearing of decorations. While it was inevitable that the Nazi salute would be forbidden, it was less clear that medals earned during the war should be banned. Doenitz invoked international law until Rooks pointed out that the relevant clauses applied to states at war and not to forces who had surrendered. For the most part decisions on who could wear what were left to local commanders.

The preoccupation with status symbols was an indication of how little there was to occupy the Northern Cabinet. Ministers had meetings, made proposals and wrote reports which were then ignored. Having completed his primary mission, Doenitz found himself adrift in a world of politics he did not begin to understand. He dreaded comparison with Prince Maximilian of Baden, the liberal aristocrat who, most reluctantly, had been drafted in to serve as Chancellor in the dying days of the First World War. Though credited with overseeing the transition of Germany from autocracy to parliamentary government, for those of Doenitz's generation and upbringing, Prince Max's leanings towards democracy had led to the Weimar Republic and to social disruption brought to an end only when Hitler re-established the strong central state and restored 'the community of our people'.

With democracy discounted as a serious option (what irony it was for Doenitz to live long enough to see his country take its place as one of the world's leading democracies) he indulged in fantastical ideas for a new Germany, including a reinvented monarchy with a European prince imported to wear the crown. He even visualised Germany being accepted into the British Commonwealth.

Refusing to make a clean break with the past, Doenitz and those around him tried desperately to justify what had been. Their efforts were greeted with derision by the American and British press. When Krosigk, interviewed by a BBC correspondent, declared his allegiance to the rule of law, did it really come as a surprise to him to be reminded that he had loyally served a state in which the rule of law had been cruelly abused? Probably it had not occurred to him. At any rate, his self-delusion carried over to his post-war memoirs, in which he excused his allegiance to Hitler 'seeing that it had been dictated solely by good will'.

Allowance must be made for a proud spirit, common enough throughout politics and the military and not just in Germany, mitigating against a confession of being totally wrong. In Doenitz's circle, until the very end, only Speer came close to it. While Doenitz and Krosigk were well aware of Jewish persecution and shared anti-Semitic prejudices, there is no reason to doubt that the extent of the horrors of the concentration camps, detailed in American newspapers carried by Friedeburg on his return from Reims, came as a shock. Even allowing for what, incorrectly, was assumed to be a large measure of enemy propaganda, Doenitz could hardly ignore or downplay the terrible sight of a shipload of concentration camp victims delivered to Flensburg.

The Anglo-American press was almost uniformly hostile to Doenitz. The anger at having endured years of purposeless destruction of lives and property was concentrated on the man who, whether he liked it or not, was now the only surviving embodiment of the old regime. Yet Doenitz could not understand why he was being singled out. Throughout his hard-fought war at sea, the enemy had given him the respect due to a formidable but inherently decent opponent. Rommel and von Rundstedt came in the same category. Yet here was the *New York Times* describing Doenitz as no more trustworthy than Himmler. Lambasting a 'fake government', the *Herald Tribune* asked why this 'grotesque comedy' had not been ended by the arrest of Doenitz. Reflecting the popular impression that Doenitz and his colleagues were doing themselves rather well at Allied expense, the Soviet *Red Star* published a cartoon of German generals and businessmen relaxing under a large sunshade. The caption, 'Flensburg idyll'.

In London, *The Times* of 9 May questioned the legitimacy of the Northern Government given that it was headed by the organiser of the U-boat war. 'If Doenitz is not already on the list of war criminals, there is a feeling that his activities fully warrant his being put there.' Three days later *The Times* declared emphatically that cooperation between Doenitz and the Allies could no longer be tolerated, while the *Daily Express* bemoaned the fact that a senior member of the military hierarchy, which the Allies had sworn to destroy, had been given 'renewed prestige and authority as Hitler's successor'.

As ever, the press wanted quick answers to complex problems. The big question was, if not Doenitz, who? Churchill hit the nail on the head when he responded to Anthony Eden's petulant reaction after General Busch took too much upon himself.

> It is of high importance that the surrender of the German people should be completed through agencies which have authority over them. I neither know nor care about Doenitz ... The question for us is, has he any power to get the Germans to lay down their arms? ... The orders [Busch's] seem to be to get the Germans to do exactly what we want them to do. We will never be able to rule Germany apart from the Germans. ... Sometimes there are great advantages in letting things slide for a while. ... It must of course be remembered that, if Doenitz is a useful tool to us, that will have to be written off against his war atrocities for being in command of submarines. Do you want to have a handle with which to manipulate this conquered people, or just to have to thrust your hands into an agitated ant-heap?

On 16 May, Hamburg Radio reported on Churchill's response to a question in the House of Commons. Asked about the future of the Doenitz government, he temporised. 'I am not sure whether any machinery of government, whether central or regional, can be said to exist at present in Germany and in any case I should prefer to speak of administrations than governments. ... In general the Germans must run their country themselves. We have no wish to burden ourselves with it.'

Doenitz was confused. How could there be administration

without government? Unless, of course, those responsible for managing the state were merely servants of the military. And was not that dictatorship by another name?

On 15 May, Jules Dorpmueller, minister for transport, and Herbert Backe, minister for food and agriculture, were flown to SHAEF headquarters, apparently for consultation. Neither returned. Backe was arrested for war crimes and hanged himself in prison. Dorpmueller did indeed lend his expertise (he had long experience of managing railways) but was desperately ill with cancer. He died in early July.

In an attempt to gain clarification, Doenitz engineered a meeting with Robert Murphy, Eisenhower's political adviser, and General Rooks. Neither was in conciliatory mood. On the very day the meeting took place, 17 May, Murphy went on record to deny any intention of recognising a German government. The approach chosen by Doenitz did nothing to improve the temper of the Americans. Failing to recognise that he was in the presence of two advocates of the 'softly, softly' approach to the Soviet Union, he launched into a tirade against Bolshevism, warning that Moscow was set on the domination of Europe.

Such was the force of his argument that Murphy and Rooks concluded that he was pushing for an anti-communist crusade with Germany working in tandem with the Western Allies. Allowing for Doenitz being essentially right in his reading of Soviet intentions, he must surely have known that he was in no position to secure a military alliance, let alone persuade the US to plan for another war. What he wanted was recognition for Germany as an independent state, capable of defending its frontiers. It was asking too much too soon. Murphy and Rooks were horrified by the prospect of reviving German militarism for whatever cause. Reporting to Eisenhower, they urged the removal of Doenitz. His makeshift government was merely an obstacle to Allied plans. Murphy noted, 'he [Doenitz] seemed totally unaware that the entire continent hated and feared Germany more than Russia'.[20]

He might have added that his political masters remained convinced that Stalin sought world peace and was amenable to reason. A revealing story was told by Kenneth Strong in his post-war memoirs. Referring to Bedell Smith as one of his 'closest friends', he recalled:

> Towards the end of the war he made a kind of solemn declaration to me. Though he would always remain my personal friend I should bear in mind that the United States regarded Russia as the country of the future and his official co-operation would be with them. Britain was old-fashioned and out of date. The war had finished her and the Americans must ally themselves with the nations of the future. I was a little surprised to hear this from Bedell Smith, but I am afraid that he was only repeating what many Americans were thinking at the time.[21]

On the afternoon of 22 May, Luedde-Neurath answered a call from the *Patria*. A British interpreter told him that Doenitz, Friedeburg and Jodl were to attend a meeting the following morning, at 9.45 'precisely'. Doenitz was under no illusions. 'Pack your bags,' he told Luedde-Neurath.

> When we stepped on to the gangway of the *Patria* things were very different from what they had been on the occasions of my previous visits to the Control Commission. There was no English Lieutenant-Colonel at the foot of the gangway to receive me, there was no presenting of arms

by any of the sentries. On the other hand there was a host of Press photographers.

On board the *Patria* Friedeburg, Jodl and I sat on one side of a table, and on the other sat the chiefs of the Control Commission, with the American Major-General Rooks in the centre and the British and Russian Generals, Foord and Truskov, to left and right of him. Feeling that our fate was inevitable, my companions and I kept perfectly calm. General Rooks declared that upon orders from Eisenhower he had to place me, the members of the German Government and the officers of Supreme Headquarters under arrest, and that from now on we were to regard ourselves as prisoners of war.

He asked me, a little uncertainly, if I wished to enter any protest? 'Comment, I retorted, 'is superfluous.'[22]

Doenitz and his colleagues were accompanied back to their quarters where they were told to get ready to fly to an undeclared destination. They were followed by armed British soldiers from the Cheshire and Herefordshire regiments and of the Fifteenth and Nineteenth Hussars. The prisoners were then marched, hands above their heads, into the courtyard where they stood for up to three-quarters of an hour to be filmed and photographed by a bevy of reporters. Not widely reported was the intimate body search for poison pills. When Krosigk protested at having to drop his trousers, a German officer waiting in line calmed him down. 'Keep smiling,' he said.

A Reuters correspondent watched the finale.

A special guard was placed in charge of General Jodl. As a car drove up to take him away he saluted his hatless Staff, who bowed in reply. Admiral Friedeburg took his last salute when a party of arrested German Marines were being marched down the road, still singing '*Wir fuehren gegen England*'. ('We're marching against England.') Further on the Marines saw Doenitz a prisoner in a car beside the road. They halted and gave a military salute which he returned punctiliously.

It was all too much for Friedeburg. 'I don't think I can stand the circus that is about to begin,' he told Doenitz. The officer who gave permission for him to go to the bathroom forgot to remove the key. Friedeburg entered, slammed the door and turned the lock. When they broke down the door it was to find Friedeburg heaving up into the washbasin. Turning, he fell back into the bath. His body was laid out on a bunk under a portrait of Doenitz.

Churchill assumed that the tragi-comedy at Flensburg had been staged by SHAEF to impress the Russians. He wrote angrily to Montgomery, 'I did not like to see German admirals and generals with whom we had recently made arrangements being made to stand with their hands above their heads.' Particularly, he objected to the involvement of British troops in staging the arrests. But his protests came too late. In his office in Whitehall, Field Marshal Sir Alan Brooke noted in his diary, 'There is no doubt that from now onwards Russia is all-powerful in Europe.'

On the evening of 23 May, Doenitz, Jodl, Speer and others in the Northern Government were driven, under escort, to Flensburg airport where they boarded an American DC-4. A gaggle of photographers were waiting for them on the tarmac.

A bumpy flight over the North Sea delivered the prisoners to Luxembourg for the rest of the journey by road to the riverside resort of Bad Mondorf where they were housed in a requisitioned hotel. The GI guards had already given the place a new name. They called it Camp Ashcan. A thousand miles away, Drew Middleton was putting the finishing touches to his lead article for the morning's *New York Times*. It began, 'The Third Reich died today'.

CHAPTER ELEVEN

It was not until 5 June that the four-power Allied Control Council, charged with the administration of Germany, came into being. It was a toothless body since all decisions were by consensus and when there was no consensus to be had, power devolved to the Commanders-in-Chief, who now became Military Governors, each with his own sector of a partitioned Germany. In the west, it was the local governor who exercised authority. Typically a middle-ranking officer of the occupying force, he was landed with the job of restoring essential services while putting in place a trusted, i.e. non-Nazi, administration.

For all the criticism thrown at Doenitz for recruiting Party members, it was instructive that the military governors almost always relied on those who had worked for the Hitler regime.

All ranks of Allied forces were subject to the non-fraternisation rule, one of the barmier restrictions imposed by SHAEF, ranking for bureaucratic mindset with the ban on political activity of whatever orientation. Both orders were imposed ahead of the entry into Germany when a long-drawn-out struggle was still in prospect with the risk of giving away vital intelligence to fifth columnists. But the determining factor was the fear of repeating the mistakes of 1918 when, it was said, the Germans had worked hard at being amiable, the better to argue later that they had been misjudged as the aggressors. As a veteran of the first German war, Montgomery was a leading advocate of the hard line, arguing that this time there must be no smokescreen put up by 'appeals for fair play and friendship'.

> It is too soon for you to distinguish between 'good' and 'bad' Germans. In streets, houses, cafés, cinemas, you must keep clear of Germans, man, woman and child, unless you meet them in the course of duty. You must not walk out with them; shake hands with them; visit their homes; make them gifts; take gifts from them; play games with them or share any social event with them ... Remember that those are the same Germans ... whose brothers, sons and fathers were carrying out a system of mass murder and torture of defenceless civilians ... A guilty nation must not only be convicted, it must realize its guilt.[1]

It was soon obvious that the non-fraternisation rule was unworkable. But it stayed in place, causing needless confusion, embarrassment and irritation all round. The Americans were more flexible than the British. GIs could not resist the importuning by small children who draped themselves over jeeps begging for chewing gum, chocolate and peanuts. From meeting children it was a short step to meeting their older sisters or widowed or lonely mothers. Non-fraternisation was wrecked on sex, admitted one senior officer, who went on to say that, to a young man 'bored and fed up with the company of other men, almost anything in skirts is a stimulant and relief'. Sixty-five dollars was the standard fine for breaking the non-fraternisation rule. Propositioning German girls became known as the '65 dollar question'. Many paid up.

Facing up to more important matters, the Allies had to cope

with a human catastrophe of massive proportions. Germany had become 'a land of the homeless, the dispossessed and the displaced'.[2] Following the migration from the East in the last months of the war came the enforced exodus of millions of German nationals from territories now under Soviet control in Eastern Europe. For civilian refugees arriving in Germany there was no respite from the horrors they had experienced on their travels. With towns and cities bombed out, families found what shelter they could in ruined buildings. In the late summer of 1945, deportees were entering Berlin at the rate of 25,000 a day. Reporting for the *News Chronicle*, Norman Clark told what it was like at a typical reception centre.

Under the bomb-wrecked roof of the Stettiner Railway Station – the Euston or King's Cross of Berlin – I looked this afternoon inside a cattle truck shunted beside the buffers of No. 2 platform.

On one side four forms lay dead under blankets on cane and raffia stretchers; in another corner four more, all women, were dying.

One, in a voice we could hardly hear, was crying out for water.

Sitting on a stretcher, so weakened by starvation that he could not move his head or his mouth, his eyes open in a deranged, uncomprehending stare, was the wasted frame of a man. He was dying too.

As I walked about the station a score of others came up to me, all ravenous and starved, for whom also nothing else could be done – until death.

Two women sanitary helpers did what they could in ministering to the small wants of the dying.

The train from Danzig had come in. It had taken seven days on the journey this time; sometimes it takes longer.

Those people in the cattle truck, and hundreds who lay on bundles of belongings on the platform and in the booking hall, were the dead and dying and starving flotsam left by the tide of human misery that daily reaches Berlin, and next day is turned back to take another train to another town in a hopeless search of food and succour.[3]

Willy Brandt, the future chancellor, saw what happened when winter approached.

A new terror gripped the city; an icy cold. In the streets it attacked the people like a wild beast, drove them into their houses, but there they found no protection either. The windows had no panes, they were nailed up with planks and plaster-board. The walls and ceilings were full of cracks and holes – one covered them with paper and rags. People heated their rooms with benches from the public parks … The old and sick froze to death in their beds by the hundreds.

All the great cities were in chaos. Of Frankfurt's 177,000 houses, only 44,000 still stood; in Nuremberg scarcely one house in ten was undamaged. Fifty-three per cent of the buildings of Hamburg had been turned into 43 million cubic metres of rubble. Cologne, the first target for a British thousand-bomber raid, was a total wipe-out. The hundreds of thousands who had been made homeless by saturation bombing lived as scavengers.

Of the newcomers from the East, the majority, reported Victor Gollancz, 'are old men, women and children'.[4] Looking now at the cinema newsreels of the period produced for German audiences, the most pitiful sight is the standard opening sequence of photographs of emaciated children appealing for news of lost parents.

When efforts were made to stop the influx into urban areas where only malnutrition and disease flourished, the refugees spilled over into the countryside where small towns and villages, hitherto untouched by war, were inundated with strangers. In Schleswig-Holstein, a village of 890 inhabitants was required to accommodate 2,300 deportees. Two years after the end of the war,

> There is not a barrack, nor a summer or garden house, not a public hall, not an air-raid shelter, not a factory room or shop, workshop or skittle-alley that has not been used as an emergency accommodation for the refugees. In one case no less than 6 families were housed in a single skittle-alley. This skittle-alley has now been vacated and the 6 refugee families have been given other quarters, but only in stables and pig-sties. These stables are dark, yet at least the walls are more solid. The families were very fortunate in being able to live there before the severe frosts of the disastrous winter of 1946–7 set in. In their first quarters they would have frozen to death.[5]

As a percentage of its pre-war population, Schleswig-Holstein had the greatest share of expellees and refugees, around 45 per cent in 1947.[6] Looting and pillaging were commonplace. Victor Gollancz found that German children were growing up with no idea of morality and with a contempt for government of every kind. The scene in Duesseldorf and other Ruhr towns, where people were living 'in holes in the ground', reminded him of 'a vile Daumier cartoon'. He was especially disturbed by the lack of shoes. Children went out into the snow barefoot.

German ration scales were invariably below subsistence level and even then were rarely honoured. The minuscule meat ration was likely to be replaced by dried fish; turnips were counted as substitutes for potatoes. Bread queues often stretched for a hundred yards. During the day, the old and very young found refuge in 'warming rooms' equipped with one small stove and sustained largely by the warmth of human bodies huddled together. If the refugee crisis was not enough of a challenge, there were the prisoners of war to accommodate and displaced persons to be sent home.

> Thousands of newly-liberated slave laborers headed everywhere. Many French were identified by their tri-color flags they had gotten someplace. They had horses, wagons, wheel barrows, baby buggies and many carried huge packs on their backs. A cry to the French of 'Vive La France!' brought cheers.'[7]

In the US zone alone, close on 8 million POWs spent days, sometimes weeks, in makeshift camps. At Rheinberg am Niederrhein, from May to July, around a quarter of a million POWs, along with civilians suspected of Nazi associations, and women who had been in the Nazi Labour Service were herded together in open fields surrounded by barbed wire. There was little to eat and nothing in the way of sanitation.[8]

But it was in the Soviet camps at Breslau where 300,000 men were clustered that the highest mortality was recorded. Most of those who survived were put on reconstruction work in the USSR. It was not until 1955 that the last surviving German POWs were repatriated.

At the end of the war, there were over 7 million homeless foreigners in Germany, many of them former inmates of concentration camps, slave labour camps and POW camps liberated by Allied armies. On 5 May Eisenhower broadcast an appeal to Displaced Persons (DPs) to stay where they were for the time being. 'Do not move out of your district. Wait for orders. Form small groups of your own nationality and choose leaders who will deal for you with the Allied military authorities.'[9]

But changed circumstances did not favour military precision. The dispossessed were liable to wander in search of food or contact with relatives. An understandable sense of grievance led to widespread looting and violent crime. This gave the military administration an added incentive to reduce the floating population. By the end of the year, some 6 million refugees had been repatriated. It was an achievement that offered the first sliver of hope that Germany would eventually work its passage back into the family of nations.

*

While the turmoil in Germany slowly subsided, Doenitz, still technically head of state, along with his former colleagues, waited to hear their fate.

The prospect of a trial of alleged German war criminals had been on the Allied agenda since 1942. Churchill was instinctively opposed to a long-drawn-out legal process but when the Big Three met in Tehran in late 1943, he reacted badly to Stalin's suggestion that, come the peace, 50,000 of the German general staff should be liquidated. Roosevelt tried to make a joke of it, revising the figure down to 49,000. There was no laughter from Churchill. Knowing full well Stalin's capability for indiscriminate brutality, he declared that his country would not stand for mass murder. His preferred option was for what he called 'executive action', the quick dispatch by the military of the big names in the Nazi hierarchy.

Roosevelt and Stalin would probably have settled for that but there was a strong body of opinion in the United States that demanded a symbolic act to show the world that aggressive militarism had had its day. Roosevelt bowed to prevailing opinion within his administration. Stalin was none too worried about spreading a message of peace and goodwill but he came round to the idea of a trial as a demonstration of raw power over his enemies. Now it was two against one.

Churchill held to his reservations. A trial would be necessarily protracted, giving more than ample opportunity for arguments to rage over points of procedure and, indeed, to cast doubts on the legality of the entire proceedings. An added point, though not one for open discussion, was the bizarre singularity of the Soviet Union pronouncing judgement on war crimes of which it was itself undeniably guilty.

In its advice to the prime minister, the Foreign Office did not hold back. 'Surely,' wrote a senior official in the German department, 'to have a Russian sitting in a case of this kind will one day be regarded as a highpoint in international hypocrisy.' As part of its ground plan to dominate other nations, the Soviet Union had embarked on 'atrocities, persecutions and deportations' on a massive scale.[10] But the Russians could not be excluded. They had suffered most from German aggression and had contributed most, in terms of lives lost, to Allied victory. The only hope was that whoever represented the Soviet Union could be persuaded to keep within the bounds of Anglo-American jurisprudence.

The leader of the American prosecution team had no doubts on that score. An associate justice of the Supreme Court, Robert H. Jackson was driven by a combination of idealism and naïveté.

Expecting everybody to share his dream of a new world order, he was frustrated by prolonged wrangling over what he regarded as petty details. Often his irritation was justified. But there was one important matter that was inevitably contentious. Who among the many candidates for arraignment was to stand in the dock? The temptation to produce a comprehensive list threatened a trial that could go on for years. Even a pared-down selection concentrating on easily recognised names looked to some to be overlong.

The British kicked off with a list of ten including Goering, Hess, Ribbentrop and Keitel. Doenitz was noticeable by his absence. This was at the behest of the Admiralty, where the view held that, for the most part, the Kriegsmarine had fought a clean war. Evidence to the contrary was hard to come by. The Americans were not having that. Doenitz had come too close to winning the Atlantic war to be let off the hook. Then there was the political dimension. Hitler's successor could not be allowed to escape retribution. For good measure, the Russians added Erich Raeder.

When the list was published at the end of August 1945, 24 names appeared. Bormann was there on the assumption that he was still at large. There were other errors, not so easily corrected. Most obviously, while it was only right for one of the Krupps to be included (the family stood accused not only of supplying the military hardware for Hitler's aggression but of using slave labour to achieve its targets), the wrong Krupp was named. Gustav was titular head of the firm but, at 75 and seriously ill, he had long since given up active management. It was his son, Alfried, sole owner of the company since 1943, who carried responsibility. Nonetheless, Gustav remained on the charge sheet, though he was dropped before the trial began. Since Bormann had not been found and Robert Ley committed suicide just before the trial, this left 21 defendants.

Another question mark hovered over Rudolf Hess. Hitler's one-time deputy had flown to Britain in 1941 under the delusion that he could negotiate peace by enlisting the support of the Duke of Hamilton. Hartley Shawcross, leading the British prosecution, commented that this 'in itself was some evidence of insanity'.[11] Since his captivity, Hess had twice attempted suicide and remained under psychiatric treatment. But, at Soviet insistence, he was declared fit to stand trial.

The Soviet legal team also pushed hard for the Germans to take the blame for the massacre of Polish officers in the Katyn Forest. The suspicion then, and the certainty now, was that the atrocity was committed on Stalin's orders. Jackson was strongly against raising the issue. In the event, the charge, though pressed, was ignored by the Anglo-American prosecutors. It failed on lack of convincing evidence of German complicity. For Shawcross this 'clearly demonstrated the hypocritical attitude of the Russians to the trial'.[12] They showed little interest in the form of the trial or in helping shape it. As eventually agreed, the indictment against the defendants ran to 18,000 words. The trial was due to start on 20 November. The venue, Nuremberg.

Shawcross took it for granted that Nuremberg was chosen because it was the only place with the necessary facilities. But this was fiction. Nuremberg was no better or worse off than any other German city that had endured saturation bombing. Still, it was an obvious choice. For those with a sense of historical irony, it was fitting that Nazi war criminals should meet with destiny where Hitler had staged his triumphalist rallies.

Each defendant was told to appoint a defence lawyer. Doenitz was one of the few who did not need to think about it. He opted immediately for Otto Kranzbuehler, a 38-year-old naval judge with a reputation for clarity of thought and argument. It was a wise choice. Appearing in court in full uniform, befitting, as he asserted, his role in defending his navy chief, Kranzbuehler's youthful good looks and powerful advocacy made him a star turn at Nuremberg.

Kranzbuehler had good reason to be confident. Of the three counts on which Doenitz was charged, the first two (conspiracy to commit a crime under international law and planning, initiating, and waging wars of aggression) failed almost entirely on time and place. Kranzbuehler was able to show plainly that Doenitz had not been present at any of the war planning conferences. He could hardly be blamed for decisions taken over his head, though it was open to debate as to whether he had waged a war of aggression. The third count, crimes against the laws of war or war crimes, was the trickiest.

Doenitz was charged with waging unrestricted submarine warfare, forbidden under the 1936 Naval Protocol to which Germany was a signatory. Specifically, Doenitz stood accused of ordering his U-boats to attack enemy and neutral ships without warning and of putting a block on rescuing survivors from ships attacked by submarines.

With his close knowledge of naval law, an advantage he had over the British prosecuting counsel, Sir David Maxwell-Fyfe, Kranzbuehler was well aware that the Naval Protocol was a shaky foundation on which to build a convincing case. Hopelessly out of date even before it was ratified, this attempt to update the rules of the sea made no concessions to the realities of submarine warfare.

The guiding principle for action against merchant ships put the onus on the commander of an assault vessel to ensure that the enemy crew, passengers and even ship's papers were in a place of safety before he moved in for the kill. For the U-boat commander this meant knowing that a rescue ship was close at hand to provide lifeboats and accommodation. It also meant a lengthy period when the submarine, unable to submerge until duty done, was vulnerable to counter-attacks.

There was a loophole. This rescue of survivors was not an absolute priority if it endangered the safety or mission of the vessel which had carried out the sinking. How far this allowed U-boats freedom of action was wide open to interpretation. It was all very vague.

The difficulties were well known to the prosecution. They had been pointed out by the British Admiralty well before the Nuremberg trial opened. Indeed, when pressed, the Admiralty warned that sinking on sight, though technically a crime, was not restricted to the Kriegsmarine. Rejecting expert advice as 'typical Admiralty whitewashing of the German navy', the Foreign Office gave the nod to persisting with the prosecution, though Maxwell-Fyfe conceded 'there was not much of a case against Doenitz'.[13]

In the event, Kranzbuehler was able to argue convincingly that merchantmen, even those sailing under neutral flags, were active participants in the war. Introducing evidence that the Royal Navy had itself sunk merchant ships suspected of being in league with the enemy, Kranzbuehler quoted from a 1938 Admiralty Handbook which ordered friendly merchant ships to report on the position of enemy ships and aircraft and to resist any attempt to capture them. Doenitz's claim that from the early days of the war British merchantmen were radioing the position of U-boats, and that they were prepared to fight even before a U-boat called upon them to stop, went unchallenged.

But the trump card played by Kranzbuehler was the testimony of Fleet Admiral Chester Nimitz, America's highest-ranking naval officer and Commander-in-Chief of all Allied land, air and sea forces in the Pacific. Responding to questions from the defence,

Nimitz conceded that the US Navy had practised unrestricted submarine warfare since December 1941. Moreover, submarines had not picked up survivors when by so doing they would have put their own vessels at risk. In other words, if he had been in Doenitz's position, he would not have acted any differently.

Kranzbuehler was careful not to overstate his case. There was no hint in his submission that the US or Britain had acted illegally or without proper regard for the decencies in what admittedly had been a brutal war. The claim was that Doenitz, in so far as he was able, had acted in accordance with recognised practice. The court sided with Kranzbuehler. The first round had gone to Doenitz.

But the prosecution was on firmer ground with the charge that Doenitz had given specific orders not to aid survivors from ships attacked by submarines, irrespective of the risk attached to the rescue operation. Critical to the case against Doenitz was the fate of the *Laconia*. At sunset on 12 September 1942, *U-156* was on patrol off Cape Town when Commander Werner Hartenstein spotted the 20,000-ton liner. A direct hit with two torpedoes caused the ship to list heavily to starboard. As *U-156* approached the liner, lifeboats could be seen. It was obvious that the *Laconia* was about to sink. With the risk of air attack, Hartenstein was eager to get away but cries for help gave him pause. The cries were in Italian. Pulling survivors aboard he soon realised what had happened. His target had been carrying prisoners of war from the North African campaign.

As Hartenstein was coming to terms with his error of judgement, the *Laconia* went down, taking the captain and 1,000 passengers with her. While continuing to lift survivors out of the water, the commander signalled Doenitz, who ordered other submarines in the area to come to the aid of *U-156*. It was then up to the naval chief, Grand Admiral Raeder to manage a touchy diplomatic issue while organising a rescue mission led by French ships from Dakar.

Hartenstein spent the night picking up more survivors. By dawn he had nearly 200 aboard a vessel designed to accommodate, in tight conditions, a crew of 50. Realising there was little more he could do, he sent out an uncoded message on several wavelengths: 'If any ship will assist the shipwrecked *Laconia*, I will not attack provided I am not attacked by ship or air forces'. Over the next three days, two more U-boats and the Italian *Cappellini* arrived to support the rescue.

On the fourth day, an American bomber flew over. A makeshift Red Cross flag was draped over the forward gun of *U-156* while a signal lamp told the aircraft that a rescue was in progress and that there were women and children aboard. The bomber flew off but half an hour later it returned to drop three depth charges. Seriously but not fatally damaged, *U-156* dived and left the area.

At Doenitz's headquarters an act of treachery was assumed. Subsequently, it became clear that the blinker signals had not been understood, though with survivors clinging to the decks of the U-boat and lifeboats in sight, it is easy to understand why the submarine command suspected the worst. Nevertheless, even after further attacks, Doenitz was prepared for the rescue operation to continue. At midday on the fifth day, French ships arrived. The final tally for the rescue was 1,091 out of 2,732. By then, Doenitz had fired off a new standing order to all U-boats.

All attempts at rescuing members of ships that have sunk, including attempts to pick up persons swimming, or to place them in lifeboats, or attempts to right capsized boats, or to supply provisions or water, are to cease. The rescue of survivors contradicts the elementary necessity of war for the destruction of enemy ships and crews.

The order for the capture of captains and chief engineers remains in force.

Survivors are to be picked up only in cases where their interrogation would be of value to the U-boats.

Be severe. Remember that in his bombing attacks on German cities, the enemy has no regard for women and children.

At Nuremberg, the prosecution used the order as evidence of incitement to murder. But on that score, it could be said, at most, that it was ambiguous. Only two witnesses could be found to give substance to the British case. Both were U-boat officers. The first claimed to have heard Doenitz tell an audience of submariners that 'crews of ships like ships themselves were a target for U-boats'. But nobody else could be found to support his contention and Kranzbuehler was able to cast doubt on the reliability of the witnesses' memories. In any case, there was a clear distinction between a prohibition against rescuing survivors, which accorded with the law, and an order to kill survivors, for which the only evidence was two ill-founded allegations.

A second hostile witness, a U-boat captain, was forced by Kranzbuehler to agree that naval standing orders urged the taking of prisoners as valuable sources of intelligence and that commanders who had defied orders on the proper treatment of neutrals had been court-martialled. After Kranzbuehler had given further indications of his wide knowledge of naval law, the British charge that U-boats had deliberately attacked rescue ships was dropped.

High-ranking naval officers from Europe and America who were in the courtroom were inclined to sympathise with their former enemy. The war at sea had been fought ruthlessly on both sides but, in so far as it could be, it was a clean war. In the witness box, Doenitz came on as the dedicated professional, one who was not responsible for initiating war but for waging it successfully once the political decision had been taken. His 120 or so conferences with Hitler were, he insisted, a military obligation. 'How in heaven's name could a commander-in-chief of a service responsible directly to the Head of State have fulfilled his duties in any other way?'

With hindsight Doenitz's argument smacks of hypocrisy. It is now generally accepted that strict neutrality in public office tends to moral corruption. 'I was only obeying orders' is no longer a justifiable excuse. But while today it is a cliché of doctrinaire stupidity, in 1945, unquestioning obedience to higher authority was deeply ingrained in the military and public service ethic. Arguably, the first big break in the tradition came with the indelible images of the opening of the concentration camps. How could the German administration, civil and military, ignore the acts of barbarity performed in their name?

In that connection, when asked by Kranzbuehler, 'Didn't anybody know anything about these things?' Doenitz shook his head and shrugged his shoulders in a gesture of sadness. Even on the safe assumption that his awareness of what Himmler and his cohorts had been up to came only after the end of the war, there remains the strong suspicion that he did not know because he did not want to know. 'It was none of my business.' That is not good enough now and should not have been good enough then.

It also counted against Doenitz that he was anti-Semitic. He was on record as declaiming against 'the poison of international Jewry'. But here an objective observer at Nuremberg might have gasped at the self-delusion and self-righteousness displayed by the Allies. What was not admitted then, and is rarely admitted even today, was the extent to which the obscene doctrine of anti-Semitism was embedded in Western and Eastern culture. Doenitz might reasonably be accused of shutting his eyes to the terrible excesses of the SS and Gestapo but it was a bit rich to tar him with a brush that could be slapped across the social fabric of all participants in the war.

Kranzbuehler's defence of Doenitz was exemplary. Maxwell-Fyfe, who was not given to unconsidered compliments, said of Kranzbuehler that he 'never put a foot wrong in ten months, which is saying a lot'. His deployment of witnesses, including Doenitz's son-in-law, Captain Hessler who was able to point out the ambiguities in the 1936 Protocol while adding that his own British interrogators had promised that no U-boat commander would be charged with criminal acts, was calculated to create the maximum impact on the court. For all the prosecution evidence mustered at Nuremberg, only five cases of criminal conduct by German U-boats came to light, a total which compared favourably with the Allied record.

But Kranzbuehler suffered a handicap that even his skilled advocacy could not overcome. With the Russians sitting in judgement along with the Americans and British, he was inhibited from introducing what is now regarded as Doenitz's strongest claim to vindication, the saving of hundreds of thousands of troops and refugees from Soviet captivity. Instead he had to face the accusation of extending the war for no better reason than death or glory.

Yet Doenitz came close to absolution. The American judge, Francis Biddle, urged acquittal. His three colleagues dissented – though, interestingly, given the Russian tendency to pronounce the death sentence as the way to settle any judicial disagreement,

Major General Nikitchenko was ready to accept a lower sentence than the 20 years handed down to Raeder.

Raeder had been easier to prosecute. Though he had retired in 1943, he was in on pre-war planning and the early stages of the war when he showed scant regard for the laws of the sea. And he was ready to lie his way to justification of illegal acts, as he had demonstrated by tampering with the log book of the U-boat which had sunk the *Athena* and falsifying the official Naval War Diary to support claims that the sinking had been a deliberate act by Britain to encourage America to enter the war. Captured documents went heavily against him while helping to put Doenitz in a relatively favourable light.

Surprisingly, given that the strongest opposition to putting Doenitz on trial in the first place had come from the British, Judge Norman Birkett pressed for a 20-year sentence while, for France, Robert Falco was ready to settle for ten years. Realising he would not get his way, Biddle eventually agreed to compromise. Found guilty of waging a war of aggression, Doenitz faced ten years in prison. Having stepped into Hitler's shoes he could hardly have expected to escape scot-free. Indeed, he may have thought himself lucky not to have joined Ribbentrop and nine others, including Keitel and Jodl, on the scaffold. (Goering pre-empted execution by taking poison.)

The First Sea Lord, Sir John Cunningham, was in court to hear the verdicts. Catching the moment, Kranzbuehler spoke to him about an appeal on behalf of Doenitz and Raeder. Cunningham advised him to send it to the British admiral on the Allied Control Commission and to say that it had been done at his suggestion. The appeal was rejected.

The nine-month-long Nuremberg trial was imperfect. How could it have been otherwise? But it did establish beyond doubt that for those in positions of power, the easy evasion of responsibility was no longer an option. And there were other lessons learned, not least by Doenitz. In his address to the court before sentence was passed, he conceded that 'the principle of dictatorship, as a political principle is false'. He went on:

> When, in spite of all the idealism, the honest endeavour and the boundless sacrifices made by the great mass of the German people, the ultimate result has been this irreparable misfortune, then the principle must be false. False because human nature obviously is incapable of making good use of the power which the principle confers, without succumbing to the temptations of the abuse of power which is inherent in it.

There was no remission. Along with his co-defendants, Doenitz served his full sentence in Spandau, a fortress-like prison in West Berlin. The four occupying powers took turns in mounting guard. In the early days, the prisoners submitted to psychiatric assessment of their state of mind. An American psychiatrist, William H. Dunn, considered Doenitz:

> Poised, affable, pleasant-spoken, with more humour than most of the others but at times it becomes barbed – particularly in speaking of the trial, which he considered dominated by politicians. Has very little in the way of dejection and suicidal ideas. Felt that if he had been before a military tribunal he would have been cleared in three hours. His conscience is clear. Felt he had fought cleanly for his country and the government in power. Demonstrates rather strikingly the attitude of the 'good' German who

feels he was only discharging his duty to the nation and was not involved in the common guilt and shame of his people.

In a game of intelligence testing, Doenitz came out top with an IQ of 138. He was classified as 'very intelligent' but politically naïve, 'feeling that he was kicked upstairs to answer for crimes he knew nothing about'.[14]

Support for the Doenitz family was provided by a fund backed by, among others, 36 former U-boat commanders. The fund was administered by a private bank in Kiel which included Eberhard Godt, the grand admiral's one-time chief of staff and operations, among its directors. The story went that Doenitz was looking to the future when he would need finance to promote his ambitions for a political comeback. But beyond the occasional and fanciful news filler there was no evidence for this. More substantial were reports of Doenitz's certainty that, sooner rather than later, he would be vindicated.

The conviction came on him during the Nuremberg trial when he read newspaper accounts of Churchill's sensational 'iron curtain' speech at Fulton, Missouri. Borrowing a memorable soundbite from Goebbels, Churchill had taken a sharp knock at American hopes for a brave new world of international goodwill by telling his audience that from 'Stettin in the Baltic to Trieste in the Adriatic an iron curtain has descended across the Continent'. In familiar rounded tones, he condemned the Soviet-sponsored dictatorships in Eastern Europe, the 'enormous and wrongful inroads upon Germany' made by the Russian-dominated Polish government and the expulsion of millions of Germans from their homelands. He concluded, 'This is certainly not the liberated Europe we fought to build up. Nor is it one which contains the essentials of permanent peace.'

Of those in the dock, Doenitz was not alone in believing that Churchill had effectively nullified the charges against them. While it was ludicrously optimistic to assume that Hitler's crimes could be so easily whitewashed, there was some satisfaction for Doenitz in the belated recognition that he had been right to warn (albeit, surely, with a sense of irony) against Soviet imperialism and right to dedicate his brief period of power to saving as many as he could from Soviet domination.

Emotionally withdrawn and possessed of the inner discipline that had driven his entire career, Doenitz adapted better than most to a severely spartan regime. It was not too long before circumstances outside Spandau favoured a lighter custodial touch. In June 1948, with the Cold War getting frostier by the month, Stalin made a bid to take over the whole of Berlin by cutting off the road and rail connections to the western sector of the city. Since the Allied share of Berlin was an island within Soviet-controlled East Germany, soon to be styled the German Democratic Republic, this was easy enough to do. But Stalin had reckoned without the ingenuity and determination of the other occupying powers. With the military governor, the bullish General Lucius Clay, ready to take the biggest gamble of his military career, West Berlin survived on an airlift of food and fuel. Over the next year, an incredible 277,500 flights delivered 2.3 million tons of supplies to the besieged city. Stalin knew when he was beaten. In early December he ordered a toning down of triumphalist propaganda. On 12 May 1949, the blockade was finally lifted. As Doenitz had expected and prophesied, Germany, or at least the western part of it, was now in the forefront of the fight against Bolshevism.

As a side effect of the ending of the Berlin blockade, the Russians proved to be more accommodating to the Spandau prisoners. Rations were increased and rest periods extended, more frequent visits were allowed and letters were no longer subject to rigorous censorship. But the new rules agreed by the US, Britain and France did not meet with Soviet approval. In one month in four, when the Russians took control, the regime tightened. When Dr Kranzbuehler, still energetically promoting the interests of Doenitz and Raeder, wrote to Maxwell-Fyfe appealing for greater liberality, he was warned that 'such action might prick the Russians into reprisals against the prisoners when they are next in the chair on the Prison Governorate'.

Doenitz kept alive his hopes of an early release. In April 1953, he had word of an opinion survey which put him at the head of a list of recent former leaders of whom the German people still had a good opinion. 'I shall soon be getting out,' he told Speer.[15] He was to be disappointed.

Life in Spandau was one long round of tedium. After five weeks in which Speer found nothing worth recording in his diary, he fell back on describing the petty details of the domestic routine.

> *February 20, 1956*   Doenitz has his favourite broom and is furious if someone else uses it. Is it worth recording that for years we have been sweeping the hall in precisely the same order? – first Schirach and I do the sides, he always working from the left and I from the right toward the centre, while Doenitz takes care of the centre. Subsequently the heaps swept up by Doenitz are picked up by Funk and Hess. Hess comes with a pail and dustpan; Funk always has the broom. Wordless motion. How well we have adjusted to our surroundings![16]

A rare, possibly the only, redeeming feature of Spandau was the garden where the inmates were free to engage their skills in husbandry. Doenitz tended his vegetable patch. His relations with the other prisoners were formal and often strained. He and Raeder refought old naval battles, disagreeing, as they had always disagreed, on how the war at sea could have been won.

Given how closely Doenitz and Speer had cooperated on the construction programme for the new generation of submarines, it is revealing that in Spandau they kept their distance from each other. The explanation was in the contrast of personality. Serving 20 years as against Doenitz's ten, Speer held his sanity by total submission to the verdict at Nuremberg. An unqualified confession cleared his conscience. By contrast, Doenitz remained convinced that he had nothing to clear. He had done his duty and was now, unfairly in his view, paying the price for unstinting loyalty. He readily admitted to errors of judgement, even to political delusions, but total abrogation was not in his nature.

Doenitz was released from Spandau at midnight on 1 October 1956, two weeks after his 65th birthday. Outside the prison, his wife Ingeborg was waiting for him in a car. The Berlin police were there in force to clear a way through the crowd of onlookers. Doenitz was the third prisoner to leave Spandau but the first to complete, to the day, his full sentence, Raeder and Neurath having been released early on grounds of ill health and old age. Left behind were Rudolf Hess, Walter Funk, Albert Speer and Baldur von Schirach.

Doenitz's first sight of Berlin since the war was on the drive to the suburb of Zehlendorf where he was to spend the night in the home of an old naval comrade, Commander Horst Else. He had a glass of wine and went to bed. The next day, he held a news conference. Refusing questions about the democratic West Germany arising from the ashes, he made a brief statement.

Do not forget that until yesterday I was in prison. In a cage.

Place yourself in the position of a man who has been separated from the outside world for eleven and a half years. I'm not in a position to pass any judgements. I have no opinion about the situation existing outside, therefore it would be foolish of me if I said anything or criticized anything, so it is my task now to be silent and to fit myself into the world again. I want to be silent today, and I shall be silent in the future.

From Berlin he flew to Duesseldorf to spend a few days with his lawyer, Otto Kranzbuehler, before beginning his retirement in a ground floor apartment outside Hamburg. He gave occasional lectures and was back in the news for a short while with the publication of his memoirs. But to the disappointment of his more vocal admirers, not to mention those who expected the worst of him, he made no attempt at a political comeback. After the death of Ingeborg in 1962, he was a lonely and isolated figure. He died of a heart attack on 24 December 1980. Among those who attended his funeral were officers of the Royal Navy.

EPILOGUE

At the 70th anniversary of the end of the Second World War, Doenitz remains a deeply controversial figure. But it is surely time to move on from the knee-jerk dismissal of him as a failed and unreconstituted Nazi.

Doenitz was in the top rank of naval strategists. The course of the war might have altered irrevocably had he been given the resources for his submarine fleet to dominate the Atlantic and to cut off Britain's lifeline to the United States. As Churchill conceded, 'The U-boat attack was our worst evil. It would have been wise for the Germans to stake all upon it.'[1]

Churchill also recognised the risks posed towards the end of the war when Germany was close to launching its new super submarines. As an innovator, Doenitz was way ahead of his time. Even today, submarine technology pays deference to the design breakthrough achieved under his command.

Then there is Operation Hannibal, the Kriegsmarine-led Baltic crossing, much of it a brilliant exercise in improvisation, which saved up to 2 million troops and civilian refugees from the Soviet advance. That Dunkirk has entered the British folklore while Hannibal is all but forgotten, even in Germany, needs explaining. Part of the reason is that while Dunkirk happened at the beginning of the war when the outcome was in doubt,

Hannibal came at the end of the war when the outcome was in no doubt at all.

Then again, in the collective memory, Hannibal has been swept into the wider movement of German refugees, a first wave fleeing overland from the Russian front in the East, the second and much bigger post-war wave of Germans expelled from territories in Eastern and central Europe by the Soviet Union.

But failure to give Doenitz his due has most to do with Allied reluctance to accept that he was right in believing the worst of Soviet intentions. It was not long after the end of the war that America came to realise that as a threat to world peace, Stalin ranked with Hitler. By then Doenitz was in Spandau, out of sight and mind.

Of course, with so much Western propaganda devoted to portraying Stalin as much more than a necessary ally, the avuncular Joe with the general interest at heart, it was impossible to throw the political machine into sharp reverse. Still, Churchill's warnings that the big-power mutual admiration society was no more than a cover for Soviet aggression should have been taken more seriously. In this, if in nothing else, Churchill and Doenitz were as one.

There remains the question as to whether it really was to the advantage of the German people that Doenitz dragged out the surrender negotiations to cover the exodus from the East. It has been argued, notably by Ian Kershaw, that the best option for Doenitz, once he had been confirmed as leader, was to have ordered troops in all areas facing the Allies simply to stop fighting.

This would have allowed the western powers to advance their lines immediately and rapidly to the east, shortening the lines to those still trapped there.[2]

Maybe. But it is surely a matter of doubt that Doenitz had the power base to make such a decision, even assuming that he thought it to be the right one, which he did not. As a naval officer, schooled in military discipline, he had a dread of a breakdown of authority. An order for an immediate ceasefire on all fronts without first testing Allied resolve would not necessarily have been obeyed by commanders in the field. Doenitz had no wish to be held responsible for social chaos and revolution, a reprise of 1918. In any case, there could be no guarantee that the Western Allies would do anything to help contain the Red Army. Quite the opposite.

Who knows how Doenitz felt on news of his elevation to head of state? As a military professional who was inclined to hold all politicians in low regard, he had no need to be told that he was ill-equipped for his new role. He must also have known that in Allied eyes he would now be seen as the standard bearer of all that was hated in the Nazi regime.

He made mistakes, not least failing to act resolutely against Himmler's malign influence. But free from Hitler's shadow he was his own man with his own policy of ending the war quickly on the best terms he could get for Germany and for those caught on the wrong side of the East–West divide. For this Doenitz deserves credit. What he got was a prison sentence handed down at Nuremberg, a penalty that, with hindsight, stands out as an example of victor's justice.

Of the 40,900 U-boat officers and men who served under Doenitz, 25,870 lost their lives. In that number were the two sons of Karl Doenitz.

BIBLIOGRAPHY

Submarines of World War Two, Erminio Bagnasco, Arms &
Armour, 1977

Defeat at Sea, C.D. Bekker, Ballantine Books, 1973

Swastika at Sea, C.D. Bekker, William Kimber, 1953

Berlin: The Downfall 1945, Antony Beevor, Penguin, 2007

Erich Raeder: Admiral of the Third Reich, Keith W. Bird, Naval
Institute Press, 2006

Hitler's U-boat War. The Hunters, 1939–1942, Clay Blair, Modern
Library, 1996

Hitler's U-boat War. The Hunters, 1942–1945, Clay Blair, Modern
Library, 1998

My Three Years with Eisenhower, Harry C. Butcher,
Heinemann, 1946

*The Chief of Staff: The Military Career of General Walter Bedell
Smith*, D.K.W. Crosswell, Greenwood Press, 1991

Operation Victory, Major General Sir Francis de Guingand,
Hodder & Stoughton, 1947

The History of the French First Army, Marshal de Lattre de
Tassigny, Allen & Unwin, 1952

The Cruellest Night, Christopher Dobson, John Miller and Ronald
Payne, Little, Brown, 1979

The Conduct of the War at Sea, Karl Doenitz, US Navy
    Department, 1946
Memoirs: Ten Years and Twenty Days, Karl Doenitz, Weidenfeld &
    Nicolson, 1958
Red Storm on the Reich: The Soviet March on Germany, 1945,
    Christopher Duffy, Routledge, 1991
Doenitz and the Wolf Packs, Bernard Edwards, Cassell, 1996
Submarine Design and Development, Norman Friedman, Naval
    Institute Press, 1984
Tales from Spandau: Nazi Criminals and the Cold War, Norman J.W.
    Goda, Cambridge University Press, 2008
Hitler, Doenitz and the Baltic Sea, Howard D. Grier, Naval Institute
    Press, 2007
Panzer Leader, General Heinz Guderian, Michael Joseph, 1952
The Schellenberg Memoirs, Louis Hagen, Deutsch, 1956
The Bridge at Remagen, Ken Hechler, Pictorial Histories
    Publishing Co., 1957
The U-boat War in the Atlantic 1939–1945, Gunther Hessler, 1951
Count Folke Bernadotte: His Life and Work, Ralph Hewins,
    Hutchinson, 1948
The Submarine and Sea Power, Arthur Hezlet, Stein & Day, 1967
The Lonely Leader: Monty, 1944–45, Alistair Horne and David
    Montgomery, 1997
Other Days Around Me, Richard Hough, Hodder &
    Stoughton, 1992
The Memoirs of General the Lord Ismay, Heinemann, 1960
Memoirs of Field Marshal Keitel, William Kimber, 1965
U-boats Destroyed. German Submarine Losses in the World Wars,
    Paul Kemp, Weidenfeld & Nicolson, 1999
Memoirs, Field Marshal Kesselring, William Kimber, 1953

Political Adventure: The Memoirs of the Earl of Kilmuir, Weidenfeld
& Nicolson, 1964

The First Casualty, Phillip Knightley, John Hopkins University
Press, 2004

Steel Ships, Iron Crosses and Refugees, Charles W. Koburger,
Praeger, 1989

Type XXI U-boat. Anatomy of a Ship, Fritz Kohl and Eberhard
Rossler, Naval Institute Press, 1991

So fiel Königsberg, Otto Lasch, Motor-Buch Verlag, 1977

Mr Churchill's Secretary, Elizabeth Layton, Coward-McCann, 1958

I Was There, William D. Leahy, Gollancz, 1950

Unconditional Surrender, Walter Luedde-Neurath, Pen &
Sword, 2010

Hitler and His Admirals, Anthony Martienssen, Secker &
Warburg, 1948

Soldier: The Memoirs of Matthew B. Ridgway, Harold H. Martin,
Harper, 1956

Nuremberg. A Nation on Trial, Werner Maser, Scribner, 1979

Eclipse, Alan Moorehead, Hamish Hamilton, 1945

Report From Germany, Leonard O. Mosley, Gollancz, 1945

CBS, On the Air – War Report, Ed Murrow, Oxford University
Press, 1946

Russia's War, Richard Overy, Allen Lane, 1998

Doenitz, the Last Fuhrer, Peter Padfield, Gollancz, 1984

1945: The Dawn Came Up Like Thunder, Tom Pocock,
Collins, 1983

Struggle for the Sea, Erich Raeder, William Kimber, 1959

Chronology of the War at Sea 1939–1945, Jurgen Rohwer and
Gerhard Hummelchen, Naval Institute Press, 1992

*The U-boat. The Evolution and Technical History of German
Submarines*, Eberhard Rossler, Naval Institute Press, 1981

The Forgotten Soldier, Guy Sajer, Weidenfeld & Nicolson, 1971

Goebbels – the Man Next to Hitler, Rudolf Semmler,
    Westhouse, 1947

Defeat in the West, Milton Shulman, Secker & Warburg, 1947

Inside the Third Reich, Albert Speer, Macmillan, 1970

We Defended Normandy, Hans Speidel, Herbert Jenkins, 1951

Capitulation 1945, Marlis G. Steinert, Calder & Boyars, 1969

Battle Beneath the Waves: The U-boat War, Robert C. Stern,
    Weidenfeld & Nicolson, 1999

Intelligence at the Top: The Recollections of an Intelligence Officer,
    Sir Kenneth Strong, Cassell, 1968

*British and Commmonwealth Merchant Ship Losses to Axis
    Submarines 1939–1945*, Alan J. Tennent, The History
    Press, 2001

Flight in Winter, Juergen Thorwald, Hutchinson, 1953

Stealth at Sea. A History of the Submarine, Dan van der Vat,
    Weidenfeld & Nicolson, 1994

The German Navy in World War Two, Edward P. Von der Porten,
    Arthur Barker, 1970

Memoiren, Lutz Graf Schwerin von Krosigk, Seewald, 1977

Finale Furioso: Mit Goebbels bis zum Ende, Wilfred von Oven,
    Grabert, 1974

Conqueror's Road: An Eyewitness Report of Germany 1945, Osmar
    White, Cambridge University Press, 2003

NOTES

Chapter One

1. Misch outlived all the other occupants of the bunker. After eight years as a Soviet prisoner of war, he returned to his family in Berlin in 1953. He died aged 96 on 5 September 2013.
2. *Memoirs of Field Marshal Keitel*, 1965; pp. 196–7.
3. Ralph Hewins, *Count Folke Bernadotte: His Life and Work*, 1948; p. 118.
4. Louis Hagen, *The Schellenberg Memoirs*, 1956.
5. Ibid.
6. Albert Speer, *Inside the Third Reich*, 1970; p. 487.
7. Speer later denied that he had said any such thing. But the story was strong enough for Doenitz to believe it and, post-war, to hold it against Speer.

Chapter Two

1. Karl Doenitz, *Ten Years and Twenty Days*, 1958; p. 300.
2. Ibid; p. 3.
3. Ibid; p. 5.
4. Twenty years later, in a protest against British involvement in the Suez war, the Swedish ambassador in London reflected 'Scandinavian opinion has never been more shocked – not even by the British German Naval Agreement of 1935'. (*International Affairs*, Vol. 64, Summer 1988)
5. Karl Doenitz, *The Conduct of the War at Sea*, 15 Jan. 1946. US Navy Department.

6. Erich Raeder, *Struggle for the Sea*, 1959; p. 136.

7. *History of U-boat Policy 1939–45*, compiled from captured records, Feb. 1946. Admiralty Records CB4501.

8. Dan van der Vat, *Stealth at Sea*, 1994; p. 180.

9. Karl Doenitz, *The Conduct of the War at Sea*, 15 Jan. 1946. US Navy Department.

10. *History of U-boat Policy 1939–45*, compiled from captured records, Feb. 1946. Admiralty Records CB4501.

11. Ibid.

12. Karl Doenitz, *Ten Years and Twenty Days*, 1958; pp. 120–1.

13. Dan van der Vat, *Stealth at Sea*, 1994; p. 199.

14. Ibid; p. 278.

15. Karl Doenitz, *Ten Years and Twenty Days*, 1958; p. 202.

16. Dan van der Vat, *Stealth at Sea*, 1994; p. 282.

17. Anthony Martienssen, *Hitler and His Admirals*, 1948; p. 139.

18. *History of U-boat Policy*, Admiralty Records; CB4501.

19. Anthony Martienssen, *Hitler and his Admirals*, 1948; p. 140.

20. Karl Doenitz, *The Conduct of the War at Sea*, 1 Jan. 1946, US Navy Department.

21. Edward P. Von der Porten, *The German Navy in World War Two*, 1970; p. 188.

22. Interview with Juergen Rohwer quoted in the 1990 edition of the Doenitz memoirs.

23. Karl Doenitz, *Ten Years and Twenty Days*, 1958; p. 311.

24. Ibid; p. 312.

Chapter Three

1. Karl Doenitz, *Ten Years and Twenty Days*, 1958; p. 357.

2. Dan van der Vat, *Stealth at Sea*, 1994; p. 310.

3. Tom Pocock, *1945: The Dawn Came Up Like Thunder*, 1983; p. 60.

4. Hans Speidel, *We Defended Normandy*, 1951; pp. 60–1.

5. Howard D. Grier, *Hitler, Doenitz and the Baltic Sea*, 2007; p. 17.

6. Karl Doenitz, *Ten Years and Twenty Days*, 1958; p. 400.

7. C.D. Bekker, *Swastika at Sea*, 1953; p. 160.

8. Guy Sajer, *The Forgotten Soldier*, 1971; pp. 515–6.

9. Ibid; p. 510.

10. Milton Shulman, *Defeat in the West*, 1947.

11. Frederick Fox, Third Army, Hoskins Library, University of Tennessee, Knoxville.

12. W. Haupt, *Heeresgruppe Mitte 1941–45*, 1968; p. 283. Quoted in Christopher Duffy, *Red Storm on the Reich*, 1991; p. 67.

13. Wilfred von Oven, *Finale Furioso: Mit Goebbels bis zum Ende*, 1974.

14. Juergen Thorwald, *Flight in Winter*, 1953; p. 90.

15. Ibid; p. 92.

16. Ibid; p. 89.

Chapter Four

1. Charles W. Koburger, *Steel Ships, Iron Crosses and Refugees*, 1989; p. 80.

2. C.D. Bekker, *Swastika at Sea*, 1953; pp. 174–6.

3. Dobson, Miller and Payne, *The Cruellest Night*, 1979; pp. 58–9.

4. Ibid; p. 61.

5. Ibid; pp. 104–5.

6. Ibid; p. 119.

7. Juergen Thorwald, *Flight in the Winter*, 1953; p. 127.

8. Charles W. Koburger, *Steel Ships, Iron Crosses and Refugees*, 1989; p. 73.

9. K. Dieckert and H. Grossmann, *Der Kampf um Ostpreussen*, 1960; p. 176. Quoted in Christopher Duffy, *Red Storm on the Reich*, 1991; p. 212.

10. Commander Arnold Schoen, *Pillau*. Bundesarchiv – Lastenausgleichsarchiv, Bayreuth.

11. Martin Bergau, Kempowski Archiv, Nartum.

12. Otto Lasch, *So fiel Koenigsberg*, 1977; p. 115.

13. M.E. Katukov, *Na Ostrie Glavnogo Udara*, 1976; p. 386. Quoted in Christopher Duffy, *Red Storm on the Reich*, 1991; p. 227.

14. Juergen Thorwald, *Flight in Winter*, 1953; p. 161.

15. H. Schaeufler, *Der Weg war weit*, 1973; pp. 241–2. Quoted in Christopher Duffy, *Red Storm on the Reich*, 1991; pp. 229–30.

16. F. Kurowski, *Endkampf um das Reich 1944–45*, 1987; p. 288. Quoted in Christopher Duffy, *Red Storm on the Reich*, 1991; pp. 235.

17. Charles W. Koburger, *Steel Ships, Iron Crosses and Refugees*, 1989; p. 88.

Chapter Five

1. US Strategic Bombing Survey, Sept. 1945.

2. William Buckley letter, 5 April 1945. Hoskins Library, University of Tennessee, Knoxville.

3. Walter Denise, Rutgers Oral History Archives of World War II.

4. Rudolf Semmler, *Goebbels – the Man Next to Hitler*, 1947; p. 169.

5. Karl Doenitz, *Ten Years and Twenty Days*, 1958; p. 427.

6. Marie Therese Fuegling, *Die Heimat*, Summer 1954.

7. Diary of Lucie Lecoq, quoted in *General Anzeiger* (Bonn newspaper), 1979.

8. Karl Hechler, *The Bridge at Remagen*, 1957; p. 114.

9. Field Marshal Kesselring, *Memoirs*, 1953; pp. 238–9.

10. Ibid; p. 238.

11. Ibid; p. 239.

12. *Eyewitness War*, 1995; p. 221.

13. A.E. Baker, Wireless Operator, 4th Squadron, Seventh Royal Dragoon Guards, Imperial War Museum; 88/34/1.

14. Richard Hough, *Other Days Around Me*, 1992; p. 119.

15. Harold H. Martin, *Soldier: The Memoirs of Matthew B. Ridgway*, 1956; p. 133.

16. Sergeant Richard Greenwood, Ninth Battalion Royal Tank Regiment, Imperial War Museum, 95/19/1.

17. Chester Wilmot, BBC, in *On the Air – War Report*, 1946; p. 342.
18. Alan Moorehead, *Eclipse*, 1945; p. 228.
19. Field Marshal Kesselring, *Memoirs*, 1953; p. 253.
20. Ibid; p. 262.
21. Harold H. Martin, *Soldier: The Memoirs of Matthew B. Ridgway*, 1956; p. 139.
22. General Heinz Guderian, *Panzer Leader*, 1952; pp. 404–5.
23. Ibid; p. 429.
24. Nuernberg Stadtarchiv.
25. Nuernberg Stadtarchiv.
26. Ed Murrow, CBS, *On the Air – War Report*, 1946; p. 387.
27. Leonard O. Mosley, *Report From Germany*, 1945; p. 72.
28. *Zehlendorfer Chronik*, 1987.
29. Ibid.
30. Ibid.
31. Heimatsmuseum Tiergarten Archive, Berlin.
32. Ibid.

Chapter Six

1. Bundesarchiv, Collection R62/2: *Flensburger Nachrichten* No. 102.
2. Walter Luedde-Neurath, *Unconditional Surrender*, 1948; p. 41.
3. *Tribune*, 2 Feb. 1945.
4. Quebec Conference, 1944.
5. Marlis G. Steinert, *Capitulation, 1945*, 1969; p. 103.
6. Ibid; p. 113.
7. Bundesarchiv, Collection R62/10.
8. Karl Doenitz, *Ten Years and Twenty Days*, 1958; p. 439.
9. Ibid; p. 441.
10. Ibid; p. 443.
11. Ibid; pp. 443–4.
12. Marlis G. Steinert, *Capitulation, 1945*, 1969; p. 73.

13. Walter Goerlitz, *The German General Staff*, 1953.
14. General Guenther Blumentritt, *Irish Defence Journal*, 1949.
15. Field Marshal Keitel, *Memoirs*; p. 226.
16. Albert Speer, *Inside the Third Reich*; p. 493.
17. Irmgard Hagemeyer, Bremen Stadtarchiv.
18. Bremen Stadtarchiv.
19. Karl Doenitz, *Ten Years and Twenty Days*, 1958; p. 437.
20. Ibid; p. 437.
21. Walter Luedde-Neurath, *Unconditional Surrender*, 1948; p. 50.
22. Marlis G. Steinert, *Capitulation, 1945*, 1969; p. 141.

Chapter Seven

1. Walter Luedde-Neurath, *Unconditional Surrender*, 1948; p. 51.
2. Trumbull Warren, *The Surrender of the German Armed Forces* (unpublished), quoted in Alistair Horne and David Montgomery, *The Lonely Leader*, 1997; p. 336.
3. Ibid.
4. Ibid.
5. Major General Sir Francis de Guingand, *Operation Victory*, 1947; p. 453.
6. Trumbull Warren, *The Surrender of the German Armed Forces* (unpublished), quoted in Alistair Horne and David Montgomery, *The Lonely Leader*, 1997.
7. Ibid.
8. Major General Sir Francis de Guingand, *Operation Victory*, 1947; p. 446.
9. Ibid; p. 449.
10. Ibid; pp. 451–2.
11. *Expressen*, 2 March 1945.
12. Karl Doenitz, *Ten Years and Twenty Days*, 1958; p. 459.
13. Walter Luedde-Neurath, *Unconditional Surrender*, 1948; p. 54.

14. Robert C. Stern, *Battle Beneath the Waves*, 1999; p. 126.
15. C.D. Bekker, *Swastika at Sea*, 1953; p. 206.
16. Leonard Mosley, *Report from Germany*, 1945; pp. 100–1.
17. Ibid; p. 101.
18. Osmar White, *Conqueror's Road*, 2003; p. 192.
19. Leonard Mosley, *Report from Germany*, 1945; pp. 102.
20. Harry Butcher, *Three Years With Eisenhower*, 1946; p. 681.

Chapter Eight
1. Albert Ricketts. BBC Archive. WW2 People's War. Article: A3537371.
2. D.K.W. Crosswell, *Chief of Staff*, 1991; p. 300.
3. Sir Kenneth Strong, *Intelligence at the Top*, 1968; p. 200.
4. Ibid; p. 200.
5. D.K.W. Crosswell, *Chief of Staff*, 1991; p. 324.
6. Karl Doenitz, *Ten Years and Twenty Days*, 1958; p. 462.
7. Sir Kenneth Strong, *Intelligence at the Top*, 1968; p. 203.
8. Ibid; p. 204.
9. Osmar White, *Conqueror's Road*, 2003; pp. 111–3.
10. General the Lord Ismay, *Memoirs*, 1960; p. 394.
11. Phillip Knightley, *The First Casualty*; p. 316.
12. William D. Leahy, *I Was There*, 1950; p. 421.
13. *New York Times*, 8 May 1945.
14. *Daily Mirror*, 8 May 1945.
15. Elizabeth Layton, *Mr Churchill's Secretary*, 1958; p. 176.
16. Marlis G. Steinert, *Capitulation, 1945*, 1969; pp. 173–4.
17. Sir Kenneth Strong, *Intelligence at the Top*, 1968; p. 208–9.
18. Marshal de Lattre de Tassigny, *The History of the French First Army*, 1952; p. 515.
19. Ibid; pp. 518–9.
20. Field Marshal Keitel, *Memoirs*, 1965; pp. 230–1.
21. Ibid; p. 232.

22. Sir Kenneth Strong, *Intelligence at the Top*, 1968; p. 211.

23. Ibid; p. 208.

24. Ibid; pp. 211–2.

25. Ibid; p. 213.

26. General the Lord Ismay, *Memoirs*, 1960; p. 402.

Chapter Nine

1. Tom Pocock, *1945: The Dawn Came Up Like Thunder*, 1983; pp. 110–2.

2. Centraal Archievendepot, Ministerie van Defensie, Doc. O.D., inv. Nr. A-53.

3. Richard Petrew, *The Bitter Years*, 1974; p. 334.

4. Charles W. Koburger, *Steel Ships, Iron Crosses and Refugees*, 1989; p. 108.

5. Howard D. Grier, *Hitler, Doenitz and the Baltic Sea: The Third Reich's Last Hope, 1944–1945*, 2007; p. 105.

6. C.D. Bekker, *Swastika at Sea*, 1953; p. 185.

7. Imperial War Museum; 92/37/1.

8. Benjamin Jacobs and Eugene Pool, *The Hundred Year Secret*, 2004; p. 67.

9. Ibid; p. 109.

10. C.D. Bekker, *Swastika at Sea*, 1953; p. 188.

11. Guy Sajer, *The Forgotten Soldier*, 1971; pp. 545–6.

12. *The Times*, 19 May 1945.

13. Richard Petrew, *The Bitter Years*, 1974; p. 358.

14. *Copenhagen Post*, 13 April 2014.

15. Kirsten Lyllof, *German and Non-German Refugees in Denmark after the Second World War*; Department of History, University of Copenhagen.

Chapter Ten

1. Omar N. Bradley, *A Soldier's Story*, 1951; p. 544.

2. Ray W. Brown, Rutgers Oral History Archives.

3. William Louis Meissner, *Life as a GI*, Hoskins Library, University of Tennessee, Knoxville.

4. Captain C.T. Cross, Imperial War Museum. Courtesy, Worshipful Company of Armourers and Brasiers.

5. Charles Whiting, *Finale at Flensburg*, 1973; p. 109.

6. Ibid; p. 110.

7. Ian Kershaw, *The End*, 2011; p. 373.

8. Omar N. Bradley, *A Soldier's Story*, 1951; p. 545.

9. Charles Whiting, *Finale at Flensburg*, 1973; p. 111–2.

10. Captain C.T. Cross, Imperial War Museum. Courtesy, Worshipful Company of Armourers and Brasiers.

11. Kempowski Archiv, Nartum.

12. W.A. Lewis, Imperial War Museum; 88/60/1.

13. James Witte, Imperial War Museum; 87/12/1.

14. N.L. Francis, Imperial War Museum; 88/58/1.

15. Montgomery, *The Memoirs of Field Marshal Montgomery*; p. 367.

16. Marlis G. Steinert, *Capitulation, 1945*, 1969; p. 193.

17. Major General Sir Francis de Guingand, *Operation Victory*, 1947; p. 456.

18. Ibid; pp. 401–2.

19. Peter Longerich, *Heinrich Himmler*, 2012; p. 1.

20. Robert Murphy, *Diplomat Among Warriors*, 1964; p. 299.

21. Sir Kenneth Strong, *Intelligence at the Top*, 1968; p. 218.

22. Karl Doenitz, *Ten Years and Twenty Days*, 1958; p. 474.

Chapter Eleven

1. Saul K. Padover, *Psychologist in Germany*, 1946; p. 211.

2. Richard Bessel, *Germany 1945: From War to Peace*, 2009; p. 247.

3. *News Chronicle*, 24 August 1945.

4. Victor Gollancz, *In Darkest Germany*.

5. Local authority report quoted in Douglas Botting, *From the Ruins of the Reich*, 1985.

6. Francis Graham-Dixon, *The Allied Occupation of Germany*, 2013.
7. James Graff, *Memoirs of the 134th Infantry, 35th Division, Ninth Army*. Hoskins Library, University of Tennessee, Knoxville.
8. Richard Bessel, *Germany 1945: From War to Peace*, 2009; p. 201.
9. Ibid; p. 256.
10. Ann Tusa and John Tusa, *The Nuremberg Trial*; p. 72.
11. Hartley Shawcross, *Life Sentence*, 1995; p. 102.
12. Ibid; p. 103.
13. Ann Tusa and John Tusa, *The Nuremberg Trial*; p. 185.
14. Jack Flashman, *Long Knives and Short Memories*, 1986; p. 26.
15. Albert Speer, *Spandau. The Secret Diaries*, 1976; p. 226.
16. Ibid; p. 287.

Epilogue

1. Winston S. Churchill, *The Second World War*, Vol. IV; p. 125.
2. Ian Kershaw, *The End: Hitler's Germany 1944–1945*, 2011; p. 176.

ACKNOWLEDGEMENTS

I am indebted to Admiral of the Fleet Lord Boyce, a distinguished submariner and former Chief of Defence Staff, for his thought-provoking introduction and for much valuable advice, not least urging me to watch the 1981 German movie *Das Boot*, a shockingly realistic portrayal of submarine warfare.

Staff at the German Historical Institute, London, the London Library, the Imperial War museum, the National Maritime Museum and the International Maritime Museum in Hamburg have gone way beyond duty to be supportive and helpful. Among those who have pointed to sources I might otherwise have missed, I am especially grateful to Claus Budelmann, chairman of the Anglo-German Club in Hamburg and to Lennart Oldenburg in Stockholm.

Once again, my long-time assistant, Jill Fenner, has achieved the miracle of interpreting my longhand scrawl, while my agent, Michael Alcock, has provided a wealth of constructive advice. At Icon, I have been blessed with the outstanding editing skills of Duncan Heath and Robert Sharman.

INDEX

JULY 1914
Countdown to War

Sean McMeekin

'A genuinely exciting, almost hour-by-hour account of the terrible month when Europe's diplomats danced their continent over the edge and into the abyss.' BBC History Magazine

'A work of meticulous scholarship … McMeekin's description of the details of life in the European capitals – small events that influenced great decisions – makes July 1914 irresistible.' Roy Hattersley, *The Times*

'Lucid, convincing and full of rich detail, the book is a triumph for the narrative method and a vivid demonstration that chronology is the logic of history.' *Independent*

'Sean McMeekin is establishing himself as a – or even *the* – leading young historian of modern Europe. Here he turns his gifts to the outbreak of war in July 1914 and has written another masterpiece.' Norman Stone, author of *World War Two: A Short History*

9781848316577 (paperback) / 9781848316096 (ebook)

STALIN'S GENERAL
The Life of Georgy Zhukov
Geoffrey Roberts

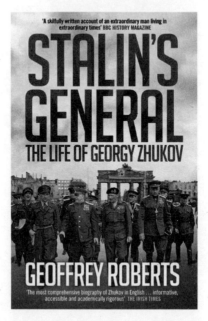

'A skilfully written account of an extraordinary man living
in extraordinary times.' *BBC History Magazine*

Marshal Georgy Zhukov is increasingly seen as the indispensable
military leader of the Second World War, surpassing Eisenhower,
Patton, Montgomery and MacArthur in his military brilliance and
ferocity. He played a decisive role in the battles of Moscow, Stalingrad
and Kursk, was the first of the Allied generals to enter Berlin, and took
the German surrender. He led the huge victory parade in Red Square,
riding a white horse, dangerously provoking Stalin's envy.

Making use of hundreds of documents from Russian military archives,
as well as unpublished versions of Zhukov's memoirs, Geoffrey Roberts
fashions a remarkably intimate portrait of a man whose personality was
as fascinating as it was contradictory.

9781848315174 (paperback) / 9781848314436 (ebook)

AND SOME FELL ON STONY GROUND
A Day in the Life of an RAF Bomber Pilot

Leslie Mann with an introduction by Richard Overy

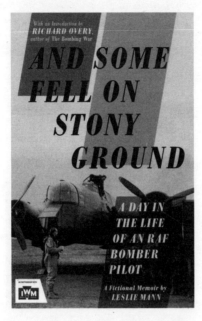

In June 1941, Flight Sergeant Leslie Mann, a tail gunner in a British bomber, was shot down over Düsseldorf and taken into captivity. After the war, wanting to record the experiences of the RAF's 'Bomber Boys', he gave voice to his private thoughts and feelings in a short novella, uncovered only after his death.

Visceral, shocking and unglamorous, this compelling story transmits as rarely before the horrors of aerial warfare, the corrosive effects of fear, and the psychological torment of the young men involved. The sights, sounds, smells, and above all the emotional strain are intensely evoked with a novelist's skill.

And Some Fell on Stony Ground is introduced by historian Richard Overy, author of the acclaimed *The Bombing War* (Allen Lane, 2013).

9781848318380 (paperback) / 9781848317543 (ebook)

BEYOND THE CALL
The True Story of One World War II Hero's
Covert Mission to Rescue POWs on the Eastern Front

Lee Trimble with Jeremy Dronfield

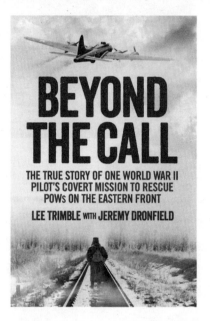

'The inspiring tale of a hitherto unknown true hero – a story
worthy of a Hollywood movie.' *Military History Monthly*

'Captivating stuff, detailing one man's courage in a seemingly impossible
situation – a brilliantly told story of a true unsung hero.' *History of War*

As the Red Army advanced across Poland in 1945, thousands of freed
Allied POWs – viewed by the Soviets as cowards or potential spies –
were abandoned to wander the war-torn Eastern Front. In total secrecy,
the OSS conceived an undercover mission to rescue them. The man
they picked to undertake it was veteran Eighth Air Force bomber pilot
Captain Robert Trimble.

Alone, Trimble faced up to the terrifying Soviet secret police and
saved hundreds of lives, all the while fighting his own battle against
the trauma of war.

9781848319417 (paperback) / 9781848318533 (ebook)